# CRISIS AND CONTROVERSY

*Also by Chris Cook*

SOURCES IN BRITISH POLITICAL HISTORY (*co-editor*)

THE AGE OF ALIGNMENT: ELECTORAL POLITICS IN BRITAIN, 1922–1929

A SHORT HISTORY OF THE LIBERAL PARTY: 1900–76

BY-ELECTIONS IN BRITISH POLITICS (*ed. with John Ramsden*)

EUROPEAN POLITICAL FACTS, 1918–73 (*with John Paxton*)

THE POLITICS OF REAPPRAISAL, 1918–39 (*ed. with Gillian Peele*)

ENGLISH HISTORICAL FACTS, 1485–1603 (*with Kenneth Powell*)

THE DECADE OF DISILLUSION (*ed. with David McKie*)

BRITISH HISTORICAL FACTS, 1830–1900 (*with Brendan Keith*)

THE LONGMAN ATLAS OF MODERN BRITISH HISTORY, 1700–1970 (*with John Stevenson*)

EUROPEAN POLITICAL FACTS, 1815–1918 (*with John Paxton*)

# CRISIS
# AND
# CONTROVERSY

*Essays in Honour of*
*A. J. P. Taylor*

*Edited by*
**ALAN SKED**
*Lecturer in International History*
*London School of Economics*

*and*

**CHRIS COOK**
*Assistant Keeper*
*Royal Commission on Historical Manuscripts*

## ST. MARTIN'S PRESS NEW YORK

# Contents

# Foreword

Alan Taylor published his first history book in 1934. Since then his works have been so widely read, his views so widely debated, that his name is now synonymous with the writing of history in this country. He has interpreted the modern history of Great Britain and of Europe with such incisiveness of mind and facility of style that his contribution to this field has been unique. No other contemporary historian has written so many major books on so many major themes. And none has brought to the writing of history such a formidable display of talents: his style is inimitable, his views, illuminating and original; he has a gift for communicating which borders on genius. Readers of this book will therefore readily appreciate that its authors have laboured under an abiding sense of humility.

It is, however, much more than as a writer of history that Alan Taylor is honoured. Most of the authors of this book have been privileged to know him either as teacher or as friend, and all of them are personally aware of his influence on many other individual historians. The editors of this volume, although working in widely differing fields, owe him a very special debt. It was he who supervised their doctoral research at Oxford and it was he who displayed that patience, tact and wisdom on which every doctoral student depends. Alan Taylor's brilliance as writer, broadcaster and journalist is well known; his talents as a teacher should also be remembered. He has been an outstanding tutor at Magdalen; his seminar in London was acclaimed as the best on modern British history.

To Alan Taylor, therefore, on his seventieth birthday, these essays are dedicated with affection. From historians of different ages and of differing fields, this volume is offered as a token of esteem to one who has inspired them all. It is offered to a historian, who, though occasionally slighted by the more blinkered members of his profession, has few equals indeed in the world of history writing.

Alan Sked
Chris Cook

# Acknowledgements

In any book of this sort, the editors must thank a variety of persons. Each contributor owes a debt to those who have helped and checked his own article. More generally, the editors owe a wider debt to colleagues and friends at the London School of Economics. Much of the typing for this book was done with unfailing enthusiasm by Eileen Pattison and Jean Eli. A particular debt is due to Harry Bawden, Deborah Dickson, Angela Dyer, and Tim Farmiloe at The Macmillan Press for their constant help in seeing this volume to publication. The index was compiled with her usual helpful efficiency by Beryl McKie.

We are indebted to Mr R. H. Ellis Davies for permission to quote from the journal of Ellis W. Davies. Our warm thanks are also due to the respective copyright holders for the Asquith, Attlee, Beaverbrook, Collin Brooks, Dalton, Eager, Elibank, Gardiner, Viscount Gladstone, Haldane, Hickleton, Lloyd George, Maclean, Nicoll, Strachey and Barrington-Ward papers. A particular debt is due to the Imperial War Museum for the papers used in Chapter 8, and to the University of Swansea Library for permission to use the Claude Stamfield papers.

The publishers have made every effort to trace the copyright-holders, but if they have inadvertently overlooked any they will be pleased to make the necessary arrangement at the first opportunity.

# Notes on Contributors

PAUL ADDISON (b. 1943) was educated at Pembroke and Nuffield College, Oxford. He was Lecturer in History, Pembroke College, Oxford, 1966–7; formerly Research Assistant to the late Randolph S. Churchill; and has been Lecturer in Modern History at the University of Edinburgh since 1967. He has contributed to *Lloyd George: Twelve Essays*, edited by A. J. P. Taylor, and to *By-Elections in British Politics*, edited by Chris Cook and John Ramsden.

CHRIS COOK (b. 1945) was educated at St Catharine's College, Cambridge, and at Oriel and Nuffield College, Oxford. He was Lecturer in Politics at Magdalen College, Oxford, 1969–70. From 1970 to 1975 he was Senior Research Officer at the London School of Economics. In January 1976 he took up his present senior appointment at the Royal Commission on Historical Manuscripts. His previous books include *The Age of Alignment: Electoral Politics in Britain* and (with co-authors) *By-Elections in British Politics; European Political Facts, 1918–73; Sources in British Political History, 1900–51; The Decade of Disillusion; British Historical Facts, 1830–1900* and *The Politics of Reappraisal*.

JOHN GRIGG (b. 1924) was educated at Eton and New College, Oxford, and was awarded the Gladstone Memorial Prize. He was editor of *National and English Review*, 1954–60, and a columnist for the *Guardian*, 1960–7. He contested Oldham West in 1951 and 1955. His previous books include *Two Anglican Essays* and *The Young Lloyd George*.

STEPHEN KOSS (b. 1940) holds three degrees from Columbia University, New York, where he is currently Professor of History. He has been a Fulbright Scholar, 1964–5, a Fellow of the John Simon Guggenheim Memorial Foundation, 1972–3, and a Fellow of the Netherlands Institute for Advanced Study, 1975–6. In 1972–3 he was also an academic visitor at the London School of Economics. His books include biographical studies of various Liberal Party figures, including *Fleet Street*

*Radical: A. G. Gardiner and the 'Daily News'*. His most recently published work is an interpretive account of *Nonconformity in Modern British Politics*. He has written numerous reviews and articles for scholarly journals on both sides of the Atlantic, and is a regular contributor to the *New Statesman* and the *Times Literary Supplement*.

ARTHUR MARWICK (b. 1936) has been Professor of History at the Open University since 1969. He was formerly Lecturer in History at Edinburgh University, 1960–9, and Visiting Professor, University of Buffalo, 1966–7. His previous publications include *The Explosion of British Society; Clifford Allen, the Open Conspirator; The Deluge: British Society and the First World War* and *Britain in the Century of Total War*.

IAN NISH (b. 1926) has been Reader at the Department of International History, London School of Economics, since 1974. He was formerly Lecturer at Sydney University, 1958–62, and Visiting Professor, Yale University, 1969–70. His previous publications include *The Anglo-Japanese Alliance, 1894–1907, The Story of Japan* and *Alliance in Decline, 1908–23*.

ALAN SKED (b. 1947) was educated at the University of Glasgow and Merton College, Oxford, and is currently Lecturer in International History at the London School of Economics. He is at present writing a book on the Habsburg monarchy and a survey of British politics since 1945.

JOHN STEVENSON (b. 1946) was educated at Worcester College and Nuffield College, Oxford. He has been Lecturer in History at Oriel College, Oxford, since 1971. His previous publications include *Popular Protest and Public Order* (edited with R. Quinault) and the *Longman Atlas of Modern British History, 1700–1970* (with Chris Cook).

DONALD WATT (b. 1928) has been Professor of International History in the University of London since 1972. He was educated at Oriel College, Oxford. He was editor of the *Survey of International Affairs*, Royal Institute of International Affairs, 1962–72, and has been Secretary of the Association of Contemporary History since 1967. Among his many publications are *Britain and the Suez Canal; Britain Looks to Germany; Personalities and Policies; A History of the World in the Twentieth Century (Part 1)* and *Hitler's Mein Kampf* (editor).

# 1 Metternich and the Federalist Myth

## ALAN SKED

It is among the peculiarities of our time [wrote Charles Morgan in 1946][1] that the introduction of Metternich's name into conversation is generally a cause of embarrassment. Few are eager to declare themselves on that subject. In the early years of the twentieth century it was easy enough. Everyone, at any rate in England and America, had persuaded himself, through many years of security, that freedom was broadening down, and would continue to broaden down, from precedent to precedent. Metternich, therefore, was comfortably written off as timid and oppressive. He had defenders but their defence of him was highly technical. How adroit he was, they said, how long the old juggler succeeded in keeping the balls in the air! That his game and the way he played it were immoral was scarcely doubted, and argument concerning his policy began with an assumption that, even from his own point of view, he failed because in the end, Liberalism was happily triumphant.

Morgan, of course, disagreed[2]—'Today criticism of Metternich as facile as that will not pass muster'—and his disagreement reflected the pessimism of the immediate post-war world. Liberalism was no longer happy and triumphant and Metternich, as a result, was no longer a spiritual outcast. Nor had he been, in fact, for some time, even in the Atlantic world, for during the pre-war decade a number of sympathetic biographies, often reflecting the outlook of the Austrian historian von Srbik,[3] had helped revise his reputation.[4] With the end of the war this process of revisionism continued and it was immeasurably aided by the onset of the 'cold war'. If Srbik himself had sometimes been willing to take Metternich's excuses at face value this predilection proved often irresistible for the many central European exiles who in the 1950s began to write 'cold war' history in America.[5] Victims of Europe's totalitarian upheavals, they were intellectually seduced by the stability of the 'Metternich system' and came to visualise the Austrian State Chancellor as a nineteenth-century John Foster Dulles, stemming the tide of red revolution in Europe.

There was, of course, always one great weakness in their arguments. Given his use of the secret police, his abhorrence of liberal and nationalist movements, not to mention his support of military interventions against such regimes, Metternich could easily be pictured as Khrushchev rather than Dulles, a parallel which often carried much more conviction. This weakness, however, was usually evaded on the part of the revisionists by the deployment of two distinct but complementary lines of defence: Metternich, according to their interpretation, had seldom exercised any influence upon internal policy; such influence as he did possess was employed in the support of efforts to create a less centralised, more federal Habsburg monarchy. At heart, therefore, he was no reactionary after all. Somewhere beneath his sneering exterior was a liberal of sorts who was struggling to get out.

Mr Peter Viereck invoked exactly this defence in the classic revisionist article of 1951:[6] 'To a great extent, the "Francis system" or the "Police Chief Sedlnitzky system" would be the proper name for the repressive side of the "system" named after a man who ruled his emperor in foreign policy but not in internal administration.'
And again:[7]

> . . . Metternich in 1817 also urged freer institutions for the rest of the empire, with an embryonic parliament which, once started, would inevitably have assumed an ever greater governing power. Possibly central Europe might even have followed England's evolutionary road of 1832 towards a freer society instead of the revolutionary road of 1848 and 1918. His plans (to summarize from two different memoranda of 1817) included a 'deliberative body of notables', partly elected by provincial diets and partly appointed to represent the country in 'scrutiny of the budget and every law'. Far-sighted, in view of the Slav and Italian revolts that were to wreck the monarchy, is his plan of separate constitutions and separate chancellors for the chief national minorities, protecting them from the oppression of Germanization.

Mr Viereck, unfortunately, had overstepped the mark. Most of the research that had been done or was still to be done on Metternich and the secret police in no way indicated that his role had been a minor one.[8] Nor did the published sources. Kübeck noted in his diary, for instance, that Sedlnitzky acted as if he were the Chancellor's manservant and that this annoyed the Emperor.[9] In 1963, however, the second line of defence was powerfully reinforced by the publication of Arthur G. Haas's book, *Metternich: Reorganization and Nationality, 1813–1818*,[10] which, based as it was on thorough archival research, appeared to confirm the revisionist interpretation of the 1817 memoranda referred to by Viereck. Haas based most of his conclusions on documents referring to Lombardy-Venetia although the book dealt also with Illyria, a subject which he has treated elsewhere.[11] According to Haas,[12] Metternich in 1817 had attempted 'to form the so badly shaken Monarchy into an inwardly balanced and stable union of constituent states with equal rights', something that constituted 'a notable example of statesmanlike foresight and intelligence'. Haas's work was well received by a number of experts.[13] Professor Berthier de Sauvigny in France for instance, agreeing that Metternich had wanted to remould the Empire, wrote in a review[14] that it had been Metternich's aim 'to bring the turbulent Hungarian nation back into line by balancing and surrounding it with other entities endowed with the same privileges and competences'. In Austria, it obviously influenced Professor Heinrich Benedikt's conception of Metternich as he appears in *Kaiseradler über dem Appenin. Die Oesterreicher in Italien, 1700 bis 1866,*[15] for there Benedikt wrote of him: 'he was in favour of a federal state, provincial diets and pointed to the dangers of centralization in the Emperor's patriarchal rule . . .' Paul Schroeder expressed some doubts about Haas's general thesis in a very short but generally commendatory review in the *American Historical Review*[16] but nowhere was the thesis subjected to a thorough-going critique. Now that the cold war seems all but over, perhaps it is time to look at the evidence again.

The federalist defence, however, did not emerge suddenly from the swishing nibs of post-war revisionists. Its birth can be documented to 1848. 'The revolution of 1848', Sir Lewis Namier has written,[17] 'was universally expected.' In the Austrian Empire, according to Professor Friedrich Walter,[18] 'it came as no real surprise to anybody'. The Archduke John, for example, was writing in December 1847:[19] '. . . the present state of affairs is beyond help, it is altogether too late'. Metternich himself by this time had reached exactly the same conclusion:[20] 'I am no prophet and do not know what will happen, yet I am an old doctor and can distinguish temporary from fatal illness; we are now dealing with the latter. We shall hold out for as long as we can, but I despair of the outcome.' When at the beginning of the following year he again surveyed events, he wrote with not a little irony:[21] 'The past year has been the most confusing of all that I have lived through. . . . The year 1848 will clear things up.' And so it did, with Metternich's vision of impending doom coming very close to fulfilment. The Austrian nobility, however, had its excuses ready as soon as the revolutions erupted. The concept they seized on was federalism: the revolution had broken out because Francis I had refused to give more power to the Diets and had persisted in his refusal even in spite of the advice of his Chancellor. The faith they placed in this federalist defence and the full implications of it can best be gauged by reference to two primary sources: the explanation of the revolutions given by the army to its troops,[22] and—more pertinent to the argument developed here—Metternich's own defence as he pleaded it to Hübner.[23]

Very soon after the outbreak of the revolutions, FML. Baron Hammerstein, an intimate of Prince Windischgrätz and chief of the Galician General Command, informed the Praesidium of the *Hofkriegsrath* in Vienna that he had distributed amongst his N.C.O.s a text designed to help them explain the causes of events to the troops.[24] He wrote:

> . . . it is necessary to instruct the men, in their mother tongues and in a manner appropriate to their intelligence, both in the causes which have led to the change in our form of government and the difference[s] between the past and present [situations]. It is necessary [also] to give them some idea of the meaning of the expressions, *Constitution* and *Freedom of the Press*, which today are on everybody's lips, in order . . . to show them that this change in the form of government involves no change in the circumstances of soldiers *of any rank*, [and] that they now as before have the same duties and are subject to the same laws.

Enclosed was a copy of the text prepared for his N.C.O.s to show just how effective a piece of propaganda it was. It began:[25]

> His Majesty, our Emperor, has, as you will know from your oath to the colours, many other lands apart from Hungary and Transylvania—e.g. Austria, Galicia, Bohemia, Tyrol, etc., etc.,—all of which when taken together make up the Austrian Empire.
>
> Since each of these lands makes up a kingdom or a duchy in itself, our Emperor does not rule them all in the same way, but after the manner laid down by previous kings or dukes. Only in Hungary and Transylvania was there the opportunity of choosing from each county or *Stuhl* deputies to attend the Diets in Pressburg or Klausenburg in order to report to a Commissioner appointed by the Emperor what had happened in the land and what its needs were. The Commissioner, having been informed by the deputies what was the best thing to do, would then report to the Emperor, who in turn would issue orders. In other kingdoms and lands no such procedures existed. Orders were issued, rather, once the reports of the governors, circle officials and magistrates had been read.
>
> In this way, as can best be seen here, things were well looked after. However, the Emperor can look after lands much better and more quickly if a certain number of intelligent men are chosen to voice the wishes and requests of a country in a Diet, as in the case of Hungary . . .

The *Leitfaden* then went on to explain that the Viennese revolution had taken place when a deputation, whose purpose it had been to secure a constitution from the Emperor, had become the focus for demonstrations and riots. The most significant point about the document, however, was the view propounded by the traditional military leadership that the chief impulse behind the revolutionary tremors then shaking the Habsburg Empire was a federalist one, that the need felt in other parts of the monarchy for institutions similar to the traditional ones of the Magyar Constitution, had precipitated the final disaster.

Metternich, *on the very eve of the revolutions* (1 March 1848), in an eloquent and famous plaidoyer, had reached what has traditionally been interpreted as the same conclusion:[26]

In 1817 I proposed to the Emperor Francis the creation at the centre of the monarchy of a deliberative body of notables from our various provinces. The memorandum in which I set out my ideas was a detailed, conscientious piece of work which went to the bottom of things. It would no longer correspond to the needs of the present but, essentially it indicated, to my way of thinking, the only possible solution to the great problem of getting the different races of the Empire to coexist within the context of an organic union. Over the years I saw my work on the desk of the Emperor who would not or could not come to a decision on this great and, in my opinion, pressing question. One day in 1826, having overcome a serious illness which had almost killed him, on finding me at his side, he suddenly said to me: 'Do you know what tormented me most when I thought I was going to die? It was the thought of leaving your report of 1817 behind on my desk. But now, this very day, I shall refer it to the State Council.' However, he did nothing about it. One day in 1835, that is eighteen years after the composition of my report, when I was offering him my regards, he himself returned to the theme, saying: 'Before the year has ended, this question shall be settled.' Two months later he died.

Without a doubt, it is indispensible to adapt our provincial diets to the needs of the time and to extend their powers. But that will not be enough. There will also be a need at the centre for a body sitting at Vienna (I leave Hungary aside for the present) composed of delegates from the provincial Diets. This would be a provincial chamber and not a chamber of deputies, a *Volkshaus* whose members would be elected in the same way as those of the provincial diets. One could not superimpose assemblies elected from the same votes one on top of the other without creating among them an antagonism that would arrest and paralyse their working.

Let us also guard against destroying the provinces as individual units and obliterating the position of the Emperor as sovereign of each one of these provinces. This would make the links that unite them with the dynasty, the personal element, disappear and with it the most effective means at the disposal of the crown to prevent conflicts and struggles between the various races that live within the monarchy . . .

Haas and Viereck, therefore, have only been presenting the excuse put forward by the Austrian nobility in 1848: the Empire succumbed to revolution because Francis I, against Metternich's advice, refused to federalise the monarchy. This is a claim which has been widely accepted; it deserves to be critically examined.

Metternich's plans for the reorganisation of the imperial government centred around two institutions which he hoped to see created—a Ministry of the Interior and an Imperial Council or 'Reichsrath'. There is some difficulty in deciding exactly how the latter was meant to operate for the simple reason that the memorandum in which Metternich originally proposed the establishment of this body to the Emperor has not survived. In spite of valiant efforts on the part of Metternich himself in the 1840s, by the editors of his *Nachgelassene Papiere*[27] and by many historians,[28] it has simply never been discovered. Nevertheless, the editors of his published papers included amongst these documents some 'comments' on this institution, composed by Metternich, significantly enough after 1848—and hence decades after the original proposal was drafted[29]—and from these, it would appear that the *Reichsrath* is the *Volkshaus* which Metternich described to Hübner:

Since I considered it an unquestionable fact that the Empire was enjoying a period of extraordinary good fortune and that the question to be settled was not whether this was so but merely how this could be exploited, the task for me was limited to discovering *for what end* and *how*. The first [question] gave rise to the idea of strengthening the central power; the other made me wonder whether this strengthening should be sought in the idea of centralization as the French think of the matter, or with respect to the basically rather separate nature of the component parts of the Empire. As far as I was concerned there could be no doubt about my verdict. It was a question of strengthening the Empire, not of transforming it, and for this reason I took my stance on the principle of a *legislative adjustment* of the parts and the corresponding *strengthening of the central power* regarding legislative and administrative matters.

Representatives of the estates existed in the parts and for this reason a representation had also to be created at the centre. At that time, in spite of the inevitable difficulties associated with such a structure, the exercise was a much easier one to plan out than it would be today. I, therefore, proposed besides a revision of the powers of the diets, the creation of a *Reichsrath* that was to consist of members appointed at the centre by the Emperor along with deputies from the estates. The jurisdiction of this newly to be created central point was

to be the examination of the budget and of those laws which concerned the generality.

In order to consolidate these proposals Metternich, according to a
memorandum of 1817, had planned to have the internal administration
of the Empire come under the jurisdiction of a Ministry of the Interior.
Once again, he seemed to be paying particular attention to 'national'
scruples because he proposed the appointment, at a level immediately
below that of the Supreme Chancellor or Minister of the Interior, of four
'chancellors' each of whom would be responsible for a specific part of the
Empire, namely one for Bohemia-Moravia-Galicia, one for Dalamatia
and Illyria, one for Austria and one for Lombardy-Venetia:[30]

> In this organization, the Minister of the Interior is the guardian and
> representative of the unity of the government.
> Each chancellor in the Ministry represents the direct local interests
> of the provinces under his jurisdiction which require consideration.
> He defends the concept of the unity of government and the govern-
> ment's principles, given the circumstances, in the most enlightened
> sense, *against* the provinces.

In another memorandum to which these proposals were attached,
Metternich described the principles which lay behind them:[31]

> Whereas the *unity of all executive organs* that an *administration* has at its
> disposal over *homogenous component parts* offers governments the most ef-
> fective and acceptable expression of strength possible, one can also be
> sure that *the complete fusing together of mutually alien parts* will result only in
> violent revolution . . . I would regard *any system of complete fusion of the in-
> dividual parts of the monarchy which would be brought about by an arbitrary act
> as an idea without substance and as an even more dangerous one today when any
> undertaking of this kind would necessitate the discussion of a Central Representa-
> tion of the Nations ( however nonsensical this might be in itself under the present
> circumstances).*

What is one to make of all this?
In the first place, it seems clear that Metternich was almost exclusively
concerned with the role of the central government whose powers he
wished to strengthen. That was the end to which all his proposals were
directed and in his 'comments' on the missing memorandum he was absolutely clear about this. The only question in his mind was how he
might achieve his objective. True to form, he was equally clear how not to
do it: there was never any question of devolving power from the centre—
the central tenet of modern federalist thinking—because, as Metternich
put it, '*the unity of all executive organs* that an *administration* has at its disposal

*over homogenous component parts* offers governments the most effective and acceptable expression of strength possible'. Hence the regional chancellors were envisaged merely as under-secretaries of a centralised Ministry of the Interior explaining government policy to the provinces they had to deal with. They were part and parcel of the central government machinery which was to be totally centred in Vienna.

The Reichsrath, too, was to sit in Vienna as part of the central government. Its exact role was not made immediately clear either in Metternich's 'comments' or in his plaidoyer to Hübner. On the other hand, it is clear that he envisaged it as an advisory body which would meet at the Emperor's request and that the provincial representatives would merely be additions to a number of imperial advisers who would already have been appointed. All of these people would have been consulted only on such matters as the Emperor saw fit to seek their advice. Meanwhile, presumably the most important advice would still have been sought in the *Staatsrath*,[32] which Metternich never spoke of abolishing. Perhaps he supposed that in any case the nominated members of the *Reichsrath*—who were there almost certainly to 'guide' their provincial colleagues—would have included members of the *Staatsrath*. Since the *Reichsrath* itself, however, had no powers whatever, this would hardly have mattered. It had a built-in government bias; it was only advisory; it could only advise when asked; and even its links with the provinces were tenuous—'one could not superimpose assemblies elected from the same votes one on top of the other'. Why then should members of the *Staatsrath* have been expected to waste their time on such a body?

These provincial delegates to Vienna would, however, have performed one invaluable function. Given their personal links with the provincial Diets, the latter would have been tempted to deal with the imperial government through them. This was the 'increase' in the power of the Diets that Metternich had really meant. Naturally, it would have been an illusion—the *Reichsrath* had no power—but Metternich hoped that the illusion itself would keep the provinces contented and let the bureaucrats get on with their jobs. Or in his own words: 'I took my stance on a *legislative adjustment of the parts* and the corresponding *strengthening of central power.*' It is difficult to believe that he ever meant to increase the powers of diets inside the provinces themselves. Certainly he never outlined any such proposals and whenever he talked of extending the powers of diets he went immediately on to the *Reichsrath*. It is safe, therefore, to assume that the two ideas were really the same. If Metternich had really wanted significantly to extend the local powers of diets, he most certainly would have made this clear both to Hübner and in his 'comments'. Fortunately, the matter is one that can be finally resolved by reference to yet another document. When in 1818 Metternich was asked to advise the Prussian government on exactly this kind of issue he gave the following advice:[33]

According to my firm conviction, the King ought to go no further than the formation of provincial Diets in *a very carefully-considered, circumscribed form*. If the idea of a central representative body, chosen from the different Diets, is referred to by me, this is because a similar idea already exists in the Royal [i.e. Prussian] Declaration, which is known to the public and is the only one possible. *Beyond this all is pure revolution. Will these very limited ideas not also lead to revolution? This question the King should ponder deeply before he decides.*

His idea of bringing provincial nobles to the capital, he told the Prussians, was conceived in the hope that they might there be '*guided aright more easily.*' He also believed that they would be '*individual, mutually hostile deputies—far from ready to unite for* ONE *purpose of state.*'

The fact that this advice was given in 1818 should also be noted, since according to Professor Haas our traditional picture of Metternich is only conceivable with regard to the years after Kotzebue's assassination in 1819.[34] Professor Haas claims to have discovered a 'new Metternich' in the years before then. Like the 'new Nixon', however, he turns out to be a purely imaginary being. The truth is that when Metternich told the Emperor that his aim was only 'the careful regulation of the reasonable long-existing differences sanctioned by speech, climate, manners and customs in the various parts of the monarchy, under a strong, well-organized government', which aim could be obtained 'with the least possible modification of the present forms of government', he was by no means attempting to mislead the Emperor into approving a grand new federalist conception of the Empire—which is what Professor Haas would have us believe[35]—but simply stating the truth as he saw it.[36]

Why Metternich believed that it was necessary to state this truth so forcefully and at such length is also quite apparent. The true origin of Metternich's proposals of 1817 was not a desire on his part to transform the monarchy. It was, rather, his fear that the Emperor Francis himself might do just that. Haunted by the suspicion that the revolutionary forces which had dominated Europe for so long had suffered only a temporary defeat and would once again arise to assail the redoubts of absolutism, Francis was deeply concerned to consolidate and strengthen his imperial position. Like Metternich he envisaged doing this by extending the powers and range of activities of the Austrian secret police; but unlike Metternich he did not reject the expedients of Josephinist or Jacobin rule. He was powerfully attracted to the notion of ruling the Empire entirely from the centre, dispensing with the diets altogether and relying solely on the police and the bureaucrats. Since 1811 he had refused to summon a Hungarian Diet and it was summoned again only in 1825. On 25 May 1814 he had Bellegarde extinguish the electoral college of the

Kingdom of Italy and he gave his reasons for doing so as follows:[37]

> Since these lands have been conquered there can be no discussion of constitution, senate or any other bodies or representations. Consequently, the electoral colleges, in so far as this has not already been done, are to be dismissed and no one, other than [Bellegarde] or the Provisional Government are to make decisions or to give orders in my name.

Metternich, therefore, had every reason to fear that Francis would adopt a system of rule that would be personal in the extreme. This is why, in his *Vorträge* he explicitly rejected *any system of complete fusion of the individual parts of the monarchy which would be brought about by an arbitrary act (Gewaltstreich)*; this is why he deliberately conjured up the spectre of a central imperial parliament; this is why he repeatedly returned to the failure of Joseph II; and why he also rejected 'the idea of centralization as the French think of the matter'. The Prince Chancellor wanted, just as much as his master, to see a strongly governed, centralised Empire. As a professional diplomat, however, he saw the expediency of retaining the Diets as monuments to the cultural diversity of that Empire; as an aristocrat he knew how they kept the local nobility employed; as a conservative, he recognised their traditionalist influence; and as a true reactionary, he was determined to render them impotent. His *Vorträge* of 1817 were, therefore, essentially the products of his diplomatic training. 'By all means centralize the Monarchy', he was telling the Emperor, 'but remember to keep up appearances.' The whole of Metternich's career was devoted to keeping up appearances and this was just another example of his doing so. The people he was trying to impress were the provincial notables. He wanted to negate their nuisance value.

The Emperor, in the end, took only half Metternich's advice: he retained the Diets in the emasculated form on which they could both agree; but after toying for a short period of time with a Ministry of the Interior, he let that idea drop; similarly, he never created a *Reichsrath*. The result was, in Metternich's eyes, that the central government was never strong enough to impose its will efficiently. That is what he meant when in his retirement he often complained that 'administration' had taken the place of 'government'. It never crossed his mind that too much power had been concentrated at the centre.

Metternich's fear that the Emperor Francis would attempt to rule without the Diets serves also to explain a lie in the documents. In his *Vortrag* of 27 October 1817, Metternich stated that he did not intend to raise the question of Hungary; yet he did have this to say:[38]

> Your Majesty has often heard outspoken references made about overthrowing the Hungarian constitution: indeed in 1811, at a time when a

similar enterprise brought about the inevitable ruin of the Monarchy, and in 1813 when, although it did not come to that, [such an enterprise] would at least have rendered impossible any show of strength by the Monarchy, this question was discussed as if it were simply a matter of a decree. When I at that time expressed my opinion in a sense very opposed to this idea, I in no way denied that it was necessary, given time and opportunity, to plan out in advance, in a spirit of cold objectivity and calm impartiality, the great work of a possible civilizing of Hungary—for that is what the question in hand really was—together with its most precise consequences.

He did not, however, pursue this point and for one good reason. When Napoleon had been at the height of his power before the Moscow expedition, Metternich had attempted, but without success, to secure the aid of Bonapartist troops in support of a *coup d'état* in Hungary.[39] With the fall of Napoleon he gave up this idea and decided instead to incorporate Hungary into a centralised but legitimist political framework. There was no point at all, therefore, in reminding Francis of his previous plans to abolish the Hungarian Diet. A major point of his new proposals was that they would help to discipline the Hungarians instead:[40]

It is obvious that as a result of this organization the Hungarian and Transylvanian chancelleries will sink from the high level at which they stand today to that of the administration in general . . . In this way, I foresee the first step towards an appropriate reformation of both lands which will have to be prepared gradually.

Metternich believed that the increase in the strength of the central government which was at the heart of his proposals would enable him to emasculate the Hungarian constitution:[41]

. . . the more the organs of the highest authority are strengthened, the less [troublesome?] will become the obstacles which today so powerfully prevent that rational alteration in the administrative and constitutional circumstances of Hungary, an alteration which would exceedingly benefit the country itself.

For this reason, the verdict of Erzsébet Andics seems a highly convincing one:[42] 'one of the fundamental aims of . . . Metternich's proposals was in reality to take away from Hungary her ancient rights and her, albeit very limited, independence; not, however, to endow other peoples with *similar* rights.' The Austrian statesman (probably Count Schnirding) who published the book *Oesterreich im Jahre 1840* began his first chapter with the words: 'The Austrian constitution in all the provinces with the exception of Hungary and **Transylvania is a purely monarchical** one.' It was always Metternich's aim—as Andics's book so convincingly demonstrates—to get rid of that exception. The Austrian Empire which he envisaged, and which his 1817 proposals entirely presupposed, was a predominantly German, aristocratic and highly centralised one in which the provinces were to be encouraged to indulge their local patriotisms so long as they obeyed the orders of the central government. In order, finally, to demonstrate the truth of this interpretation, let us examine Haas's evidence with regard to Lombardy-Venetia.

### The Case of Lombardy-Venetia

The only comprehensive modern work on Austrian rule in eighteenth- and nineteenth-century Italy is Professor Heinrich Benedikt's *Kaiseradler über dem Appenin*. Professor Benedikt, as has been noted,[43] has accepted Haas's thesis that Metternich '. . . was in favour of a federal state, provincial diets and [that] he pointed to the dangers of centralization in the Emperor's patriarchal rule . . .' Yet he evinces a certain reluctance to approve the federalist position:[44] 'Perhaps it would have been better to strengthen the diets at the cost of the imperial power; perhaps Francis I secured his Empire for a longer time through centralization than would have been the case with a federal solution.'

Moderation, however, is not always a virtue. Had Professor Benedikt examined the evidence more carefully he would have discovered that Haas is as wrong on the Italian provinces as he is on the Empire as a whole. His 'less known Metternich . . . capable of submitting original ideas or reshaping the empire's inner structure'[45] is just as absent in the history of Lombardy-Venetia as he is in the history of Austria.

As Professor Haas would have it,[46] 'Metternich's conception of nationality in the post-war years was cultural as well as political, although what may be considered his national policy went beyond a concern for cultural autonomy in making provisions for administrative and even political home rule.' The professor concedes that:[47] '. . . as perceptive as such a policy might have been in most parts of the empire, in Lombardy-Venetia it was already behind events.' Truth to tell, however, in Lombardy-Venetia, it was so far behind events that it never in fact existed. There is no evidence at all that Metternich ever wanted political or administrative home rule for the north Italian provinces and where Haas finds the evidence on which to base his opposite conclusions is just about as clear as his following statement:[48]

> Metternich must be credited with having the ideas and striving to open the emperor's eyes to an admirably sensible program—a program almost fascinating in the way it anticipated much of what was arrived at in futile hindsight decades—even a century—later.

About three decades after 1817 the Habsburgs lost Lombardy; about four decades later they lost Venetia; about one century later they lost their empire altogether. Even his worst detractor would not accuse Metternich of having wanted to anticipate these events.

On one matter, of course, Professor Haas is absolutely right. Metternich did encourage cultural autonomy and nearly all the evidence that Haas's book contains is evidence in support of this cultural policy. The motives behind it, however, were in no sense new or enlightened. Quite the opposite. Metternich intended, to quote Professor Rath,[49] 'to use the traditional Habsburg policy of *divide et impera* in coping with the new liberal and national spirit prevailing in certain quarters in Lombardy'. That this was so is clearly demonstrated by Metternich's letter of 15 May 1814 to the Austrian commander in Milan, Marshal Bellegarde,[50] in which he expressed great anxiety about 'the so-called Italian spirit' which was being stirred up and instructed Bellegarde that he should 'in no manner' favour it. 'The best counterpoise against this Italian pretension', wrote Metternich, 'is without doubt to be found in parcelling out Italy'.

As far as Austrian Italy was concerned, the Chancellor remarked:

> For several centuries many local animosities and jealousies have existed in Italy. These hatreds have never allowed the union of all the diverse elements [found in the peninsula] and they have survived. The territory allotted to Austria is bounded by the *Ticino* and the *Po*; nothing, therefore prevents us from attempting to revive the *Lombard* spirit.

If Metternich believed that 'one cannot coin everything with a German stamp', he was equally determined that there would be no Italian one either. In a similar fashion it was also his policy 'to make people [in Galicia] think of themselves as true Galicians first in order to stop them thinking of themselves as Poles'.[51] In both cases his was an anti-national policy explicitly thought out as such.

In Italy, moreover, Metternich had another reason to pursue such a policy. Austria had accepted Lombardy towards the end of April 1814, only about a fortnight before the arrival in Paris of the Lombard deputation, and had done so with some reluctance. The Archduke John, for instance, noted in his diary:[52]

> I am not at all pleased with the division of territory. Austria has received a great deal in Italy to its misfortune. I would never have placed boundaries beyond the Po and the Chiese. I would have given Lombardy to the King of Sardinia as King of the Lombards, because it would be useful to have a powerful prince there, as it is in Holland in the north.

Metternich told Cardinal Consalvi[53] that at first the Austrians did not want Lombardy but had been forced to take it 'for the sole reason . . . *of killing Italian Jacobinism in Milan'*. Milan, according to Metternich, was the centre of radical agitation for the unification of the whole peninsula under constitutional government. To secure her Venetian territories, therefore, Austria had required Lombardy. During the whole of his career, however, Metternich had only one remedy for centres of Jacobinism or radicalism—he brought them under his tightest control.

The real motives behind Metternich's policy towards northern Italy had very little, therefore, to do with the home rule of national minorities. Yet Professor Haas has chosen to ignore this evidence[54] and clutches instead after straws. For example, he points out that when the deputation sent to Paris by the Provisional Government (which came to power in Milan after the 'revolution' there on 20 April 1814 and which was in nominal charge until Bellegarde proclaimed Austrian rule on 12 June) met with Metternich on 6 May, the latter encouraged the belief that an autonomous kingdom under an Austrian archduke 'might well be permissible'.[55] One wonders whether Professor Haas at times knows the difference in meaning between 'autonomous' and 'separate' but be that as it may, he fails to put this incident into its proper context. The deputation had been sent to Paris with specific instructions to secure from the powers 'the absolute independence of the new Italian state', along with 'the greatest possible extension . . . of boundaries' and a 'liberal constitution'.[56] Metternich had to tell them—what until then they surely did not know—that there was to be no independent state and that Lombardy instead would become part of the Austrian Empire. He could obviously foresee their disappointment so that when Count Litta reacted to his news by proposing as second best the formation of an autonomous Italian kingdom under an Austrian prince, Metternich did all he could to soften the blow by foreclosing none of the options. His sympathy, however, was purely diplomatic. He knew, as the Lombards did not want to know, that between a possibility and a likelihood there is all the difference in the world. The dirty work, in any case, he could safely leave to others. Francis I received the delegation on 7 May and on the twenty-seventh and at first even he was prepared to offer sympathy. On 7 May he told the delegates that they would receive much that would make them proud to be Austrians. By the end of the month, however, he had stiffened his tone:[57] 'Emperor Francis's words at the interview showed that the Habsburgs intended to be absolute master of both Venetia and Lombardy. The deputies could turn to them only as docile subjects beseeching their paternal ruler to grant their wishes'. He said: 'You belong to me by right of transfer and conquest.' The deputies were quick to see the point. Confalonieri, one of their number who had taken up the issue with the British representative Lord Bentinck, a man whose sympathy for the Italian cause was well known, wrote:[58] 'We will do what we can but we have no bayonets . . . it is a question of seeing what a master will be willing to grant us . . . we have come to ask for the independence of a country that has already been sold.' Metternich had also put pressure on the British to bring the Lombards round.[59] Bentinck told Confalonieri:[60] 'Austria has a government against which its citizens have less right to revolt than any other; in the history of this house, right up until the present there has been no sign of abuse of power or of force . . . I will do nothing, nor can I do anything opposed to Austria; I will do everything to get you to agree, to make you see well in her.' And so the message got home. Metternich knew exactly what sort of a reception the delegates were in for; it was not in his interest to provoke them into immediate and intransigent opposition; and for this reason he sought to mollify their reactions. He made no promises, no commitments. He merely wanted them to get used to the idea of becoming Austrians. There was plenty of time to let them have the details when these were worked out later, even if, as must have been the case, he knew what Francis's views were in the meantime. Curiously, Professor Haas, who elsewhere attributes every word of Metternich's to diplomatic persuasion, is altogether loath to consider that he might ever have flattered the Italians.

When Haas states his principal theme, however, he at first appears to be on slightly firmer ground—if only at first. The nationality problem, he writes,[61] centred around 'specific, semi-political institutions which symbolized a special *national* status: the Italian chancellery in Vienna, an Italian supreme court for the Lombardy-Venetian kingdom and the Italian Viceroy in Milan'. He has, in fact, very little to say about the supreme court, which in any case could not have been expected to play an independent part in a monarchical state. The point at issue was whether it should sit in Vienna or Verona and that, in the final analysis, was a matter more of cultural policy than of political import and is not a matter for contention. Metternich would have preferred to have seen the legal traditions of Lombardy given much more support and opposed for instance the introduction of the Austrian civic code. With regard to the Italian Chancellery in Vienna, however, this was part of a scheme designed by Metternich to make central government stronger and more efficient. It was never meant to be a means of 'making Italian affairs relatively independent of central administration' or of assuring 'a separate status for the Italian possessions . . . on the highest level'.[62] Metternich was too well aware that in the final analysis the same men at the very top advised on internal policy for the monarchy as a whole. The Lombardo-Venetian Chancellor after all was to be only one under-secretary to a Minister of the Interior, who himself had no executive power. That, all of it, rested with one man who took all the decisions of any importance for all parts of the Empire—the Emperor himself. Thus there would have been little if any point in the creation of a 'separate status' for the Italian possessions in the heart of the bureaucracy. It could not have corresponded with reality. Metternich, in effect, had merely been streamlining the filing system—an important consideration in a mammoth bureaucracy. It was an important consideration also, if really an extraneous one, that Italians were happy to think that as a result of his streamlining, their correspondence with Vienna would land on the desks of a particular section of the bureaucracy. This might well have happened anyway. Metternich's reorganisation would only have made this more certain. An Italian as Chancellor also meant that the section's chief would have had some familiarity with the land he was dealing with. Yet, once again, this would probably have been so in any case. Finally, there would have been no guarantee that he would have been predisposed on account of his origins to adopt a 'nationalist' line on policy—Francis only chose men who were 'patriots for him'. The Italians, therefore, as Metternich well knew and appreciated, would have been gaining little from the chancery other than the adjective—and that, as Professor Haas should have noted—was 'Lombardo-Venetian', not 'Italian'.

At this stage, Haas's case is left resting with the Viceroy. That this is so, he explains, is due to the fact that, 'In Italy there was a more recent tradition of direct home-rule and thus the viceroy was always more important than the provincial congregations.'[63] The latter bodies—and probably he means to refer to the *central* congregations which came to be the local form of diets in Lombardy and Venetia—did not figure, therefore, in the professor's list of 'specific, semi-political bodies which symbolized a special national status'. Professor Haas, it should be pointed out, only dismisses these with an *assertion*. He cannot *prove* that they did not matter to the Milanese because they did. When the Austrian Emperor abolished the electoral colleges of the Kingdom of Italy, the Provisional Government protested that it would have to receive a 'national representation' of some kind to replace them.[64] Moreover, by that it did not mean a viceroy, but elected delegates. However, there is, unfortunately, no evidence from this period—none at least that Professor Haas has been able to find—to prove that Metternich was supporting these efforts—a curious omission in the light of Haas's general thesis—and one suspects that it is on this account that the professor has seized on the office of viceroy.

With admirable consistency he manages to misinterpret this position also. He writes:[65] 'At best the "nationality minded" who turned to Austria necessarily or willingly had hoped for an independent realm ruled over by a Habsburg prince. At least they desired an autonomous entity governed by an Austrian archduke-viceroy whose position and status was equal to Eugene's. Upon this latter wish, Metternich came to form his policy for Lombardy-Venetia.' It must be remembered at this point, however, that in this context Professor Haas has already referred to Lombardy's 'more recent tradition of direct home-rule',[66] so that altogether his reader is left to suppose that Metternich wanted to see Lombardy-Venetia established as a self-governing unit under the Viceroy. There are only two problems concerning this argument. In the first place, there never had been any 'direct home rule' under Eugene; secondly, there is no evidence at all that Metternich ever wanted to give any real power to the Viceroy.

> Highly centralized as the government of the Kingdom of Italy was [writes Professor Rath][67] it is evident that all ultimate power lay in the hands of the King of Italy, Napoleon himself . . . With Eugene as Viceroy, Napoleon's own position was to be the executive and the administrator; Eugene his chief spokesman and lieutenant . . . Napoleon never took pains to conceal from his viceroy that his interest in Italy was wholly confined to what the Italian people 'could furnish him in money and men for his European wars.' He admonished Prince Eugene to bear in mind that he was always to consider 'France above all' and that he was to make Italy's interests 'inseparable to those of France'.

A quick dip into Napoleon's letters confirms this. When Eugene was first appointed to the post, Napoleon told him:[68]

> The public decree that I have signed defines the powers I am delegating to you. I am reserving for myself the most important of all—the power of directing your operations. Send me an account of your doings every day. It is only by degrees that you will come to understand how I look at everything . . . Keep my household and stable in order and make up all my accounts at least once a week; this is all the more necessary as they have no idea how to manage things here.

Napoleon at that time was writing from Milan. The same letter includes the following sentence: 'There is only one man here at Milan who really matters—the Minister of Finance: he is a hard worker and knows his job well.' The Minister concerned was Etienne Méjan, former secretary to the prefecture of the department of the Seine. So much for 'direct home-rule' in an 'autonomous entity'.

In any case, Metternich never intended to give the Austrian Viceroy any real authority at all, or at least there is no evidence to prove that he did. Like the Emperor himself he had a distinct vested interest in keeping power out of the hands of the Archdukes. They were members of the imperial family and therefore difficult to control. Status, on the other hand, was a different matter altogether; status they had to have, and Metternich was genuinely disappointed in the end when the Viceroy got none. This and this alone accounts for his remark[69] that 'the Milanese must first of all be convinced that the Viceroy shall be left with a really sufficient elbow-room for his activity in order to be good there . . .' The activity referred to by Metternich, however, was not 'political activity' in any sense save one. The Viceroy's job was that of putting on a show, keeping up appearances, showing the flag—very much indeed like the activity of a modern constitutional monarch, or better still a modern governor-general. Napoleon had been concerned to familiarise Eugene with exactly the same rules of public relations:[70]

> Learn their language; frequent their society; single them out for special attention at public functions; like what they like and approve what they approve . . . Nothing is so advisable as to get to know all their names and families. Don't show too much attention to foreigners: there is nothing to gain by it.

It was to be just one big deception:

> Show respect for the nation you govern, and show it all the more as you discover less ground for it. You will come to see in time that there is little difference between one nation and another. The aim of your administration is the happiness of my Italian peoples, and the first sacrifice you will have to make will be to fall in with certain of their customs you detest. In any position but Viceroy of Italy you may boast of being a Frenchman: but here you must forget it, and count yourself a failure unless the Italians believe you love them . . .
>
> Don't show my letters to a single soul, under any pretext whatsoever. It ought not to be known that I write to you or even that I write at all. Keep one room to which no one is admitted—not even your private secretaries.

The words were Napoleon's but they might just as well have been Metternich's with 'Austrian' in place of 'Frenchman'. The trouble was that Francis I was less interested in public relations, and his brother the Archduke Rainer was sent to Italy to do exactly this kind of job, but with less power and money and no tuition at all. As a result, the Austrian court at Milan became an exclusive, impersonal society run distinctly on the cheap, and even before the Viceroy's arrival Austrian protocol had offended everyone. Lord Stewart wrote to Viscount Castlereagh from Milan on 4 February 1816:[71] 'The brilliant court that was held here by the Viceroy Eugene has been succeeded by a System of Ceremony so rigid and seclusion so absolute that the Italians who pay nearly the same *Impôts* are discontented not to receive the same Engagements and Festivities.'

Rainer was not even allowed to correspond officially with other Italian sovereigns, something which Metternich objected to, not as Professor Haas seems to believe, because he wanted the Viceroy to conduct an independent foreign policy, but because he was thus deprived of a useful would-be source of diplomatic gossip. Metternich had hoped to have a reliable subordinate from the *Staatskanzlei* become Rainer's diplomatic secretary. In the end, however, Rainer was limited to pinning on medals and doling out a few minor pensions, and public relations were neglected. Austrian rule was based on bread *rather* than circuses; not the two together. This was all right until 1848 by which time even the bread ran out.

Metternich put his faith, therefore, not into any sort of 'specific, semi-political institution which symbolized a special *national* status'—all of these had propaganda value only—but in that traditional servant of the central bureaucracy, the provincial governor:[72] 'If Lombardy and Venetia were governed here under a *strong* governor and in line with principles announced and controlled—of course (of course!)—in Vienna, then Your Majesty will have repose, happiness and peace spread over the lands beyond the Alps.'

By *strong*, however, Metternich did not mean that the governor of Lombardy should have any more powers than those endowed upon an Austrian governor in any other province. Why favour the Italians in this way? A 'strong' governor was a man of strong personality and years of experience, one who was intimately acquainted with central government policies and attitudes, who was in agreement with them and who could be relied upon to override any opposition in the provinces themselves. He could, therefore, (or so Metternich believed) be relied upon to spare Vienna much of the paperwork which so clogged the works and which had in fact spurred Metternich to think of bureaucratic reform in the first place:[73] 'The whole question reduces itself actually to the following: should Vienna be bothered every month with 500 or only fifty issues from here? In the first case there would be a back-log of 400 which would cripple the course of things here.'

Metternich was much more concerned with the devolution of paper than the devolution of power for in an Empire as bureaucratic as the Habsburg one, there was no real correlation between the two. A strong provincial governor, in Metternich's opinion, could reduce the paperwork by three-quarters without in any way gaining in power thereby. Considering how trivial were many of the matters dealt with personally by the Emperor, this was an argument that Metternich wanted badly to exploit.

On 3 November 1817 Metternich reminded the Emperor how important it was to put some life into the bureaucratic machinery of the Kingdom of Lombardy-Venetia which had been in a state of some uncertainty regarding its future for the past three years.[74] He again stressed how important it was 'to meet the national spirit and amour-propre of the nation' and to prove to the Italians that they would not be treated 'in exactly the same way as, or rather be merged into the German provinces of the Monarchy'. He added, however:

> I do not doubt that it should be possible to attain this very useful end without encountering any great difficulties, even indeed without having to deviate from the general principles which serve as a basis for administering the other parts of the Monarchy, principles which indubitably must be retained for its well being, but which in practice can be easily modified in form.

The 'principles' he was referring to were those of centralisation. When he said that they had to be retained, he meant exactly that—Professor Haas notwithstanding. He realised of course that others, especially in the provinces, were less enthusiastic about his principles than he himself. He also feared that they perhaps might turn to nationalism. Dissimulation, however, rather than concession was his response and it took the form of a careful plan to display the institutions of early modern Europe to their best advantage in the nineteenth century. Always the pessimist, probably even he despaired of getting away with it but he was prepared to have a go. Moreover, as head of the Austrian imperial diplomatic service he was exceedingly well placed to balance appearance against reality. His essential function when all is said and done was to create an illusion of power on Austria's behalf in international affairs. Who can wonder, therefore, that he was similarly tempted to balance appearance against reality in domestic affairs? Were he alive today, he would be very amused to find his method retaining effect.

## Notes

1 Charles Morgan, *Reflections in a Mirror*, 2nd ser. (London, 1946) p. 39.

2 Ibid.

3 Heinrich Ritter von Srbik, the author, in particular, of the monumental *Metternich: der Staatsmann und der Mensch*, 2 vols (Munich, 1925).

4 See e.g. Arthur Herman's *Metternich* (London, 1932) and Hélène du Coudray's *Metternich* (New Haven, 1936); but cf. R. W. Seton-Watson's article 'Metternich and Internal Austrian Policy', *Slavonic Review*, XVII (1939) 539–55 and XVIII (1939) 129–41.

5 The revisionist process continued after the war with the publication of biographies such as Algernon Cecil's *Metternich, 1773–1859: a Study of his Period and Personality* (London, 1947) and Constantin de Grunwald's *Metternich* (London, 1953; originally published in Paris in 1938 as *La Vie de Metternich*). The 'cold war' period can be represented by Peter Viereck's *Conservatism Revisited* (New York, 1949) and his article 'New Views on Metternich', *Review of Politics*, XIII (1951) 211–28, even more so by Henry Kissinger's *A World Restored: Metternich, Castlereagh and the Problems of Peace, 1812–1822* (Boston, 1957) and Robert A. Kann's 'Metternich: a Reappraisal of his Impact on International Relations', *Journal of Modern History*, XXXII (1960) 333–9. Just how effective this process of revisionism was can be gauged from Hans Kramer's remarks on Metternich in *L'Europe du XIX^e et du XX^e Siècle. Interprétations Historiques*, ed. Max Beloff et al., 2 vols (Milan, 1959) Vol. II, pp. 995–6.

6 Viereck, *New Views on Metternich*, pp. 214–15.

7 Ibid., p. 225.

8 See in particular the work of Julius Marx, *Die österreichische Zensur im Vormärz* (Vienna, 1959). Also his 'Die Zensur der Kanzlei Metternichs', *Oesterreichische Zeitschrift für öffentliches Recht*, new ser., IV (1951) 170–237 and 'Metternich als Zensor', *Jahrbuch des Vereins für Geschichte der Stadt Wien*, XI (1954) 112–35. But note too Josef K. Myr's *Metternichs Geheimer Briefdienst* (Vienna, 1935) and more recently Paul W. Schroeder in his article 'Metternich Studies since 1925', *Journal of Modern History*, XXXIII (1961) 225, lists several other works which, he concludes, 'help to fill out the picture and reinforce the general impression that in respect to censorship and secret police, at least, Metternich, despite his disclaimers, did rule Austria'.

9 *Tagebuch des Carl Friedrich Freiherr Kübeck von Kübau*, ed. Kübeck (Vienna, 1909) Vol. 1, pt 2, pp. 622, 674.

10 Wiesbaden, 1963. Cf. the comments of Enno E. Kraehe in Kraehe (ed.), '*The Metternich Controversy*' (New York, 1971) p. 110.

11 A. G. Haas, 'Kaiser Franz, Metternich und die Stellung Illyriens', *Mitteilungen des Oesterreichischen Staatsarchivs*, XI (1958) 373–98, and *Metternich und die Slaven. Gedenkschrift Martin Göhring* (Wiesbaden, 1968) pp. 146–61.

12 Haas, 'Kaiser Franz', p. 397.

13 Professor John Rath, curiously enough, in his book *The Provisional Austrian Régime in Lombardy-Venetia, 1814–1815* (Austin, 1969), has nothing to say about Haas's work, even in passing.

14 In *Revue d'Histoire*, Vol. 12 (1965) 72.

15 Vienna and Munich, 1964; see p. 113.

16 Vol. 36 (1964) 341–2.

17 See his *1848: The Revolution of the Intellectuals* (London, 1962) p. 3.

18 See his *Die österreichische Zentralverwaltung* (Vienna, 1964) 3rd Part, Vol. 1, p. 1.

19 Ibid., p. 2.

20 Ibid., p. 1.

21 Ibid.

22 Vienna, *Kriegsarchiv, Centralkanzleiakten, Präsidialreihe* (1848) no. 150. FML. Hammerstein to Hofkriegsrath Praesidium, Lemberg, 28 March 1848.

23 *Le Comte de Hübner: Une Année de Ma Vie* (Paris, 1891) pp. 16–21.

24 See note 22 above.

25 Ibid.

26 Hübner, *Une Année de Ma Vie*, pp. 16–21.

27 Richard von Metternich and Alfons von Klinkowström (eds), *Aus Metternichs nachgelassenen Papieren* (Vienna, 1880–4). (Hereafter cited as *N.P.*)

28 See Alfred Stern, 'L'Idée d'une représentation centrale de l'Autriche conçue par le Prince de Metternich', *Revue Historique*, XXXI (1886) 313–26.

29 *N.P.*, Vol. 3, pp. 74–5.

30 Ibid., Vol. 3, p. 72.

31 Ibid., Vol. 3, p. 68.

32 The Council of State; the most senior body of civil servants advising the Emperor.

33 *N.P.*, Vol. 3, doc. 305. In the quotations that follow the italics are the author's.

34 Haas, *Metternich: Reorganization and Nationality*, p. 157.

35 Haas, *Metternich*, p. 10: 'It was one thing to have *brilliant* ideas; it was quite another to submit them in a manner acceptable to the Emperor. Thus Metternich's proposals for changing the administration of the interior were cut to assure the monarch that his minister's suggestions in no way involved exactly what they did involve—reform . . . Kaiser Franz regarded any reform with deepest suspicion . . . it could be taken into consideration only as a carefully-planned and minimal *re-forming* of that already at hand . . . hence Metternich's obvious and continuous lip-service.' (author's italics).

36 *N.P.*, Vol. 3, p. 68.

37 Ibid., p. 30. But see also R. J. Rath, *The Fall of the Napoleonic Kingdom of Italy (1814)*

(New York, 1941) p. 199.

Haas also writes (*Metternich*, p. 30), without fully appreciating the implications for his thesis, that '. . . for the emperor the prerogative of the monarch could only be conceived of as cloaked with unchallenged authority, and because all authority and initiative could emanate only from the monarch, no sort of independent political initiative could be tolerated. Provincial assemblies or estates were allowed to exist only through the pleasure of the monarch and only with the right to approve imperial measures . . . Furthermore, any other self-asserted rights or claims to legitimacy based on tradition or continued existence, as well as demands for the re-establishment of former assemblies of *national* chancelleries for Italy or Illyria, were discounted on the grounds that conquest by the emperor's armies had in effect created a *tabula rasa* . . .'

38  *N.P.*, Vol. 3, p. 64.
39  Erzsébet Andics, *Metternich und die Frage Ungarns* (Budapest, 1973) pp. 24–5.
40  *N.P.*, Vol. 3, p. 72.
41  *N.P.*, Vol. 3, p. 64.
42  Andics, *Metternich und die Frage Ungarns*, p. 32.
43  See note 15 above.
44  Ibid., p. 113.
45  Haas, *Metternich*, p. 6.
46  Ibid., p. 15.
47  Ibid.
48  Ibid., p. 152.
49  Rath, *Fall of the Napoleonic Kingdom*, p. 204.
50  Ibid., pp. 203–4.
51  Ibid.
52  Ibid., p. 189, footnote 34.
53  Ibid., pp. 189–90.
54  See Haas, *Metternich*, p. 28.
55  Ibid. But see also Ettone Verga, 'La deputazione dei collegi elettorali del regno d'Italia a Parigi nel 1814', *Archivo Storico Lombardo*, xxxi (1904). Also Rath, *Fall of the Napoleonic Kingdom*, pp. 192ff.
56  Rath, *Fall of the Napoleonic Kingdom*, p. 131.
57  Ibid., pp. 197–8.
58  See Cesere Spellanzon, *Storia del Risorgimento e dell'Unità d'Italia*, 4 vols (Milan, 1934–51) Vol. 1, p. 600.
59  Rath, *Provisional Austrian Régime*, p. 176.
60  Spellanzon, *Storia del Risorgimento*, p. 607.
61  Haas, *Metternich*, p. 9.
62  Ibid., pp. 84–5.
63  Ibid., p. 9.
64  Rath, *Fall of the Napoleonic Kingdom*, p. 199.
65  Haas, *Metternich*, p. 26.
66  Ibid., p. 9.
67  Rath, *Fall of the Napoleonic Kingdom*, pp. 18–19, 22.
68  *Napoleon's Letters*, ed. and translated by J. M. Thompson (London, 1964) pp. 123–6.
69  Haas, *Metternich*, p. 145.
70  Thompson (ed.), *Napoleon's Letters*, pp. 172–3.
71  Haas, *Metternich*, pp. 172–3.
72  Ibid., p. 86.
73  Ibid., p. 85.
74  *N.P.*, Vol. 3, p. 90.

# 2 Liberals on Trial
## JOHN GRIGG

What are we to think of the Liberal regime that held office for the best part of a decade before the outbreak of war in 1914? Was it a truly radical regime which achieved great things and would have achieved still greater but for a combination of human and divine malevolence? Or was it an organised hypocrisy, half-hearted in its approach to social reform, cynically traditionalist in its foreign policy, and stumbling at length into a calamity in which it deservedly perished? These questions have been, and remain, the subject of lively debate.

Any attempt to answer them must begin with a look at the electorate in the early years of the century. One necessary implication of representative government is that politicians, however radical, cannot move much farther or faster than the electors desire them to move; and the Liberals in 1905–14 had to reckon with an electorate that excluded not only all women but also about 40 per cent of adult males. Disraeli's Reform Act in 1867 enfranchised a section of the industrial working class, and Gladstone's in 1884 gave the vote to most agricultural workers, but between those two measures and the establishment of a truly democratic franchise in 1918 the electorate still remained disproportionately bourgeois. If Liberal leaders had all been firebrands with a mission to transform society their party would not have been a serious contender for power, let alone the party of government through three general elections. The inescapable difficulty was that people who had the vote tended not to want drastic social change, whereas most people who wanted drastic social change did not have the vote.

Another obstacle, of course, was the House of Lords, which since the Home Rule split had contained an overwhelming anti-Liberal majority. The Lords were usually careful not to block any Liberal legislation that was likely to be popular with the English masses, but felt that they could safely oppose measures subversive of the Constitution or the Established Church. They knew that England had no time for Irish Home Rule or Welsh Disestablishment, and they doubted the efficacy of Nonconformist anathemas against the 1902 Education Act. On the other hand they did not wish to alienate Labour, of whose growing power they were afraid, and which they also regarded as a potential ally against the Liberals. Consequently, during the first two or three years of Liberal rule they were skilfully selective in their use of the unfettered power of obstruction that they still possessed.

The huge majority won by the Campbell-Bannerman Government at the election of January 1906 did not, to put it mildly, reflect a mood of undiluted radicalism in the electorate, or even in the country at large. Reaction against the Tories was partly due to the Boer War, whose cost in life and treasure the public had had time to evaluate, with the result that the Liberals were able to make a strong appeal as the party of peace and sound finance. More important still was their conservative appeal as the defenders of Free Trade against Joseph Chamberlain's radical policy of Tariff Reform. Though there was, also, a whiff of genuine radicalism in the air—for instance, in the commitment of most Liberal candidates to old-age pensions—the Liberals' programme in 1906 was far less radical than the Newcastle Programme on which they had fought and won the election of 1892.

Nor was the personnel of the Campbell-Bannerman Government such as to strike much terror into the hearts of the respectable. Sir Henry himself was a reassuring figure; elderly, easy-going and rich. Morley and Bryce were eminently safe and were anyway parked at the India and Irish Offices. Birrell at Education was a genial belletrist, and the Government contained its quota of broad-acred peers. Above all, the so-called Liberal Imperialists were in good positions; Asquith as Chancellor of the Exchequer, Grey as Foreign Secretary and Haldane as War Minister. Haldane, in fact was one of the few advanced thinkers in British politics, and Asquith was rather more radical than he seemed. But as a group the Liberal Imperialists had endeared themselves to the Centre and Right for their 'patriotism' during the Boer War, and that reputation stood them in good stead even though public opinion on the merits of the war had significantly changed.

Only two members of the Cabinet could be seen as potential threats to the social order, John Burns and Lloyd George, but even they soon provided evidence of being less dangerous than was feared. In Burns's case the impression was not misleading. The 'Man with a Red Flag' proved, as President of the Local Government Board, to be a thoroughly incompetent minister and a bulwark against change. His talents were for agitation, not for executive action, and his feud with Keir Hardie helped to move him away from the extreme Left towards a rather staid form of Liberalism. In 1914 he resigned in protest against Britain's declaration of war, but did not campaign for peace and disappeared from politics for the rest of his long life. (He was still alive in the early years of the Second World War.)

Lloyd George was a very different sort of man. Though never, as Burns had been, a socialist, he was by temperament and conviction a full-blooded radical reformer. Suggestions to the contrary, which still persist, are based either upon the mistake of equating radicalism with socialism, or upon a misunderstanding of Lloyd George's flexible way of working towards consistent objectives. From boyhood onwards his dedication to social reform can be clearly and irrefutably documented, but he was always a pragmatist, more concerned to achieve results than merely to expound noble theories. Moreover, he was just as gifted for conciliation as for controversy, and was ever on the look-out for means of disarming enemies and resolving disputes.

When he became a Cabinet Minister after fifteen stormy years as a backbencher, he wisely decided that his first task was to show that he could run a department and legislate responsibly in the national interest. As President of the Board of Trade he promoted a number of useful reforms, but in so doing sought agreement and co-operation both from his political opponents and from the business community. Though at the same time he frequently made challenging party speeches in the country, the chief effect of his performance at the Board of Trade was to soften his image; and this effect was calculated partly to win the goodwill of self-made financiers and captains of industry, whom he regarded as potential allies against Britain's antique, superannuated strongholds of privilege.

Ironically, some of the Campbell-Bannerman Government's most radical legislation was put through by one of its least exciting members, the Home Secretary, Herbert Gladstone. Gladstone was a good party man who had the sense to recognise that strict adherence to his father's doctrine of non-interference by the State would ill serve the cause of Liberalism in the new century. Thus he encouraged Charles Masterman to become a Liberal candidate despite Masterman's socialistic doubts (rather as Archbishop Randall Davidson ordained the young William Temple, disregarding his unsoundness on the Virgin Birth); and between 1906 and 1908 Gladstone carried a Workmen's Compensation Act and an Eight Hours Act (for coal-miners), as well as instituting the Borstal system, children's courts and the Court of Criminal Appeal. These important reforms were not obstructed by the House of Lords, which also accepted the Government's Trade Disputes Bill—a measure designed to undo the effects of the Taff Vale judgment and largely dictated, in its final form, by Labour.

The idea that the Campbell-Bannerman Government got very little done is sheer fantasy, whether those who assert it are trying to prove that the Government had no serious interest in reform, or that its reforming efforts were serious but frustrated by the House of Lords. Actually, it was a more radical Government than some of its members would have wished it to be; and if to the legislation already mentioned we add (among other things) Haldane's sweeping Army reforms and Asquith's differentiation, in his 1907 Budget, between earned and unearned income, we can hardly maintain that the first two years of Liberal rule were barren of achievement. All things considered, the record is one of unusual activity and substantial success. Yet the myth dies hard that the Liberals' constructive programme was entirely wrecked by the peers.

To the extent that the peers did exercise their veto it is true, however, that they did so on matters that were peculiarly sensitive for the Government. Though Nonconformity was far more strongly represented than Labour among its parliamentary supporters, it was in the embarrassing position of being able to do quite a lot to please Labour but virtually nothing to please the Nonconformists. No Welsh Disestablishment Bill was introduced, because it seemed pointless to waste the Commons' time on a measure that the Lords would be bound to reject. Instead, the Government played for time by setting up a Royal Commission and Lloyd George had to appease the wrath of his compatriots, which he did without much difficulty but at a considerable cost in time and patience. On education, progress was made wherever sectarian controversy was not involved—for instance, in the measure permitting school meals—but the Nonconformist grievance about religious teaching could not be removed. The House of Lords forced the Government to drop Birrell's Bill, and two further attempts to settle the matter by legislation also had to be abandoned. The Lords were able to defy the Liberals on that issue because the Nonconformist grievance, though eloquently and passionately voiced by the leaders of Dissent, was of diminishing interest to ordinary chapel-goers and of no interest at all to other members of the public.

By the spring of 1908, when Campbell-Bannerman was succeeded by Asquith—and when Lloyd George took Asquith's place as Chancellor of the Exchequer—the Liberals were facing a menace that was deadly in itself and also likely to encourage the Tory Opposition to take a more militant line. Trade was slumping and unemployment was rising. The prosperity which had served, in 1904–5, as such a powerful argument for the champions of Free Trade was now giving way to conditions equally serviceable to the exponents of Tariff Reform.

Radicalism, never a monopoly of the Liberal Party, had become less so than ever when Joseph Chamberlain and his Liberal Unionists allied themselves with the Tories on the Home Rule issue, and more especially when Chamberlain launched his Tariff Reform campaign in 1903. He was the outstanding radical of his generation and his new gospel, linking social reform with Imperialism, was aimed at the masses as well as at industrialists feeling the pinch of foreign competition. There were only two weaknesses in it as an instrument of mass conversion. One was that Chamberlain's proposed scheme of Imperial Preference would involve the taxing of British food imports ('stomach taxes'), and the other that the state of the British economy when his campaign was launched, and for several years afterwards, seemed to belie his predictions of doom. In 1908 the second flaw at least was disappearing, but unfortunately for his cause Chamberlain himself was no longer able to act as its fighting general and evangelist, because in 1906 he had suffered a debilitating stroke. He could only issue orders and advice from the seclusion of his home, in speech which, though still coherent, was slurred. Had he retained his oratorical faculties until the economic climate shifted in his favour, who can say which of the two rival radicalisms—his or Lloyd George's— would have prevailed?

That the two men were on opposite sides was a tragic irony, since the young Lloyd George had undoubtedly derived inspiration from Chamberlain rather than from Gladstone, though it was to Gladstone that the overwhelming sentiment of Welshmen had compelled him to give formal allegiance. On social policy he was Chamberlain's disciple, and on the Irish question his private opinion was closer to Chamberlain's than to Gladstone's. Yet he dissented strongly from Chamberlain's form of Imperialism as manifested, above all, in the provoked conflict with the Boers. Himself no less of an Imperialist, he believed in Imperial unity through devolution and conciliation. On the fiscal issue, though never a bigoted Free Trader, his instincts were anti-Protectionist and he regarded the necessity for food duties as a fatal objection to Chamberlain's scheme of Imperial Preference. Moreover, since he was relentlessly opposed to the House of Lords and all that it stood for, the spectacle of Chamberlain in league with the Lords disgusted him; for Chamberlain, though as innocent as Lloyd George of any 'sneaking kindness for a lord', was driven by the exigencies of politics into making tactical use of a body that he despised and had, in the past, savagely denounced.

Lloyd George was determined to provide a radical alternative to Tariff Reform, and to revive the drooping fortunes of the Liberal Party. After listening to Asquith's 1908 Budget speech he wrote to his brother William: '. . . it leaves the coast clear for me to initiate my own schemes. It is time that we did something that appealed straight to the people . . .'[1] During the summer recess he visited Germany to study the Bismarckian system of social insurance, and it has been alleged that this visit marks the beginning of his interest in social reform, whereas in fact it was undertaken because he was at last in a position to do things that he had long aspired to do. Characteristically, he turned his attention to the practical details only because he knew that he would before very long be able to take practical steps.

Apart from his far-reaching schemes of social reform, he had other reasons for planning a substantial increase in revenue from taxation. There was a large anticipated deficit for 1909–10, partly due to the Old Age

Pensions which Asquith had announced and which it was one of Lloyd George's first tasks to introduce. Moreover, by the time his 1909 Budget was in preparation it was clear that, so far from being able to impose any cuts upon the Service departments, as he had originally hoped to do, he would have to allow for heavy new expenditure by the Admiralty. Public alarm at the scale of Germany's naval construction made it possible for the First Lord, Reginald McKenna, to resist the Chancellor's demand for economy. When he spoke, at the end of June 1908, of having to find new hen-roosts to rob, Lloyd George may have been thinking of Service cuts as well as more and higher taxes. A month earlier he had told a Welsh M.P. of fairly advanced views that he was 'not inclined to increase income tax & death duties in case of rich', and that he was hopeful of being able to 'carry on without further taxation if economy exercised by various departments'.[2] But by early 1909 he knew that his schemes would have to be financed by new taxation alone. (At the time he shared Asquith's view that the National Debt should on no account be added to, but, if possible, reduced.)

In any case it is hardly likely that he would have imposed no additional taxes. At the very least it was to be expected that he would launch a fiscal attack on land values, because he was under strong pressure to do so from the land tax lobby, and because his own prejudices equally strongly inclined him in that direction. The Lords had thrown out the Government's Scottish Land Valuation Bill, which could be regarded as a pilot measure. But more serious was their rejection, at the end of November, of the Government's Licensing Bill, which was done with Balfour's full encouragement. This measure meant a great deal to Nonconformists and, unlike the Government's Education Bills, had the support of most Anglican bishops. But the liquor trade was a Conservative vested interest, and the Opposition also knew that temperance was not a popular issue with the working class. The Government would hardly have dared to dissolve on it even if conditions generally had been favourable for an election. Yet the Lords' act of aggression had to be countered, and Winston Churchill's furious comment presaged the form that the Government's riposte would take: 'We shall send them up such a Budget . . . as shall terrify them, they have started the class war, they had better be careful'.[3]

Churchill at this time, and for the next two or three years, was Lloyd George's most enthusiastic ally. His interest in social reform, which had been latent and not very obvious until the early part of 1908, was chiefly inspired by Lloyd George; and the suggestion, occasionally put forward, that it was Churchill who made the running, is simply absurd. But his mind was so resourceful and original that his relationship to Lloyd George could never be that of a mere lieutenant. The two men stimulated each other, and there was, inevitably, an undercurrent of rivalry in their collaboration.

Lloyd George's 1909 Budget was certainly a class-war Budget, as well as one designed 'to wage implacable warfare against poverty and squalidness'. About 75 per cent of the proposed additional taxation was calculated to fall upon those paying income tax, who represented little more than one-third of the electorate, restricted though it still was. Moreover, the steepest increases were applied to only a small proportion even of those who paid income tax; only 12,000 people were liable to the new super-tax, and only 80,000 to the increased death duties (out of one million income-tax payers). But was the Budget framed with a view to its being rejected by the Lords, so that the issue of the Lords' veto would be forced on ground relatively advantageous for the Liberals? The answer is, yes and no. Ministers, including Lloyd George, were well aware that even fighting on the Budget they would be unlikely to retain their overall majority, and would therefore in the next Parliament be at the mercy of their allies, more especially of the Irish Nationalists. They had little enthusiasm for appealing to the country at a time of economic recession, and did not underrate the deferential factor in British politics, which would inevitably benefit the Lords. On the whole, therefore, they would have preferred to defeat their enemy without the necessity for an election. If, in accordance with tradition, the Lords felt obliged to pass the Budget, they would be stultifying their veto on at least two other issues, since the liquor taxes would be an answer to their rejection of the Licensing Bill, and the land taxes would compel them to accept a valuation of land.

Chamberlain from the first took the view that they should throw the Budget out, but it was not until August that Balfour came to the same conclusion. According to Lord Esher and J. L. Garvin the balance was tipped by Lloyd George's Limehouse speech on 30 July, but it is hard to believe that the Tory leader would have decided differently if Lloyd George had been conciliatory instead of provocative at that stage. Pressure from the well-organised Tariff Reformers, and a general feeling among Tories that the tide was running their way, would have made it virtually impossible for Balfour to impose a policy of moderation. Lloyd George for his part cannot justly be accused of reckless and premature demagogy. The Limehouse speech was delivered three months after the Budget, during which time opposition to his proposals had been gathering momentum. He counter-attacked at Limehouse because it seemed that there was nothing to gain, and much to lose, from continued restraint.

There is, however, a wider criticism—that his polemical style damaged the Liberals in the January 1910 election; that but for him the Unionists would not have regained so much of their lost ground. This is the sort of might-have-been question that can never be resolved, one way or the other, but in fairness to Lloyd George it should be said that not only his Budget, but also the brilliance of his campaigning for it, roused the Government's supporters from despondency to exaltation. The percentage turn-out in January 1910 was higher than in 1906, and the Liberals polled even more votes than in that landslide year. Though Lloyd George's attacks on the peerage may have contributed to the Liberal collapse in the shires—where deference was still very strong, and where the House of Lords was seen by countrymen at all levels as their protector against the towns—nevertheless it was those very attacks that diverted attention from Tariff Reform and made the Budget's opponents appear ridiculous.

Even so the Liberals would probably have been defeated if economic conditions had remained adverse. As it was, trade and employment revived during the latter part of 1909, and the improvement was not affected by the onset of winter. Hence the Liberals' narrow victory, which the Opposition accepted as popular endorsement of the Budget. Unfortunately the Liberal leaders had not prepared themselves for the ensuing situation, in which radicals and Irish Nationalists united in a demand for action against the House of Lords. Before the election Asquith gave a pledge on Irish Home Rule, which many English Liberals regretted, and he also gave the impression that he had secured guarantees from the King concerning use of the prerogative to overrule the Lords' veto. In fact, he had obtained no such guarantees; the King had expressly said that he would not feel justified in creating the necessary number of peers until after a second general election. The Government was thus committed to the Irish, and dependent upon their votes in the new Parliament, yet unable to carry a Home Rule Bill without again risking its life at the polls.

In parenthesis, one should mention that the Irish 'veto' in British politics, which resulted from the January 1910 election, was based upon gross over-representation of Ireland at Westminster—a relic of the pre-Famine period. Whereas the Liberals had 275 M.P.s elected by 2,880,581 votes, and the Unionists 273 M.P.s elected by 3,127,887 votes, the Irish Nationalists had 82 M.P.s elected by 124,586 votes. Even when 55 unopposed Irish returns are taken into account, the disproportion is staggering. For the number of Irish M.P.s to have reflected accurately the 1910 population of Ireland it would have been necessary to reduce the total by forty or so; and if at the same time the representation of other parties in the United Kingdom had been made to reflect population more accurately, there would have been no Irish 'veto' in the critical years 1910–14. When the enormities of Unionist opposition to Home Rule are rehearsed, that rather material point is seldom mentioned.

It would probably have been better if the problem of the Lords had been tackled during the Liberals' honeymoon period; that is to say, within a year or so of the 1906 election. Lloyd George and Grey alone, apparently, among members of the Campbell-Bannerman Cabinet favoured a showdown when the Lords sabotaged Birrell's Education Bill in December 1906. The relative unpopularity of the measure might then have been offset by the general popularity of the Government, and there would have been a chance of dealing with the Second Chamber without in the process destroying the Liberals' independent majority and so raising once again the supremely contentious Irish issue. But when the moment of truth did arrive in 1910 the Liberals were no longer free agents, and to make matters worse they were fundamentally divided on what to do about the House of Lords.

There was then (and is still) a strong case for reforming the House on a non-hereditary basis, but if it was to remain hereditary the logical and proper course would have been to deprive it altogether of power to wreck or reject measures passed by the elected Chamber. Since one hereditary figure within the Constitution—the Sovereign—had been reduced, in effect, to a consultative role, there was surely no good reason why five hundred men ('chosen'—in Lloyd George's not wholly fair, but deadly, phrase—'accidentally from among the unemployed') should continue to exercise substantial power, even if it were to be limited. Yet the policy that emerged, after agonising debate within the Cabinet, was to limit the Second Chamber's powers without altering its composition. To implement this policy the Government had to fight another election, having first obtained from the new King (George V) guarantees which should have been obtained from his father before the earlier election—if, indeed, it was true that the Sovereign could constitutionally refuse to create peers when advised to do so by his Ministers.

All things considered, the Liberals were lucky to come through the election of December 1910 as successfully as they did. The result largely reproduced that of January, and once again the state of the economy helped the Liberals. It is likely, too, that they retained enthusiastic mass support for their achievement in discrediting the House of Lords, for which they had Lloyd George chiefly to thank. Until recently it was assumed by historians of the period, including even the great Elie Halévy, that the electorate was apathetic during the December 1910 election, because the percentage poll fell from 86·6 per cent to 81·1 per cent compared with January. But Dr Neal Blewett has shown that this assumption was due to a crude misreading of the statistics. The lower percentage in December was mainly caused by an increase in the number of uncontested seats and by the fact that the election was conducted (except in Scotland) on a stale register. It did not reflect any significant loss of interest on the part of the voters.[4]

The Parliament Act of 1911 is described by R. C. K. Ensor in his volume of the Oxford History as 'the most decisive step in British constitutional development since the franchise extension of 1867'. This may well be true, but it must also be said that the measure had grave defects. Its most admirable feature is the least well known—that it reduced the statutory life of Parliaments from seven to five years. But in other respects it is open to a variety of objections. Mr Roy Jenkins has explained that the subsequent docility of the Lords 'owed more to a change of political climate than to the legal provisions of the Parliament Act', and has further argued very convincingly that the scope for delay which the Act afforded had disastrous consequences in 1912–14. Moreover, the provision that money bills should pass virtually without any delay at all—obviously intended to prevent any repetition of what the Lords did to the 1909 Finance Bill—seems rather absurd in the light of Speaker Lowther's statement that he would not have been able to certify that bill as a money bill within the meaning of the Act. According to Mr Jenkins, there have since been numerous occasions when Finance Bills have not received the Speaker's certificate.[5]

Granted the situation in 1910, the Liberals could not have chosen to reform the House of Lords without at the same time ensuring that its power to obstruct Liberal legislation was removed. The Irish would not have allowed such a policy, which would also have been repugnant to English radicals. But two courses were open to the Government, either of which would have been preferable to the one it adopted. It could have departed from the cautious formula put forward by Campbell-Bannerman in 1907 (that the will of the Commons should be made to prevail 'within the limits of a single Parliament'), by proposing instead that the Lords should have no power to delay Commons' measures of any kind, beyond the right to suggest amendments which the Commons could either accept or ignore. Alternatively, the Liberals could have insisted upon a mass creation of peers so that they would have controlled both Houses of Parliament at least for the next few years. In the absence of either of these solutions they were doomed to a period of frustration more bitter and embittering than anything they had experienced in the earlier phase of their long regime.

Lloyd George, sensing the dangers to which not only the Government but the State itself would be exposed through an escalation of party strife, made in August 1910 his remarkable private suggestion that there should be a national government to settle a number of outstanding, and vital, national questions. Though he may subsequently have exaggerated, with hindsight, his apprehension of the growing crisis in Europe, that was undoubtedly one of the motives for his memorandum. His initiative failed, and was probably bound to fail, because both personal conviction and political circumstances inhibited Balfour and more or less ensured his refusal to co-operate. Moreover, even if he had agreed, and had then been able to carry his party with him, Asquith would have had great difficulty in persuading his own rank-and-file to accept the package. If the federal Home Rule that Lloyd George had in mind for the whole United Kingdom was a hard morsel for Conservatives, the introduction of compulsory military training on the Swiss model would have been no less hard for Liberals. All the same, Lloyd George's move was imaginative and patriotic, and he deserves rather more credit for it than at least one distinguished writer has been willing to give him.[6]

After the constitutional struggle the Liberals' record seems on the whole barren, with the conspicuous exception of Lloyd George's National Health Insurance Act. But is the impression of barrenness true or false? Historical study of the last phase of Liberal rule before the outbreak of war in 1914 has been immeasurably influenced by one book— *The Strange Death of Liberal England*[7]—which argues that the fault was in themselves rather than in their stars. Most people who have since written about the period have been concerned either to endorse or to refute Mr Dangerfield's argument, which is a sure sign of its importance.

*Strange Death*'s career is worth a brief digression, because it illustrates both what an amateur historian can achieve and how unobtrusive an influential work can be at the time of its first appearance. Mr Dangerfield left England in 1930 and settled, to begin with, in New York (he now lives in California). He had never read Modern History but became enthralled by the atmosphere of pre-war Britain, in which his childhood was spent. *Strange Death* was the result of intense research in the New York Public Library, reminiscent of Karl Marx's in the British Museum. It was published in the United States in 1935. The critical reception was on the whole friendly, but emphasised the book's vividness rather than the novelty of its approach. Sales were minimal, partly because the firm that published it went out of business almost immediately afterwards.

A year later the book was published in England, by Constable, though with strictly limited discussion of the Larne gun-running (for fear of libel proceedings by Major Crawford) and without the last chapter, 'The Lofty Shade' (which the publisher considered irrelevant). The edition did not sell well and is now out of print, but the book received some notice in the press.

In 1961 Capricorn Books, a paperback branch of Putnam, brought out an edition of the book which continues to sell about 2500 copies a year. A few years later a second hardback edition appeared in England, published by MacGibbon and Kee, with a preface by Paul Johnson; and in 1971 the same edition was brought out in paperback by Paladin Books. Finally, in 1972 a *de luxe* edition was published in Switzerland, in a series entitled 'The March of History'. Apart from *Victoria's Heir*, published by Constable in 1941, Mr Dangerfield has since written no other book.

In his preface to *Strange Death* Paul Johnson says that it was commended to him by his tutor at Magdalen College, Oxford, 'as an example of how, in the writing of history, vividness and readability need be no obstacle to truth'. The tutor in question was none other than Alan Taylor, whose own work—as Mr Johnson adds—strikingly illustrates the precept. There is, indeed, much truth in Mr Dangerfield's picture of pre-1914 England, though in common with some of the greatest historians—Gibbon and Macaulay, for instance—his colourful style is sometimes used, unintentionally, to promote prejudice rather than truth.

The Liberal England whose autopsy he is conducting was not simply the Liberal Party, but a social, political and cultural establishment which, in his view, was dying—and deserved to die—before the Great War killed it. Apart from the problem of, as it were, identifying the body (because the concept of Liberal England, however interpreted, is not without ambiguity or imprecision), it may also be thought that Mr Dangerfield has exaggerated the morbid symptoms and overlooked the symptoms of health. Moreover, it is by no means clear that the institutions and values whose demise he is recording were, in fact, killed even by the war. Liberalism in the strict party sense may have been a casualty, but liberalism in the wider sense, including 'the illusion of progress', is even now far from defunct.

Nevertheless *Strange Death* conveys to us with incomparable subtlety and skill the feeling of an *élite* losing control of itself and of events; and the narrative is illuminated with a wealth of telling detail. The author concentrates upon the threats to Liberalism from Ulster, the suffragettes and militant trade unions, each of which he describes as a rebellion, and to none of which, he suggests, did the Liberal Government or the society it represented have an effective answer.

Beyond question, the Irish issue proved too much for the Liberals, and their mishandling of it compounded the folly of Gladstone's initial commitment to Home Rule. Under Parliament Act procedure enacting their Home Rule Bill was an appallingly slow business, and while the Bill was being debated and re-debated the situation in Ireland was getting out of hand. Official Opposition support for Ulster's prospective defiance of the law was a grave constitutional lapse, but Bonar Law at least was of Ulster Protestant extraction; his playing of the 'Orange card' was far less cynical than Lord Randolph Churchill's. Since the Liberals appeared to be the prisoners of the majority Irish faction, it could plausibly be argued that the Tories had a right to give their backing to the minority. In any case, even if the Tories had not supported the Ulster revolt, the Government would have been unable to suppress it, because the Ulstermen had no intention of being coerced.

The women's 'rebellion' was in one sense less serious, and less incompetently handled by the Government. The resort by the Womens Social and Political Union to violence alienated moderate opinion, but might all the same have endangered the whole fabric of law and order if the campaign of arson had been directed against public buildings and factories rather than against private houses, and if, particularly in London, the W.S.P.U. had organised menacing mass demonstrations by working-class women. As it was, the tactics employed were extremely troublesome but not uncontrollable. Yet in another sense the Government's handling of the women's suffrage question did more than anything to damage its liberal credentials. From 1906 onwards there was strong rank-and-file pressure, in Parliament and outside, for a measure of female enfranchisement. But the Government failed to act while the movement was entirely peaceful, and so provoked the militancy of the W.S.P.U. This in turn led to the exclusion of women from meetings to be addressed by Liberal Cabinet Ministers, which often did not avert trouble and was anyway a very bad advertisement for 'the party of progress'. One reason for the Government's refusal to make a gesture was that Asquith himself was, in his way, a fanatical anti-feminist. Another reason was that to enfranchise women on a qualified franchise was thought likely to benefit the Conservative Party. But these were not adequate or worthy reasons, and it remains a serious blemish on the Liberals' record that they did not at an early stage of their regime introduce a proper Bill to give women the vote.

Labour as a political movement had been very successfully contained by the Liberals at the two 1910 elections, mainly because of the radical appeal of Lloyd George and Winston Churchill, both as orators and as practical reformers. But trade unionism was a growing force, and syndicalism a growing force within the trade unions. Despite high employment (by contemporary standards), real wages were not significantly rising. Moreover, despite legislation to mitigate the Osborne judgment, despite the effect of Churchill's labour exchanges, despite payment of Members, and despite Lloyd George's varied reforming activity, Labour was often hostile to the Government and the working class was conscious of being, still, only partly enfranchised. The Reform Bill of 1912 would have added two and a half million male voters to the register—and was also declared by the Government to be susceptible of amendment in the interest of women's suffrage. But early in 1913 the Speaker ruled that much of the Bill was out of order, including the amendments to enfranchise women; and the Government then tamely withdrew the Bill. Asquith was privately well content that the cause of women's suffrage should have received this setback, and it is hard not to be suspicious that the blow to further working-class enfranchisement was equally welcome. In the event, it was the achievement of full manhood suffrage (together with a large measure of women's suffrage) in 1918 that gave the Labour Party formidable representation in Parliament and made it seem, for the first time, an independent competitor for power.

Apart from mixed motives on the franchise, the Government suffered—through its own fault—from a lack of Parliamentary time. Home Rule was not the only long-running show that the Parliament Act inflicted; Welsh Disestablishment was another. All the same, the barrenness of the Liberals' immediate pre-war record is, in at least one respect, more apparent than real. Lloyd George's land campaign and his 1914 Budget should not be forgotten. The 1914 Budget, in particular, was a major exercise in radical reform, second only to the Budget of 1909. It contained the innovation of a graduated income tax on earned incomes, and lowered the super-tax exemption limit from £5000 to £3000 a year. By 1914 Lloyd George, the Marconi scandal well behind him, seemed to be regaining the initiative for Liberalism.

The First World War, however, has overshadowed the 1914 Budget in history books, and has in general given to the last years of peace the appearance of a doom-laden phantasmagoria. Was the war inevitable? Two schools of thought, very different in other ways, unite in believing that it could and should have been avoided. The belief is held by those who argue that Britain could have maintained her independence as a great naval power free from Continental entanglements, and it is also held by radical pacifists to whom the balance of power seems a wicked and barbarous concept. But there are others, probably a majority, who take the view that so long as power exists in the world it is safer balanced than unbalanced, and who consider that wars are caused not when the balance of power is asserted but when it is neglected. There are many, too, who will not easily be convinced that Britain should have allowed Germany to conquer Europe and Russia in 1914, as might well have happened but for British intervention. A German empire stretching from Brest to Vladivostok would have posed a mortal threat to Britain and her world-wide interests, which she would have been forced to grapple with sooner or later on terms far less advantageous than in August 1914.

Might the Germans have been deterred if British obligations towards France and Belgium had been more clearly defined? The evidence strongly suggests that they would not have been deterred, but it was, all the same, very unfortunate that British public opinion was so little prepared for the crisis, and that the Cabinet itself gave so little consideration to the problems of peace and war in Europe. Foreign policy was still regarded as an arcane matter which only experts could understand, and it would anyway have been difficult for Grey to discuss it with his Ministerial and party colleagues, because so many of them were ignorant and prejudiced. Even if he had been able to discuss it, there is no reason to suppose that war would have been averted. The conspiracy theory of Britain's involvement in 1914 is a canard. Parliament, in effect, took the decision to go to war, and took it because of a general and genuine feeling that Britain's vital interests were at stake.

The decision was certainly disastrous for the Liberal Party, but any other decision would probably have been far more disastrous for the country. The Liberal regime that led Britain into war should not, on that account, be judged a traitor to the liberal cause, nor should its fine, if imperfect, record through nearly eight years of peace be underrated by people today who are, often unknowingly, its beneficiaries.

## Notes

1 David Lloyd George to William George, 6 May 1908 (quoted in William George, *My Brother and I*). By agreement with Lloyd George, Asquith introduced the 1908 Budget though he was already Prime Minister.

2 Journal of Ellis W. Davies M.P., entry for 20 May 1908.

3 Lucy Masterman, *C. F. G. Masterman, a Biography* (London, 1968) p. 144.

4 Neal Blewett, *The Peers, the Parties and the People: the General Elections of 1910* (London, 1972) pp. 379–80.

5 Roy Jenkins, *Mr. Balfour's Poodle* (London, 1968) Epilogue, pp. 186–195.

6 G. R. Searle in *The Quest for National Efficiency* (Oxford, 1971) ch. VI. Mr Searle says that 'Lloyd George's deviousness ultimately proved self-defeating'. But surely such a delicate and precarious negotiation required the sort of diplomatic finesse that is seldom, if ever, compatible with perfect candour.

7 G. Dangerfield (London, 1966).

8 R. C. K. Ensor, 'History Like a Novel', *Manchester Guardian*, 3 July 1936.

# 3 Labour and the Downfall of the Liberal Party, 1906–14

## CHRIS COOK

In 1906, the Liberals returned to power after a triumphant electoral landslide. Less than twenty years later, the party had been reduced to a mere forty members after an electoral humiliation almost unprecedented in British history. By October 1924, the downfall of the Liberal Party was complete.

The causes and course of the Liberal downfall continue to fascinate historians. Indeed, as Kenneth Morgan has written: 'today, British historians of the twentieth century seem almost as obsessed by it as were Tudor and Stuart historians a few years ago by the rise or decline of the gentry.'[1]

Kenneth Morgan continued:

> It is not hard to see why the 'strange death' of Liberalism should exercise such fascination. There is the personal drama associated with the schism between Asquith and Lloyd George. There is the sociological interest of the rise to political maturity and power of the working class. More generally, the decline of the Liberal Party has been popularly equated with the decline of a whole civilization, with the erosion of the liberal ethic, of the optimism and the certainty of moral values which the tensions and disillusionments of British society since 1914 have so largely undermined. In a sense, the decline of Liberalism has been taken as a parable of the decline of modern Britain.

It is a debate which remains far from over. Historians continue to differ as widely as ever over the causes and course of the events which led Labour to supplant the Liberals. Recently several important studies have attempted to transfer the emphasis of this debate from the pre-1914 period. For Trevor Wilson, the onset of war marked the crucial period in the downfall of the Liberal Party.[2] Other attempts have been made to shift the emphasis towards Liberal fortunes after 1918.[3] But it is the period from 1906 to 1914 which still generates most controversy.[4] The argument on the degree of Labour's advance and the nature of the Liberal decline in these years remains as unresolved as ever. It is with the electoral fortunes of Labour and Liberals during these crucial years that this essay is concerned.

The debate on the relative electoral fortunes of Labour and the Liberals has hitherto concentrated almost exclusively on the performance of the parties in general elections and parliamentary by-elections. This essay attempts to look at what was happening in the constituencies, using the hitherto largely untouched material on municipal elections each November as evidence.

These annual municipal contests were seen by contemporaries to be of considerable importance, for they were often the only occasions when local Labour Parties put up candidates. Hence, they were in many ways taken more seriously in some constituencies than parliamentary contests.[5] And since the influence of Head Office fell less weightily and less often on municipal candidates, constituency parties were consequently more eager to nominate them.

There are, however, problems in analysing municipal elections during this period. Despite the fact that local elections were increasingly contested on party lines in many towns, particularly in the smaller boroughs and more residential areas, local elections were not contested on overt party issues. Barnsley and Darlington are examples of such towns. Even in London, elections in such boroughs as Stoke Newington and Hampstead were not fought on party lines.[6] Even in those provincial boroughs where such contests as occurred were on party issues, many wards went uncontested each year as the Liberals and Conservatives sought to avoid wasteful expenditure. Thus in 1912, there were no contests in any of the wards in West Bromwich, Wednesbury, Exeter, Darlington or Barnsley. Indeed, when elections were held in every ward in Smethwick in 1913, it was the first occasion since 1899. In 1913, when a municipal 'general election' was held in Reading, and the size of the council increased to fifty-two, only two contested elections were held. Few contested elections occurred in such North-East towns as Sunderland or South Shields.[7] Only Labour fought elections in the Pottery towns on party lines.[8]

A further factor which must be considered when analysing local election material is the extent of the franchise. Although figures for the proportion of the population who possessed the local government franchise in 1913 varied from town to town, rarely does this figure seem to have exceeded 20 per cent.[9] Curiously, though the limited franchise obviously hindered Labour, those voters who possessed the vote exercised it in large numbers. No doubt the 96 per cent poll in Clitheroe in 1913 was an exception. But many of the major cities produced consistently high turnout figures. Turnout reached 70 per cent in Leeds in 1909, and 74 per cent in Nottingham in 1908, whilst no fewer than 83 per cent voted in elections in Wigan and Northampton in 1913.

Though there are these difficulties in analysing local election results, the effort is well rewarded. From even a brief examination of municipal politics, it is easy to assemble evidence that supports the view that the Liberals were in difficulties and Labour advancing. After the gains of the period 1902–5, largely inspired by opposition to the Government's Education Act and tariff proposals, the period after 1906 had seen the Liberals not merely on the defensive, but suffering some severe reverses. Thus in 1908, Liberals suffered heavy losses throughout Lancashire as well as losing control of a variety of provincial boroughs. Conservatives gained control of Sheffield, Nottingham and Leicester in 1908. These were serious defections; Leicester had been in radical control since 1835; Nottingham for forty years. They were joined by others: in 1909, Coventry fell to the Conservatives for the first time in twenty years. In 1911, Burnley was won by the Conservatives for the first time in its history. In 1912, Liberals lost control of Bradford. In 1913, the Conservatives wrested Huddersfield from the Liberals, the first time they had won control of this Nonconformist stronghold since the incorporation of the borough in 1868.

At the same time that these former radical citadels were falling to Conservative control, Labour appeared to be increasing its council base each year. McKibbin cites the following figures for Labour's council advance after 1909.

TABLE 1    Labour in municipal politics, 1909–13[10]

| Year | No. of Lab candidates | Elected | Gains | Losses | Net gains |
|------|------|------|------|------|------|
| 1909 | 555 | 122 | 55 | 32 | 23 |
| 1910 | 330 | 113 | 52 | 19 | 33 |
| 1911 | 367 | 157 | 95 | 17 | 78 |
| 1912 | 596 | 164 | 63 | 21 | 42 |
| 1913 | 494 | 196 | 106 | 21 | 85 |

These figures, however, are somewhat misleading. They very much conceal the fact that, in 1908, Labour suffered a serious reverse, losing as many seats as it gained in 1907 and 1909 combined. Labour's gains in 1911 were thus to some extent only regaining wards won in 1902 or 1905 and lost in 1908. Further, these figures disguise the very nature of municipal victories—a ward won in one year would of course be won again for the following two years, even if the party's performance stayed static. To this extent the gains of 1912 and 1913 were consolidations of earlier victories as much as any real advance by Labour into new areas.

These overall figures of net gains and losses each November, even when qualified, are perhaps less useful than a more detailed examination of the annual results. A very different picture is painted if the results are looked at more closely from 1908 to 1913. Labour's reverses and rebuffs feature far more prominently than its years of advance.

Certainly, the 1908 elections produced a serious rebuff for Labour. Although Labour secured its first-ever seat on Portsmouth council, elsewhere the party suffered a series of losses. At Bradford, all three retiring Labour councillors were defeated; none of Labour's nine other candidates was successful. At Liverpool, Labour's only representative on the council was defeated; in Salford, Labour lost three seats, two to Conservative and one to an Independent. In Glasgow, where thirteen Labour candidates had been brought forward, none was successful. In both Preston and Crewe, five Labour candidates were brought forward, but none secured election, whilst the only Labour nominee at Reading was heavily defeated. As *The Times* commented on the outcome of the voting, 'The most pronounced feature of the elections has been the number of reverses sustained by the Labour and Socialist candidates.'[11]

Although Labour fared a little better in 1909, their results were distinctly unimpressive. 'The strong Socialist attack made in several big towns has uniformly failed', *The Times* declared.[12] There was evidence to support this view; none of Labour's eleven candidates in Bradford was successful. The six Labour candidates in Aston met a similar fate. All the Labour candidates in Stockport and Preston went down to defeat. Of the eight Labour candidates in Glasgow, only two were successful.

In 1911, Labour achieved its most impressive municipal advance so far. Cole calculated that the party had secured 78 gains, compared to 33 in 1910 and only 23 in 1909.[13] In some towns, Labour's advance was impressive.

Despite a net gain of 43 seats in the 1912 elections, in many boroughs Labour's challenge met with a pronounced setback. Thus in Liverpool, no Labour candidate was successful (in striking contrast to the six gains achieved by the party in 1911). In Hull, none of Labour's five candidates was elected and the party lost the one seat it was defending. In the industrial towns of South Yorkshire, Labour fared little better: at Wakefield, only one Labour candidate came forward and was hopelessly defeated; at Pontefract, all the Trades Council candidates were defeated and the composition of the town council was divided between thirteen Conservatives and eleven Liberals. In such other boroughs as Preston, Walsall and Gillingham no Labour candidates were elected.[14]

Though Labour achieved some impressive results in 1913, even in this peak year of their success, their performance revealed as many signs of weakness as strength. Thus in the North West, in Liverpool, the scene of Labour's six-seat victory in 1911, the party failed to win a single seat. In Lancashire, indeed, Labour had a disastrous year. At Rochdale, Labour's sole representative on the council went down to defeat. The party was now unrepresented on the council. Elsewhere in the country,

Labour faced a series of rebuffs: all five Labour candidates in Keighley were unsuccessful; at Chesterfield the Socialists were 'badly beaten all round'. In Cardiff, where Labour was still not represented on the council, none of Labour's candidates enjoyed any success—a fate shared by the Labour challenge in such boroughs as Grimsby and Ipswich. Even where Labour achieved its most marked successes, as in Glasgow, the scale of their achievement should not be exaggerated—for Glasgow's 37 wards, Labour fielded only 13 candidates and elected only 6 councillors, losing 2 of the seats being defended.

Nor could Labour comfort themselves with many successes in three-cornered contests. In Mànchester, Labour came bottom in the only three-cornered contest, Liberals seizing the seat from them in Blackley and Moston. In the two triangular contests in neighbouring Salford, Labour again came bottom. At Oldham the *Manchester Guardian* found that 'the greatest surprise was the success of the Liberals in the two wards in which Labour candidates meant three-cornered contests.'[15] Indeed, in 1913 there is definite evidence that Labour's successes in three-cornered contests were few and far between.

Thus in Northampton, where in 1912 eight of the eleven contested wards saw three-cornered contests, Labour had little cause for comfort. None of Labour's candidates was successful in three-cornered contests.[16] In every case, the Labour nominees were in third place. Though these Labour candidates denied the Liberals victory in such wards as St Edmunds, none were remotely near winning a seat. Indeed, the *Northampton Mercury* found the Liberal poll 'very satisfactory', whilst noting 'a big drop' in the Socialist vote.[17] Compared to 1909 (the last year the town had seen many three-cornered contests), Labour had indeed slipped back.

TABLE 2   Municipal voting in Northampton, 1909–12

| Party | 1909 | | Party | 1912 | |
| | Votes cast | Percentage | | Votes cast | Percentage |
|---|---|---|---|---|---|
| Con | 5875 | 44·2 | Con | 6404 | 47·0 |
| Lib | 4104 | 30·9 | Lib | 4294 | 31·5 |
| Lab | 3305 | 24·9 | Lab | 2930 | 21·5 |
| | 13,284 | | | 13,628 | |

These examples, from such towns as Northampton or Oldham, are useful for putting Labour's advance into perspective. Even Labour's definite success in 1912 and 1913 was patchy and far from uniform. Even when this is said, and even allowing that in some industrial cities Labour had made substantial gains in the years up to 1913, the overall results of their advance had hardly been dramatic or even impressive, as the table below indicates:

TABLE 3    Composition of town councils in November 1913

|  | Con | Lib | Lab | Others |
|---|---|---|---|---|
| Norwich | 33 | 25 | 5 | 1 |
| Halifax | 20 | 24 | 7 | 1 |
| Oldham | 14 | 22 | 1 | — |
| Burnley | 28 | 29 | 3 | — |
| Barrow | 18 | 5 | 8 | 1 |
| Leeds | 34 | 18 | 16 | — |
| Sheffield | 32 | 30 | 2 | — |
| Northampton | 17 | 14 | 5 | — |
| Coventry | 26 | 16 | 4 | 1 |
| Nottingham | 37 | 25 | 2 | — |
| Bradford | 32 | 31 | 20 | 1 |
| Wolverhampton | 25 | 17 | 3 | 3 |
| Birmingham | 87* | 25 | 8 | — |
| York | 24 | 16 | 6 | 2 |
|  | 427 | 297 | 90 | 10 |

*Includes 42 Liberal Unionists.

These figures provide a useful corrective to those who see in pre-1914 England an inexorable march of Labour. In none of these large boroughs was Labour yet in power;[18] only in Barrow was it yet the second largest party. Whereas, in these fourteen boroughs, Conservatives had 427 seats (51·9%) and the Liberals 297 (36·0%), Labour's tally amounted to a mere 90 (10·9%). And yet these were the major industrial towns. In the smaller boroughs, in the county towns and cathedral cities, Labour's impact had been virtually non-existent (see pp. 56–8). Not only had Labour really failed to break through prior to 1913, but a most noticeable feature of Labour's progress in this period was its uneven march. Labour would make a limited breakthrough in a particular town; but the next year it might fail even to take a single seat. The two cities of Birmingham and Liverpool provide excellent case studies of this phenomenon.

In Birmingham, Labour's road to municipal success was a slow one. The Birmingham and District Labour Representation Council was formed in 1902, and the first councillor 'on a distinctly Socialist ticket' was elected in Bordesley in November 1902. But few other successes followed: in 1907 all three Labour candidates for municipal election were badly defeated. Labour's first real breakthrough came in 1911. A miniature municipal 'general election' was held that year following the extension of the town boundaries. Labour fielded no less than fifteen candidates, six of whom were successful. Labour's best results came in Saltley, Washwood Heath, Duddeston and Nechells and Rotton Park.

In 1912 Labour failed abysmally to repeat its success. One retiring Labour councillor (in Rotton Park) was re-elected,[19] but no other ward returned a Socialist—even though Liberals were not attacked by Labour, and Liberal votes presumably went to Labour candidates. The council remained overwhelmingly in right-wing control.[20]

By 1913, Labour's drive had lost its momentum. Only nine of the thirty wards in the town were contested. Labour's vote remained virtually static, although it gained two Tory-held seats in Rotton Park and Duddeston and Nechells.`

Labour's inability to repeat its 1911 success, and its almost total eclipse in 1913, was closely paralleled in Liverpool. In 1911, following a bitter strike in the city, Conservatives and Liberals agreed on a municipal truce for the November election. Neither party opposed the other's candidates in any of the wards. Labour, however, put forward a large field of fifteen candidates, only one of these (James Sexton) a retiring councillor. Labour's efforts met with what the *Manchester Guardian* acclaimed as 'a great triumph'.[21] Labour secured six gains, sweeping the Liberals from Everton, Garston and Brunswick wards and taking three Conservative working-class wards. But Labour's success was short-lived. In 1912, thirteen Labour candidates fought in Liverpool. None was elected and the *Manchester Guardian* found the results 'decidedly unfavourable'. A similar total lack of success occurred in the municipal elections of November 1913.

Nor were Birmingham and Liverpool isolated exceptions. Such towns as Rochdale or Sheffield provide equally close parallels.[22] Perhaps the most extreme example of Labour's rise followed by slump was to be found in Belfast.[23]

Thus, prior to 1913, Labour often achieved a spectacular victory but failed very noticeably to repeat it. The examples of Birmingham and Liverpool provide useful evidence on another overlooked factor of Labour's municipal progress prior to 1914.

As often as not, Labour's advance in municipal elections prior to 1914 was at the expense of *Conservatives* rather than Liberals. The 1913 results in Birmingham neatly demonstrate the point. At first sight, Labour made two gains whilst the Liberals suffered two losses. The *details* are very different: Liberals lost two seats (Sparkhill and Erdington North) to the *Conservatives*. The Conservatives lost two seats (Duddeston and Nechells, and Rotton Park) to Labour—Labour had not even challenged any Liberal seats. These Birmingham results can be paralleled in 1911 in Liverpool, where Labour won such Tory-held working-class wards as Low Hill, Edge Hill and Domingo.

Paradoxically there is little doubt that many of Labour's municipal success stories prior to 1914 were not *against* Liberals, but in harness *with them* against Conservative strongholds. Not surprisingly, Lancashire provides a variety of such pacts.

A perfect example of a successful Lib-Lab *entente* in municipal politics prior to 1914 can be seen in Wigan. For the elections of November 1913, thirteen Conservative candidates found themselves opposed in straight fights by eight Labour and five Liberals.[24] The outcome was a Progressive triumph, with five Labour gains and one Liberal. For the first time since 1864, Conservatives lost control of the council. Working-class wards, such as St Catherine's, with a tradition of Conservatism, went Labour.[25] The Progressive vote totalled 7205, against 5486 for the Conservatives—leaving Labour hopeful of capturing the Parliamentary seat at the next general election. Lancashire was not alone in demonstrating the value of the 'progressive alliance'. In 1913, Wakefield was a similar scene of Progressive triumph after twenty years of Conservative domination in the council.[26] The railway town of Derby saw very close Lib-Lab municipal co-operation prior to 1914 with benefits to each partner in the 'progressive alliance'.[27]

Whilst the success of municipal Lib-Lab alliances is an interesting comment on pre-war politics, the crucial thesis that has to be tested is Labour's progress in the key cities of provincial England. For representative purposes, this essay looks at five such towns: the three Yorkshire industrial centres of Bradford, Leeds and Sheffield and the two Midland towns of Nottingham and Leicester.

Of the Yorkshire boroughs in which Labour's advance was most pronounced, Bradford occupied a pre-eminent place. Labour, who had first secured representation on the council in the 1890s, had seen their membership grow to eleven in 1906. By 1913, with twenty members, they had become a powerful force:

TABLE 4   Composition of Bradford Council, 1906–13

|      | Con | Lib | Lab | Others |
|------|-----|-----|-----|--------|
| 1905 | 31  | 42  | 10  | 1      |
| 1906 | 34  | 38  | 11  | 1      |
| 1908 | 42  | 30  | 10  | 2      |
| 1912 | 35  | 31  | 17  | 1      |
| 1913 | 32  | 31  | 20  | 1      |

Not only had Labour achieved a secure grip on such working-class wards as Bradford Moor, Manningham and Tong, but they had made a determined effort on the Liberal and Conservative strongholds. Thus, in the elections of November 1913, of Bradford's 21 wards, 18 were contested.

In 17 of these, Labour were fielding candidates, leaving only the residential North ward unattacked. And in the immediate pre-1914 period, Labour's assault was rewarded with successes. In 1912, Labour's main victims had been the Liberals, who lost four seats to Labour in a contest dominated by Labour's proposals for a municipally controlled supply of coal. The following year, in November 1913, the feature of the election was Labour's three gains at the expense of, this time, the Conservatives. But though the Conservatives had lost more seats, the Liberals had suffered equally badly. The *Yorkshire Post* commented: 'the chief fact of the Bradford polling is the demonstration of the loss of strength by the Liberal Party as a whole.'[28.] With the Liberals at the foot of the poll in three-cornered contests in such wards as Heaton and South, it was indeed clear how far the party had slipped.

Faced with a mounting Labour challenge, a highly significant coming-together of the Conservative and Liberal Parties in local 'anti-Socialist pacts' began to take place. It is not clear who initiated such local alliances, but most probably the Liberals were to the fore. Certainly, the *Yorkshire Post* found that the leaders of municipal Liberalism 'have been most emphatic in their declarations against the Socialists'.[29] Labour, not surprisingly, dubbed the Liberals and Conservatives the 'Blue and Yellow Tories' and, rather less graciously, linked them together as 'fossil-hunting liars'.[30]

By 1913, Bradford had already seen the older parties join in effective alliance in the industrial working-class wards of South and East Bradford. The nature of the anti-Socialist pact in the industrial wards can be seen in the table below:

TABLE 5   The anti-Socialist alliance in Bradford

|  | 1910 | 1911 | 1912 | 1913 |
|---|---|---|---|---|
| Allerton | L v Lab | L v Lab | C v Lab | L v Lab |
| Bradford Moor | L v Lab | C v Lab | C v Lab v L | L v Lab |
| Great Horton | C v Lab | L v Lab | L v Lab v C | L v Lab |
| Manningham | C v Lab v L | Lab v L | Lab v L | C v Lab |
| West Bowling | Lab v L | Lab v L | C v Lab v L | C v Lab |
| North Bierley E. | L v Lab | C v Lab | L v Lab | L v Lab |

As Table 5 indicates, in such working-class wards as Allerton and Manningham, Labour rarely faced three-cornered contests: the older parties had already combined against it. The anti-Socialist pact reached its peak in 1913. In that year, Labour's seventeen candidates faced no less than twelve straight fights, six against Liberals, six against Conservatives. Three-cornered fights were restricted to such wards as Heaton and Thornton. As we have seen, these tactics failed to halt

Labour's advance. Even more significantly, there is evidence to suggest that such anti-Socialist tactics by middle-class Liberals only served to alienate their working-class support. Thus, in the West Bowling ward, the local Liberal Association stood down to give the Conservatives a clear run in a ward won by Labour in November 1912. Labour, however, retained the seat, capturing much of the old radical Liberal vote. As the *Yorkshire Post* sadly concluded, 'a goodly proportion of Liberal voters are not amenable to dictation by their leaders.'

Certainly, no amount of local alliances had halted the growth in Labour's share of votes cast in the November elections.

TABLE 6    Growth of Labour vote in Bradford, 1905–13

|      | *Lab* | *Lib* | *Con* | *Ind* |
|------|-------|-------|-------|-------|
| 1905 | 22·0  | 34·6  | 41·3  | 2·0   |
| 1906 | 26·6  | 26·3  | 37·8  | 9·2   |
| 1907 | 30·5  | 31·3  | 31·7  | 6·5   |
| 1908 | 30·0  | 32·7  | 32·9  | 4·5   |
| 1909 | 31·3  | 30·2  | 29·5  | 9·2   |
| 1910 | 35·2  | 31·4  | 33·0  | 0·4   |
| 1911 | 31·0  | 33·6  | 32·0  | 3·5   |
| 1912 | 42·0  | 26·0  | 32·0  | —     |
| 1913 | 43·1  | 29·7  | 27·2  | —     |

By 1913, Labour had surpassed quite easily the polls cast for Liberal or Conservative opponents. After an almost uninterrupted rise, over 40 per cent of all votes cast in contested elections were secured by Labour candidates.

It was perhaps fitting that Bradford, where Keir Hardie had established the Independent Labour Party in 1893, and where such leaders of municipal socialism as Fred Jowett received their political baptism, should be in the vanguard of Labour's municipal advance. But Bradford's rival town of the West Riding was not lagging far behind.

In Leeds as in Bradford the decade prior to 1914 witnessed a major and significant decline in Liberal council strength. In a city in which the Liberals had been the dominant party during the Victorian period[31] a transformation occurred, as is shown by Table 7 (see p. 48).

In common with most other towns, Liberals (and indeed Labour) had suffered badly in 1907 and 1908—a time of national unpopularity for Liberals. A partial recovery of Liberal fortunes occurred in 1910, but from then onwards Labour's advance began to hit the Liberals—most especially their working-class wards such as Holbeck, Bramley and

South. In this sharp Liberal decline, the worst single year had been 1912. In a Conservative triumph that year, the Conservatives had returned thirteen members, compared to four Labour and a mere two Liberals. There had been seven Conservative gains and one Labour.[33]

The rise of Labour in Leeds was a relatively swift process. In November 1902, no direct Labour representation had been achieved. As Hennock has written, the representation of the working class was still of insignificant proportions and channelled entirely through the Liberal Party.[34] By 1912, exactly ten years later, one council member in ten was a manual worker or trade-union official. They belonged (with a solitary

TABLE 7    Composition of Leeds City Council, 1906–13[32]

|      | Con | Lib | Lab | Ind |
|------|-----|-----|-----|-----|
| 1906 | 21  | 34  | 9   | —   |
| 1907 | 28  | 26  | 10  |     |
| 1908 | 36  | 23  | 4   | 1   |
| 1909 | 34  | 23  | 6   | 1   |
| 1910 | 31  | 26  | 6   | 1   |
| 1911 | 26  | 28  | 10  | —   |
| 1912 | 34  | 23  | 11  | —   |
| 1913 | 34  | 18  | 16  | —   |

exception) to the Labour Party. Labour's rise had hit the Liberals particularly hard—not merely in Liberal seats lost to Labour, but Liberal seats lost to Conservatives through Labour intervention.[35] By 1913 it was becoming an all-too-common occurrence for Liberals to find themselves bottom of the poll in areas in which they had once been strong.[36] The *Yorkshire Post*'s observation in 1913 that 'Liberalism was on the wane in Leeds' had much justification.[37] In the six three-cornered contests in the city, the Liberals had polled less than either of the other parties.[38] It was perhaps symbolic of the decline of Liberalism in Leeds that in November 1913, if aldermanic creations are excluded, for the first time the number of Labour councillors had overtaken the Liberals. In Leeds, as in Bradford, Labour was providing a growing challenge to Liberals at this local level.

In marked contrast to both Leeds and Bradford, municipal politics in Sheffield prior to 1914 saw nothing like the same rate of growth by the Labour Party. Whilst Labour was still doing battle at local level, the scale of its challenge was also far weaker than in either Bradford or Leeds. Unlike these two towns, Liberalism in Sheffield had also less of a tradition behind it, for the town was something of a centre of working-class Conservatism.[39]

Municipal politics in Sheffield thus display several distinct features:

but the overlying trends of a town in which municipal elections had long been fought on party lines are very worthy of analysis.[40] Certainly, in common with other cities in the West Riding, the Liberals were a declining force prior to 1914.

TABLE 8   Sheffield Council composition, 1900–13

|      | Con | Lib | Lab | Others |
|------|-----|-----|-----|--------|
| 1900 | 34  | 30  | —   | —      |
| 1901 | 31  | 33  | —   | —      |
| 1902 | 30  | 34  | —   | —      |
| 1903 | 31  | 33  | —   | —      |
| 1904 | 33  | 31  | —   | —      |
| 1905 | 29  | 34  | 1   | —      |
| 1906 | 29  | 32  | 3   | —      |
| 1908 | 34  | 27  | 3   | —      |
| 1909 | 35  | 26  | 3   | —      |
| 1910 | 33  | 29  | 2   | —      |
| 1912 | 31  | 33  | —   | —      |
| 1913 | 32  | 30  | 2   | —      |

The Liberals, who had regained control of the council in 1905, never enjoyed the same degree of success again, yet they had hardly suffered a serious decline. Partly, no doubt, because of Labour's very curious lack of progress in Sheffield.

Labour's first major success in Sheffield had come in 1905, when the first avowedly Socialist representative was returned for Brightside. Labour had followed up this victory by taking both Brightside and Darnall wards in 1906. A year later, Brightside had become a completely Labour ward. By 1908, Labour was polling over 7000 votes in the November elections. But thereafter, Labour's advance was to go very rapidly and decisively into reverse.

After serious setbacks in 1909 and 1910 (when they lost the only seat they were called on to defend), Labour representation on the city council by 1912 had been completely wiped out. The old era of Gilbertian politics had been restored. Indeed, 1912 was little short of a total Labour humiliation. Of Sheffield's sixteen wards, contested elections occurred in no less than fifteen. With a mere four candidates, Labour's challenge was conspicuous only by its absence. In the three-cornered contests, Labour finished bottom in each case, losing their defending seats in each case. To add insult to humiliation, Labour finished bottom of the poll even in their Brightside stronghold, which the Conservatives won by one vote over a Liberal.

Although Labour to some extent recovered lost ground in 1913 (by winning back both Attercliffe and Brightside wards) in the only three-cornered contest in the city (in Broomhall ward) Labour finished a poor

TABLE 9    Labour and local elections in Sheffield, 1906–13

|  | Lab candidates | Lab vote | Lab percentage | Lab elected | Lab on council |
|---|---|---|---|---|---|
| 1906 | 6 | 5638 | 15·9 | 1 | 3 |
| 1907 | 5 | 5555 | 14·3 | 1 | 4 |
| 1908 | 6 | 7048 | 14·7 | 1 | 3 |
| 1909 | 4 | 4861 | 11·6 | 1 | 3 |
| 1910 | 2 | 1308 | 3·4 | 1 | 2 |
| 1911 | 4 | 4545 | 11·5 | — | 2 |
| 1912 | 4 | 2817 | 6·4 | — | — |
| 1913 | 4 | 5190 | 11·3 | 2 | 2 |

third. In these three three-cornered contests, Labour in fact had polled worst of the three major parties.[41] In the town as a whole in 1913, Labour contested only five wards, nowhere coming within real range of victory.

In terms of ward representation, the following table shows how Sheffield municipal politics remained very much a monopoly of Conservatives and Liberals:

TABLE 10    Party allegiance of Sheffield wards, 1906–13

| Ward | 1906 | 1907 | 1908 | 1909 | 1910 | 1911 | 1912 | 1913 |
|---|---|---|---|---|---|---|---|---|
| Attercliffe | Lib | Lib | Con | Lib | Lib | Con | Lib | Lab |
| Brightside | Lab | Lab | Lab | Lab | Lib | Lib | Con | Lab |
| Broomhall | Lib | Con | Con | Con | Con | Lib | Con | Con |
| Burngreave | Con | Lib | Lib | Lib | Lib | Lib | Lib | Lib |
| Crooksmoor | Lib | Lib | Lib | Lib | Con | Lib | Lib | Con |
| Darnall | Lib | Lib | Lib | Lib | Lab | Lib | Lib | Lib |
| Eccleshall | Con | Con | Con | Con | Con | Con | Con | Con |
| Hallam | Con | Con | Lib | Con | Con | Lib | Con | Con |
| Heeley | Con | Con | Con | Con | Con | Con | Con | Con |
| Hillsborough | Con | Con | Lib | Con | Lib | Lib | Con | Lib |
| Neepsend | Lib | Con | Con | Lib | Lib | Lib | Lib | Lib |
| Park | Con | Lib | Con | Con | Lib | Con | Con | Lib |
| St Peters | Con | Lib | Con | Lib | Con | Con | Con | Con |
| St Philips | Con | Con | Con | Con | Con | Con | Con | Con |
| Sharrow | Con | Con | Con | Lib | Con | Lib | Lib | Con |
| Walkley | Lib | Lib | Con | Lib | Lib | Lib | Lib | Lib |

Reducing this chart to figures, Conservatives won 65 seats at the November elections (50·8% of the total), Liberals secured 56 (43·7% of the total) while Labour managed a mere 7 (5·5%). There could hardly be more conclusive evidence of Labour's weakness.

Certainly, Sheffield politics hardly provides evidence to support a rapid rise by Labour prior to 1914 even if, in common with other Yorkshire towns, it reveals the Liberals in difficulties. Equally, in none of these three Yorkshire cities is there evidence to corroborate Clarke's important findings for Lancashire.[42] In Yorkshire, Liberalism in the large cities in 1913 was far weaker than for many years.

But was Yorkshire somehow a special case? Or was Lancashire more representative of Liberal fortunes? The old radical Liberal strongholds of the Midlands provide an area that has not hitherto been the subject of detailed research at this local level. Although there were significant differences, particularly in the scale and success of the Labour challenge prior to 1914, the major towns of the Midlands reveal many similarities in their electoral politics.

Of the former radical Liberal strongholds, Leicester provides a good example of municipal Liberalism in difficulties in the 1906–14 period. For Leicester Liberals, the municipal elections were important in two directions: a declining Liberal strength on the council, together with the problem of relations with the Labour Party.

The decline of Liberalism in Leicester was symbolised in the municipal elections of November 1908. For, prior to that date, Leicester had been a Liberal-controlled council since 1836. For over seventy years, Leicester had been a radical stronghold.[43] In 1908 Conservatives captured control with three net gains. The *Leicester Journal* commented on the Conservative triumph: 'The Liberal monopoly on the Town Council is now broken for the first time for 70 years . . . Liberalism is a dying cause here; it has been dying hard ever since Mr. MacDonald rode to Westminster on the backs of the Bishop St. caucus.'[44]

The 1908 Liberal reverse was followed by more setbacks. In 1909, a determined Labour attack gained four seats, three of these from the Liberals who also lost a further seat to the Conservatives. In 1910, another Liberal ward was lost to Labour, although with only four contests in the whole of Leicester the electoral excitement of the previous years was over. In statistical terms, during the period 1906 to 1913, Labour's advance was pronounced.

Though the Liberals had returned more councillors than either of their rivals (41·4% of the total), Labour had won 25·8% of all seats—an important achievement since they had the largest number of councillors returned in *contested* elections (see Table 11). Even more important for the future (as Table 12 shows) was the fact that by 1913, not a single ward had consistently returned a Liberal at every election since 1906. In contrast, Labour was tightening its grip on the working-class wards. As the *Leicester Daily Post* commented in 1913, St Margaret's and Aylestone were already established as Socialist strongholds.[45] Labour influence

TABLE 11    Candidates for council elections in Leicester, 1906–13

|     | *Elected unopposed* | *Elected* | *Total elected* |
|-----|-----|-----|-----|
| Con | 30 | 12 | 42 |
| Lab | 13 | 20 | 33 |
| Lib | 34 | 19 | 53 |
|     | 77 | 51 | 128 |

was growing in Newton, Latimer and Castle. The local press noted particularly Labour's all-year-round activity in the wards, in marked contrast to Liberal neglect of their own seats.[46]

Beneath the surface of the Liberal gains and losses each year, by far the most important question for the Liberals was their relations with Labour. Although, for Westminster, the Lib-Lab pact had returned Ramsay MacDonald in harness with a Liberal, at local elections relations were becoming increasingly strained. The *Leicester Journal*

TABLE 12    Party allegiance of Leicester wards, 1906–13

| *Ward* | *1906* | *1907* | *1908* | *1909* | *1910* | *1911* | *1912* | *1913* |
|-----|-----|-----|-----|-----|-----|-----|-----|-----|
| St Margarets | Con | Lab | Lab | Lab | Lab | Lab | Lab | Lab |
| Newton | Lib | Lib | Lib | Lab | Lib | Lib | Lab | Lib |
| Castle | Lib | Lib | Lib | Lab | Con | Lib | Lab | Con |
| St Martins | Con | Con | Con | Con | Con | Con | Con | Con |
| Wyggeston | Lab | Con | Lab | Lab | Con | Lib | Lab | Con |
| Latimer | Lib | Lab | Lib | Lab | Lab | Lib | Lab | Lab |
| Charnwood | Lib | Lib | Con | Lib | Lib | Con | Lib | Lib |
| Wycliffe | Lib | Con | Con | Con | Con | Con | Con | Con |
| De Montfort | Con | Con | Con | Con | Con | Con | Con | Con |
| Westcotes | Lib | Con | Lib | Lib | Lib | Lib | Lib | Lib |
| Abbey | Lib | Lab | Lib | Lib | Lab | Lab | Lib | Lab |
| Belgrave | Lab | Lib | Lib | Con | Lib | Lib | Lab | Lib |
| Humberstone | Lib | Lib | Lab | Lib | Lib | Lab | Lib | Lib |
| Spinney Hill | Lib | Con | Lib | Lib | Con | Lib | Lib | Con |
| Knighton | Lib | Lib | Con | Con | Lib | Con | Con | Lib |
| Aylestone | Lab | Lib | Con | Lab | Lab | Con | Lab | Lab |

remarked in 1906 that 'Liberals have begun to find it impossible to run with the hare and hunt with the hounds'[47]—a reference to 1905 when Labour had fought and won the St Margaret's ward from a Liberal. By 1907, Liberals and Labour were open enemies. On 18 October 1907, Liberals announced they would oppose Labour candidates. Of the nine subsequent contested wards, Labour opposed Liberals in six of them. During the campaign, relations became increasingly strained. One Labour candidate accused the Liberals of not having 'ideals, method or programme'. Liberals retorted that all Labour could do was to spend other people's money.

Both Liberal and Labour suffered by opposing each other in 1907— the Conservatives gaining two seats. The *Leicester Journal* was delighted at the Lib-Lab split. Its editorial went on: '. . . the Liberals of Leicester have at length been brought to a frame of mind which enables them to smile on Conservative victories so long as they mean Socialist defeats.' Liberal-Labour relations worsened in 1908 (the year the party lost control in the council) and again in 1909 when Labour captured Liberal seats. Thereafter, scattered opposition occurred with the Liberals less keen to challenge Labour.[48]

This uneasy relationship between Liberals and Labour was a feature of pre-war municipal politics in the neighbouring Midland city of Nottingham. Certainly, by 1910, there was evidence that Liberals were looking in two directions at once. As the *Nottingham Guardian* found, radicals and socialists were curiously mixed up as friends in one quarter and foes in another.[49] But though Liberal relations with Labour were a serious problem, the real plight of Nottingham Liberalism lay in the rapidly revived fortunes of the Conservatives. Here, the decisive year—as in Leicester—was 1908. In November 1908, Conservative net gains from Liberals (plus a Liberal loss to Labour) transformed the municipal politics of the town. Control of the city council passed to the Conservatives for the first time in a generation. Thereafter, Conservatives rapidly tightened their control (see Table 13).

TABLE 13    Council composition in Nottingham, 1906–13

|      | Con | Lib | Lab | Others |
|------|-----|-----|-----|--------|
| 1906 | 23  | 41  | —   | —      |
| 1908 | 33  | 29  | 2   | —      |
| 1911 | 34  | 26  | 3   | 1      |
| 1912 | 35  | 27  | 2   | —      |
| 1913 | 37  | 25  | 2   | —      |

By 1913, Conservative representation had grown to a record 37, a high-water mark for the decade prior to 1914. In marked contrast, the Liberals had sunk to 25 members (39 per cent of the council) compared to 41 members (64 per cent) as recently as 1906. The decline of Nottingham Liberalism was an incontestable phenomenon. Indeed, so far had the Liberals in Nottingham declined that not a single ward in the city consistently returned a full Liberal complement prior to 1913 (see Table 14 below).

TABLE 14    Party allegiance of Nottingham wards, 1906–13

| Ward | 1906 | 1907 | 1908 | 1909 | 1910 | 1911 | 1912 | 1913 |
|------|------|------|------|------|------|------|------|------|
| Forest | Con | Con | Lib | Con | Con | Lib | Con | Lib |
| Mapperley | Lib | Con | Con | Lib | Con | Con | Con | Con |
| Castle | Lib | Lib | Con | Lib | Con | Con | Con | Con |
| Robin Hood | Con | Con | Con | Lib | Con | Con | Lib | Con |
| St Ann | Con | Con | Lib | Con | Con | Lib | Con | Con |
| Market | Con | Con | Con | Con | Con | Con | Con | Con |
| Sherwood | Con | Lib | Con | Con | Lib | Lib | Con | Lib |
| Bridge | Lib | Lib | Con | Lib | Lib | Con | Lib | Lib |
| Broxtowe | Lib | Lib | Con | Con | Lib | Con | Con | Lib |
| Trent | Con | Con | Con | Con | Lib | Lib | Con | Lib |
| Manvers | Con | Con | Lab | Con | Con | Lab | Con | Con |
| Byron | Con | Con | Con | Con | Con | Con | Con | Con |
| Wollaton | Lib | Lib | Lib | Con | Lib | Lib | Lib | Lib |
| Meadows | Lib | Lib | Lib | Lib | Lib | Lab | Lib | Con |
| St Mary | Con | Con | Con | Con | Con | Con | Con | Con |
| St Albans | Lib | Lib | Lib | Lab | Lib | Lib | Lib | Lib |

As can be seen, the decline in Liberal fortunes had relatively little to do with the rise of Labour. For unlike Bradford or Leeds, Labour's advance in Nottingham prior to 1914 was never conspicuous or indeed very real. Only on four occasions in a November election were Labour councillors successful (Manvers ward, 1908 and 1911, St Albans in 1909 and Meadows in 1911).

In terms of seats won, Labour's challenge was thus negligible (see Table 15). Even in terms of candidates fielded, Labour was far behind. Only eighteen Labour candidates came forward, six of these in 1912. In the six years from 1906 to 1911 inclusive, Labour fielded only eleven candidates, an average of less than two per year. In fact there is evidence that in some wards the Labour vote was in fact on the decline in the immediate pre-war years. In the Manvers ward, with its large proportion of miners, the *Nottingham Guardian* commented in 1913 that Labour had seen 'a heavy slump in its erstwhile stronghold.'[50] However, though

Labour was almost totally unable to *win* seats by its own efforts, its nuisance value in thwarting Liberals was at times very great. In all, in Nottingham as in Leicester, in varying ways and with varying success, Liberals faced the problems of increasingly difficult relations with Labour at a time when municipal Conservatism had rarely been stronger.

TABLE 15    Seats won by party in Nottingham, 1906–13

|  | Total | Percentage |
|---|---|---|
| Con | 75 | 58·6 |
| Lib | 49 | 38·3 |
| Lab | 4 | 3·1 |
|  | 128 | 100·0 |

It is hardly an exaggeration to say that, by 1913, municipal Liberalism in the major cities hardly presented the healthiest of forces. Birmingham was effectively a lost cause; in Liverpool, sectarian politics had already forced the Liberals to the sidelines. Manchester remained firmly in Conservative hands. In Glasgow, the anti-Socialists had all joined forces since 1899 in an anti-Labour Moderate Party. In the large cities of Yorkshire, in the old radical towns of the Midlands, Liberals were on the defensive. Nor was there much of comfort for the Liberals in the municipal politics of the capital. For in London, the plight of the Progressives had by 1912 become quite desperate and indeed made the difficulties of Liberals in the provincial boroughs seem relatively unimportant. On the London County Council, the decline of the Progressives (as the local Liberals were known) had already assumed dramatic proportions.

TABLE 16    Party composition: London County Council

|  | Municipal reform | Progressive | Lab | Others | Total |
|---|---|---|---|---|---|
| 1901 | 36 | 101 | — | — | 137 |
| 1904 | 39 | 98 | — | — | 137 |
| 1907 | 89 | 47 | — | 1 | 137 |
| 1910 | 75 | 57 | 3 | 2 | 137 |
| 1913 | 81 | 53 | 1 | 2 | 137 |

The Progressives on the L.C.C. had, by 1913, been broken. As Thompson has written of their fate:[51]

In the early 1900s the most successful Progressive Party was on the L.C.C. In power since 1889, securing trade union support through its 'labour bench' and fair labour principles, justly proud of its improvements in London housing and the tramway system, holding Nonconformist allegiance through its temperance policy, the Party had been returned in the 1904 election by an overwhelming majority. Yet in 1907, a bare year after the General Election triumphs of the Liberals, it was crushed. In spite of a strong recovery in 1910, it was never again able to secure a majority on the Council.

If the plight of the Progressives on the county council was serious, at borough level the situation was little short of desperate. As Thompson has written, the Progressive parties in the borough councils were much less successful than on the L.C.C. in combining the various Liberal elements, and never met with such general success at elections. Even in 1903, when the Liberal revival was well under way, only ten of twenty-eight boroughs were controlled by Progressive parties. In 1906, the only Progressive councils to withstand the Municipal Reform attack had been Battersea and Bethnal Green. By 1909, only four councils had a Progressive majority; before the 1912 elections, Progressives still controlled Bethnal Green, Hackney and Southwark. Eight Municipal Reform gains lost the Progressives control of Hackney in 1912, and Southwark was barely held. In part compensation, Progressives regained Battersea. But by 1912, the Progressive forces could number only 272 councillors out of 1362 in the metropolitan borough councils. As the table below shows, Municipal Reform had an overwhelming preponderance after 1906, at least until Labour's 1919 landslide.

TABLE 17    Metropolitan borough council results, 1906–19

|  | Municipal reform | Progressive | Lab | Ind | Total |
|---|---|---|---|---|---|
| 1906 | 959 | 272 | 34 | 97 | 1362 |
| 1909 | 977 | 251 | 41 | 93 | 1362 |
| 1912 | 1002 | 252 | 48 | 60 | 1362 |
| 1919 | 598 | 131 | 573 | 61 | 1362 |

The evidence that municipal Liberalism was in difficulties, often serious difficulties, prior to 1913 is very great. The capital provided the worst example; the industrial North was equally bad; and there was little comfort in the Midlands. With some notable exceptions, the trend was true of the smaller municipal boroughs. But, as in some of the larger boroughs already examined, this Liberal decline was *not* accompanied by a rise of Labour. In the quiet market towns, in the university and cathedral towns, the old order of municipal politics went on undisturbed.

Of the smaller towns in which, prior to 1914, Labour made repeated efforts to achieve council success with virtually nil reward, Oxford provides an admirable example.

TABLE 18     Wards won by party in Oxford, 1906–13

| Ward | 1906 | 1907 | 1908 | 1909 | 1910 | 1911 | 1912 | 1913 |
|------|------|------|------|------|------|------|------|------|
| North | CCC | I CC | CCC | CCC | CCC | CCL | CCC | CCC |
| South | CCC | CLL | CLL | CLL | CLL | CLL | CLL | CLL |
| East | CLL | CLL | CCL | CCL | CLL | CLL | CCL | CLL |
| West | CLL | CCL | CCL | CCL | CCL | CCC | CCC | CCC |

C = Conservative, L = Liberal, I = Independent.

Prior to 1913, with the solitary exception of an Independent elected in the North ward in 1907, Oxford politics was an exclusive Liberal-Conservative monopoly, an undisturbed continuation of the Gilbertian age. As the table below shows, the North and West wards were Conservative, the South and East more evenly balanced.

|  | North | South | East | West | Total |
|------|------|------|------|------|------|
| Con | 22 | 10 | 11 | 18 | 61 |
| Lib | 1 | 14 | 13 | 6 | 34 |
| Other | 1 | — | — | — | 1 |
|  | 24 | 24 | 24 | 24 | 96 |

In terms of candidates fielded, Labour's total lack of success and the increasing Conservative predominance are set out below:

TABLE 19     Candidates for council election in Oxford, 1906–13
(including unopposed returns)

|  | Candidates | Seats won |
|------|------|------|
| Con | 77 | 61 |
| Lib | 56 | 34 |
| Lab | 17 | 0 |
| Other | 5 | 1 |

In Oxford, as in other small non-industrial towns, Labour's total lack of progress was not merely confined to the pre-war period. In 1921, Labour launched a major attack for the town council. Both in votes cast and seats won, the venture was a disaster (see Table 20).

In Oxford, as elsewhere, Labour's weakness and Liberal difficulties went together. As the *Oxford Chronicle* commented on the loss of a Liberal seat in East ward in 1908:[52]

> . . . the moral of his defeat is the one that has so often been emphasised at Oxford municipal elections. The Liberal and Labour parties ought to work together, not separately; and so long as they work separately, Liberal interests will suffer, and there will be no chance at all of any direct representative of Labour getting a seat on the Oxford City Council.

The remarks of the *Oxford Chronicle* were a fitting comment on Labour's weakness and the dangers of splitting any 'Progressive Alliance'.

TABLE 20    Municipal elections in Oxford, November 1921*

| Party | No. of candidates | Total vote | Percentage share |
|-------|-------------------|------------|------------------|
| Con | 9 | 12,525 | 40·7 |
| Lib | 11 | 13,115 | 42·6 |
| Lab | 11 | 5143 | 16·7 |
| | 31 | 32,783 | 100·0 |

* See Cook, *Age of Alignment,* pp. 67–8.

The almost total lack of Labour success in Oxford was not unique to that university city. For virtually all the smaller boroughs, the old county towns and cathedral cities with no major industrial sector, Labour's rise to power was not even beginning prior to the First World War. Detailed studies of Edwardian politics in such market towns as Banbury or cathedral cities such as Exeter confirm this fact.[53] In a few towns, such as King's Lynn, won in a notable victory by the Liberals in 1913, the sole working-class councillor was a Liberal nominee. This fact cannot be emphasised too much: outside a very few heavily industrialised wards of major cities, Labour's municipal advance prior to 1914 was either negligible or non-existent. In such boroughs as Yarmouth and Grimsby, no Labour representation on the council at all was achieved until 1918. In such towns as Canterbury, there were no Labour councillors until the 1930s.

But Labour's lack of success in the smaller towns—and indeed in some larger ones—was of little comfort to a hard-pressed Liberal Party.

For the statistics of town councils lost to Conservatives, the yearly tally of wards lost each November, were all figures which disguised some more fundamental Liberal weaknesses in these pre-war years. The first was the fact that the Liberals had not established a *modus vivendi* at municipal level in their relations with Labour. Liberal associations at local level tended to look in two directions. Some sought an accommodation with Labour; others looked to an anti-Labour alliance with the Conservatives. Close Liberal-Labour relations were, as we have seen, a feature of pre-war municipal politics in a variety of towns.[54] In these cases, Liberal-Labour relations were not only close and harmonious, but produced electoral benefits that were extremely pleasing, as in 1913 in Wigan and Wakefield. Equally, there were towns where Liberals sought an accommodation with Labour, but nothing concrete was achieved. In Coventry, for example, between 1907 and 1914 the local Liberals made repeated efforts to secure an agreement with Labour, but little was achieved. Thus in 1912 the minutes of the Coventry Liberal Municipal Committee recorded that: '. . . a letter was read from the secretary of the Coventry Labour Party agreeing to meet and confer with the Committee on the selection of candidates for the forthcoming Municipal Elections'.[55] On 7 May, the Liberals resolved to talk with Labour, but no agreement was subsequently recorded in the minutes. In the elections of 1912, Coventry Liberals suffered further reverses. The town council, captured by the Conservatives in 1908 (the first time for many years), remained firmly in Conservative control.[56] By 1918, Liberal attitudes had changed. In the first post-war municipal elections (in 1919) the Liberals entered into an anti-Socialist pact with the Conservatives.[57]

It was perhaps symbolic of Liberalism in this period that there were boroughs in which Liberals tried all three roads to salvation simultaneously. One such borough was Lambeth, a large metropolitan borough ranging from prosperous middle-class suburbs to poverty-stricken back-to-back housing along the riverside. In Lambeth, all varieties of Liberal municipal politics were to be found. As Thompson has written:

. . . at the wealthiest end, compromises with the Conservatives; a middle belt of Nonconformist influence; and in the working class wards, either arrangements or three-cornered fights with Labour. But tactics of this variety prevented a coherent policy, and even if the labour vote was not lost through direct conflict it was as likely to be lost through apathy.[58]

Lambeth was not alone in reflecting the chaos of Liberal politics. Like Lambeth, Nottingham also exhibited a peculiar mixture of *entente* in one ward and war in the next. Thus the *Nottingham Guardian* in 1910 found 'radicals and socialists curiously mixed up as friends in one quarter but foes in another.'[59] Such confusion arose from the particular social composition and political outlook of the ward concerned. The increasing tendency, however, of hard-pressed Liberals seeking an accommodation with Conservatives to exclude Labour seems to have grown considerably prior to 1914. Certainly in London, there was in this period 'a new tendency in boroughs where the Labour Party provided a threat for a "Municipal Alliance" to be formed.'[60] Partly, no doubt, the weakness of the Progressives accounted for this eagerness to come to terms with the

Conservatives. Such municipal alliances took root in such Socialist strongholds as West Ham, Poplar and East Ham.

West Ham provides a model example of such a municipal alliance. In 1898 Labour gained control of West Ham council, the first borough to fall under Socialist control. The formation of the 'Municipal Alliance' in 1899 was a direct response to this event. All shades of Conservative and Liberal opinion joined in the new organisation. The aims of the Municipal Alliance were clearly defined. The organisation sought to curtail municipal trading, promote economy wherever possible, attack the 'degrading and demoralising' Poor Law and conduct public affairs 'for the common good'.[61]

The Municipal Alliance was a borough organisation: at ward level, the Alliance fostered the growth of local ratepayers associations. These met regularly, usually at monthly intervals, and performed the important function of preventing overlapping anti-Socialist candidates in the November elections. The 'Municipal Alliance' in West Ham provided the model and the inspiration for similar anti-Socialist pacts in East Ham and Poplar.

Such was the weakness of London Liberalism that these municipal pacts extended far beyond the Socialist strongholds of the East End. Thus in Hammersmith, Liberals fought local elections after 1906 as part of a ratepayers association which had strong Conservative support—and had earlier joined forces with the Conservative Association in arranging joint lists for the Guardian's elections. In 1909, the Conservatives rebelled against their Liberal allies; nearly every former Liberal was defeated. As Thompson concludes, Hammersmith Liberalism, as a local political force, was dead.[62] A similar Liberal-Conservative alliance occurred in North Kensington, a constituency with many poor working-class districts but a wealthy residential area. The Liberals lost much working-class and Labour support over the Boer War. Thereafter the middle-class Liberal rump joined forces for local elections with the Conservatives after 1900.[63] Similar co-operation occurred in parts of Paddington. In many of the outer London suburbs (such as Croydon) and in such Kent towns as Gillingham, municipal politics by 1914 was already the issue of Labour versus the rest.[64]

Nor were these anti-Socialist alliances confined to London. In a variety of English provincial boroughs there was increasing evidence prior to 1914 of local Conservative-Liberal accommodation. In individual wards, this has already been seen in Bradford and Leeds. Parts of Nottingham displayed a similar leaning. Some of the smaller Lancashire towns (such as Leigh in 1911) also showed co-operation.

There were some unexpected examples of Liberal-Conservative co-operation, as in the railway town of Crewe. Here, Labour had achieved its first representation on the council in November 1902. By 1908, the

Labour group's strength had risen to five. In 1908, however, a municipal 'general election' took place in which the Liberals entered into an anti-Labour 'pact' with the Conservatives. This pact, the forerunner of an inter-war alliance in the Crewe Progressive Union, proved disastrous to Labour whose rpresentation on the new town council was totally removed.[65] Not until 1911 was Labour able to secure the return of any representative to the council.

Meanwhile, in Scotland, where municipal Liberalism like parliamentary Liberalism was to the right of its counterpart south of the border, Glasgow elections had long been fought by Labour against its combined opponents—grouped since 1898 as the Glasgow Moderates. Many of the smaller Scottish burghs repeated this pattern.

To concentrate unduly on such examples of Liberal-Conservative co-operation would be unfair. They were still very much the exception rather than the rule. But they were a significant forerunner of the development of national politics after 1918 and they were undoubted evidence of Liberal municipal weakness prior to 1914.

The dilemma of Liberal relations with Labour was part of a wider problem—the age, outlook and social class of the great bulk of municipal Liberal candidates. In Edwardian England the party was increasingly being seen to be fielding older candidates, and was equally seen to be unwilling to put working-class candidates in the field. At the same time the policies offered by Liberal candidates for municipal election were becoming either out-dated or contradictory.

The age of municipal Liberal candidates is not an easy subject on which to assemble detailed figures. When a Labour candidate at the 1911 municipal elections in Leicester ungraciously accused the Liberals of being able to field only 'worn-out old veterans' there was no doubt much exaggeration.[66] However, recent studies of both Wolverhampton and Leeds have confirmed that Liberals consistently fielded older men, usually businessmen and shopkeepers entering the council chamber as the crowning success of their careers.[67] Thus in Leeds, the average age of new members of the city council prior to 1914 showed considerable variations between the parties:

TABLE 21   Average age of new council entrants: Leeds City Council[68]

|         | 1888/1903 | 1903/14 |
|---------|-----------|---------|
| Lib     | 42·8      | 43·9    |
| Con     | 42·2      | 43·4    |
| Lab     | 39·6      | 32·5    |
| Average | 43·1      | 43·3    |

In each period, the Liberals were the eldest, Labour the youngest. The youth of the Labour entrants in the 1903–19 period is interesting.

Perhaps even more significant than the age and attitudes of these Liberal councillors was their class background. The Liberals not only fielded older candidates, but very rarely were they working-class men. The party relied almost exclusively on the higher and middle classes. Two examples of the Liberal inability, or unwillingness, to field working-class candidates can be seen in Leeds and Wolverhampton. Of twenty-seven elected Liberals in Leeds during the period 1906–18 whose occupations can be traced, not one was from the working class. Of thirteen newcomers to the Council in the 1919 to 1928 period, not a single working-class representative was to be found. In each group manufacturers, professional men and small shopkeepers were the most numerous. Over the whole period 1888–1935, no less than 153 of 158 new Liberal councillors were from the upper or higher-middle classes.[69]

The occupation and social class of the Liberal councillors in Wolverhampton closely follows the pattern of Leeds. Of the thirty-two new Liberal entrants between 1888 and 1919, thirteen were shopkeepers, nine were manufacturers and five were in the professions. By contrast, of the thirteen Labour entrants, eleven were working class.

What are the explanations behind this drift at municipal level towards co-operation with erstwhile enemies? Clearly, the motives and issues which had brought Liberals on to the councils had begun to disappear.

Two issues had dominated the councils, separating Conservative and Liberal, before 1900: religion and economy.[70] With the old religious cleavage beginning to disappear, Liberals were not separated on principle from Conservatives: in the face of Labour, Liberal and Conservative policy was virtually indistinguishable, and, indeed, invisible. Almost certainly, a major factor contributing to the eventual fall of the Liberal Party was its failure to produce a constructive municipal policy that went beyond such negative demands as economy. In local politics, the Liberal Party had no *raison d'être*.

At Wolverhampton, Jones has written: 'The Anti-Socialist groups possessed no distinctive policy. Neither the Liberals nor the Conservatives had a municipal programme—merely the need to resist Socialist dictation and to oppose wild and extravagant schemes. Alone of all the parties, Labour had a distinctive municipal policy.'[72] Jones was writing of the inter-war years: but his comments were increasingly of relevance to the years up to 1914.

The conclusions of this municipal study can be simply stated: the Liberals were in decline—in some places serious decline—in municipal elections prior to 1914. London, where the party's roots were weak, was perhaps the worst example. Thompson's conclusion that the party was 'rotting at the roots' is sustained by the evidence he brings forward. Of the large provincial cities of England, as we have seen, Manchester was firmly in Conservative control. Liverpool and Birmingham were already Liberal wastelands. The major cities of the north, such as Leeds and Bradford, had passed from Liberal control. In the Midland towns of Nottingham and Leicester, the old Radical supremacy had been challenged successfully. The few individual studies of pre-1914 politics for specific towns bear out these general conclusions. Of Stockport politics, as one historian has written, 'the chief interest of urban politics before the 1st World War was the weakening of the strength of the Liberals.'[73] And of Wolverhampton George Jones has written that the Liberal decline was 'a trend observable on the outbreak of the war in 1914'.[74]

There were symptoms of Liberal decline far deeper than the superficial tally of party gains and losses. The tendency to electoral pacts with erstwhile Tory foes, the age and attitudes of candidates fielded, the party's varying friendship and enmity with Labour were all evidence of malaise. Yet this is not to exaggerate the Liberal decline nor to suggest that it was in any way irreversible. Indeed, after nearly a decade of continuous Liberal government, such unpopularity at the grassroots—if that had been the only symptom—would not have been too disturbing. This Liberal decline, however, was not paralleled by a simultaneous rise to power of Labour. The principal beneficiaries were the Conservatives. To this extent the municipal elections confirm the lesson of the parliamentary by-elections. Their most constant feature was not primarily the Liberal decline (real though that was) nor the rise of Labour (patchy and unimpressive as this often was) but rather the strength of Conservatism. By 1913, the Conservatives had rarely been stronger in the councils of the land, or indeed more poised for success in a forthcoming General Election.

In this sense, this essay on the rise of Labour has a conclusion that even A. J. P. Taylor would appreciate. For the only conclusive and ubiquitous trend in electoral politics during this period is the one theme on which historians have yet to write. It is the growing ascendency of Conservatism: or, as George Dangerfield might prefer, the strange revival of a Tory England in the major cities and towns.

## Notes

1  Kenneth Morgan, 'The Forging of the Left', in *Times Literary Supplement*, 14 Mar 1975.

2  See Trevor Wilson, *The Downfall of the Liberal Party* (London, 1966).

3  See Chris Cook, *The Age of Alignment: Electoral Politics in Britain, 1922–1929* (London, 1975).

4  For this period the most useful recent study is R. McKibbin, *The Evolution of the Labour Party, 1910–24* (Oxford, 1975). See also P. F. Clarke's recent article 'The Electoral Position of the Liberal and Labour Parties, 1910–14', *English Historical Review*, xc (Oct 1975).

5  McKibbin, *Evolution of the Labour Party*, pp. 84–5.

6   P. Thompson, *Socialists, Liberals and Labour: The Struggle for London, 1885–1914* (London, 1967).

7   In 1913, only 1 ward out of 16 was contested in Sunderland; only 4 out of 14 in South Shields.

8   In 1912, only 3 of the 26 wards in Stoke were contested.

9   The figures in 1911 were Leicester (19·6%), Sheffield (18·5%), Manchester (17·1%), Leeds (19·7%), Bristol (18·3%), Cardiff (14·8%), and Swansea (16·2%). After 1918, these proportions approximately doubled. Compiled from *London County Council: Comparative Municipal Statistics* (London, 1912–13) Vol. I, pp. 124–5. See also B. Keith-Lucas, *The English Local Government Franchise* (Oxford, 1952).

10   McKibbin, *Evolution of the Labour Party*.

11   *The Times*, 4 Nov 1908.

12   Ibid., 2 Nov 1909.

13   G. D. H. Cole, *A History of the Labour Party* (London, 1948) pp. 442–60.

14   *The Times*, 2 Nov 1912.

15   *Manchester Guardian*, 3 Nov 1913.

16   Labour's solitary success was in the North Ward in a straight fight with a Conservative.

17   *Northampton Mercury*, 7 Nov 1913.

18   Of the boroughs in Labour control in 1913, West Ham was the most prominent. It had been first won in 1898 (see p. 60).

19   Rotton Park was a strongly working-class ward, centred on the Dudley Road and Winson Green area.

20   Of the council of 120, 46 were Conservatives, 41 Liberal Unionists, 26 Liberals and a mere 6 Labour; 1 ward was vacant.

21   *Manchester Guardian*, 2 Nov 1911.

22   For Sheffield, see pp. 48–51.

23   For a detailed discussion of Belfast politics, see I. Budge and C. O'Leary, *Belfast: Approach to Crisis* (London, 1973).

24   *Wigan Observer*, 1 Nov 1913.

25   Ibid., 8 Nov 1913.

26   For Wakefield, see *Yorkshire Post*, 3 Nov 1913.

27   Thus in Derby in 1913, Conservatives faced straight fights with 2 Liberals and 4 Labour.

28   *Yorkshire Post*, 3 Nov 1913.

29   Ibid.

30   *Bradford Pioneer*, 8 Nov 1912.

31   Liberals were in control of Leeds from 1835 to 1895; Conservatives from 1895 to 1904; Liberals briefly from 1904 to 1907; Conservatives after 1907.

32   See B. M. Powell, *A Study in the Change and Social Origins, Political Affiliation and Length of Service of Members of the Leeds City Council, 1888–1953*, unpublished M.A. thesis, Leeds, 1958, p. 167.

33   *Yorkshire Post*, 2 Nov 1912.

34   E. P. Hennock, *Fit and Proper Persons: Ideal and Reality in Nineteenth-Century Urban Government* (Montreal, 1973) p. 270.

35   See, for example, the West ward in 1912, where Liberals lost the seat to Conservatives through Labour intervention.

36   In 1913, Liberals came bottom in three-cornered contests in the North East, East, South and Armley and Wortley wards.

37   *Yorkshire Post*, 3 Nov 1913.

38   These figures were: Conservatives, 8573; Labour, 7243; Liberals, 7014.

39   On this point, see H. Pelling, *Social Georgraphy of British Elections* (London, 1967) pp. 231–4.

40  For the background to Sheffield municipal politics, see H. K Hawson, *Sheffield: The Growth of a City* (Sheffield, 1968) pp. 286–93.

41  The figures were: Labour 3459 (31·5%), Liberals 3493 (31·8%), Conservatives 4024 (36·7%).

42  For this important study, see P. Clarke, *Lancashire and the New Liberalism* (Cambridge, 1971) *passim*.

43  For the electoral policies of Victorian Leicester, see A. Temple Patterson, *Radical Leicester* (Leicester, 1954) *passim*.

44  *Leicester Journal*, 6 Nov 1908. Bishop Street housed the Leicester Liberal Club and was the local party headquarters.

45  *Leicester Daily Post*, 3 Nov 1913.

46  For Labour's constant attention, see *Leicester Journal*, 5 Nov 1909. For Liberal lethargy, see ibid., 6 Nov 1908.

47  Ibid., 26 Oct 1906.

48  In 1912, however, there were four Lib-Lab contests. *Leicester Daily Post*, 2 Nov 1912.

49  *Nottingham Guardian*, 2 Nov 1910.

50  Ibid., 3 Nov 1913.

51  Thompson, *Socialists, Liberals and Labour*, pp. 179–80.

52  *Oxford Chronicle*, 27 Nov 1908.

53  For Banbury, see M. Stacey, *Tradition and Change: A Study of Banbury* (Oxford, 1960). For Exeter, see R. Newton, *Victorian Exeter, 1837–1914* (Leicester, 1968).

54  See p. 46.

55  Minutes, 7 May 1912, Coventry Liberal Municipal Committee, quoted in B. R. Bentley, *Conventions in Local Government: A Study of the Party System in Coventry*, unpublished thesis, p. 47.

56  In 1913, the council was composed of 26 Conservatives, 16 Liberals and 4 Labour.

57  See Cook, *Age of Alignment*, pp. 58–9.

58  Thompson, *Socialists, Liberals and Labour*.

59  *Nottingham Guardian*, 2 Nov 1910.

60  Thompson, *Socialists, Liberals and Labour*, p. 83.

61  C. H. Ward (ed.), *The Book of West Ham* (London, 1923) p. 197.

62  Thompson, *Socialists, Liberals and Labour*, p. 188.

63  Ibid., p. 173.

64  See, for example, the local elections in Croydon and Gillingham in 1911.

65  See W. S. Chaloner, *Social and Economic Development of Crewe* (Manchester, 1950) p. 168.

66  For this accusation, see *Leicester Daily Post*, 24 Oct 1911.

67  For Wolverhampton, see G. W. Jones, *Borough Politics: A History of Wolverhampton Borough Council* (London, 1969).

68  Statistics from Powell, *Study in Change*.

69  Ibid., p. 151.

70  Jones, *Borough Politics*, Table XXIV, p. 380.

71  J. Bulpitt, *Party Politics in English Local Government* (London, 1967) p. 6.

72  Jones, *Borough Politics*, p. 57.

73  J. M. Lee, *Social Leaders and Public Persons: A Study of County Government in Cheshire* (Oxford, 1963) p. 49.

74  Jones, *Borough Politics*, p. 53.

# 4 Asquith versus Lloyd George: the Last Phase and Beyond

## STEPHEN KOSS

The careers and reputations of H. H. Asquith and David Lloyd George—like those of Fox and Pitt, or Gladstone and Disraeli, or Churchill and Chamberlain—are inextricably entwined. That they had been collaborators before they were antagonists has tended to be forgotten. In the view of posterity, they appear as inveterate opponents, vying for influence and power, representing antithetical interests and traditions, and triumphing (when they could manage it) largely at each other's expense. To praise or to criticise one is, if only by implication, to pass converse judgement on the other.

Over the past half century, the stock of each man has fluctuated continually, and always in inverse relation to that of his rival: when Asquith has been 'up', Lloyd George has been 'down', and *vice versa*. The phenomenon, begun during their lifetimes, has survived them both; it shows no sign of abating. Although earlier traces of an antipathy between them can be discerned with the benefit of hindsight, their competition for public favour officially started in December 1916, when Lloyd George supplanted Asquith in the premiership. During the next few years, Lloyd George stood at the height of his popularity, Asquith at his nadir. In the 'khaki' election of 1918, Lloyd George won a tremendous personal victory, while Asquith was rejected by the electors of East Fife, whom he had represented since 1886. Returned to Westminster in a 1920 by-election at Paisley, Asquith was again defeated in 1924. This time, he was forced to take sanctuary in the House of Lords as the Earl of Oxford and Asquith. He died in 1928, in his seventy-sixth year.

Despite his adversity, or possibly because of it, Asquith was revered in certain select circles as the worthier of the two men, the victim of a wicked intrigue that had ousted him from office, excluded him from the House of Commons, and thereby deprived the nation and the world of his sage counsel. Idealistic young intellectuals (like John Maynard Keynes and Harold Nicolson) and disillusioned old-timers (like Professor Gilbert Murray, J. A. Spender, and A. G. Gardiner), equally appalled by the moral bankruptcy of the Lloyd George ascendancy, clustered around his pedestal and adulated him as 'the last of the Romans'. It went without saying, though there were those who made the point explicit, that, if Asquith was the reincarnation of Caesar, Lloyd George was the latter-day Brutus. Or, to substitute another historical metaphor, Lord Haldane observed with no less amazement than amusement the way that the residents at The Wharf, the Asquiths' Berkshire retreat near Abingdon, had been transmogrified into the 'Holy Family'.[1] If Asquith was the Saviour, come again and predictably rejected, there was no doubt who was the Judas. The Asquithians were too few and too peripheral to restore their hero to office, ultimately even to sustain him at the helm of party affairs. Nevertheless, they compensated in pertinacity for what they may have lacked in numbers, and in eloquence for what they may have lacked in logic. Zealously assisted by Lady Violet Bonham Carter, who kept vigil at her father's shrine, they succeeded in fostering an image of him which, only recently, has come seriously into dispute.

Lloyd George was not nearly so fortunate. Toppled from power in 1922, a half dozen years after he had displaced his old chief, he joined Asquith on the sidelines, where he was fated to remain for the rest of his life. He was attended in the wilderness by friends, Free Church divines, and innumerable private secretaries, including Frances Stevenson who became his second wife. Yet he conspicuously failed to attract admirers as distinguished or as persuasive as those who adhered to Asquith. The more influential of his associates either failed (like H. A. L. Fisher) to speak out on his behalf or (like Dr Thomas Jones) spoke out equivocally. Lloyd George, too, had a devoted daughter. But, as the champion of her father's cause, Lady Megan was no match for Lady Violet. She had her own parliamentary career to consider and eventually, by going over to Labour, broke with his tradition. Lloyd George's bold economic policies during the depression won him a few converts from Asquithian ranks, most notably Keynes, but failed to impress either the electorate or the custodians of the National Government. In his final years, when the country was engaged in another, more deadly struggle against Germany, he may have derived consolation from the flattering references to his methods of organisation during the First World War. He remained, however, a distrusted and discarded figure. Created Earl Lloyd-George of Dwyfor in January 1945, he died weeks later at the age of eighty-two. The memoirs that appeared in proliferation afterwards—one of them by his son, the second Earl—revealed aspects of his private life that added to his discredit. 'The very name of Lloyd George, it seemed, had become synonymous with private and public decadence', Dr Kenneth O. Morgan has written. 'He seemed to have become a kind of universal pariah, pilloried for the various ills under which twentieth-century Britain laboured.'[2] He was especially misprised by Liberal Party fundamentalists, who had little to offer save their respectability, and who dared not acknowledge him as one of their forbears. They traced their ideological descent from Gladstone and John Bright, from Sir Henry Campbell-Bannerman and Asquith, occasionally even from Sir John Simon and Stanley Baldwin, but pointedly omitted any mention of Lloyd George, a renegade and a reprobate.[3]

The tide began to turn during the early sixties, and it could not be arrested by the publication in 1964 of Roy Jenkins's elegant biography of Asquith. Written during Lady Violet's lifetime, and with her assistance, the book fell short of a critical assessment and left the impression, perhaps unwarranted, that facts had been suppressed. It became increasingly common to regard Asquith as a pitiably inadequate war-time leader who, whatever his previous merits, ought to have stepped down gracefully before it finally became necessary to thrust him aside. By the same token, it came to be argued that Asquith bore or, at any rate, shared the responsibility for splitting the party in 1916 and for keeping its ranks divided thereafter, thus inviting its eclipse by Labour.

As Asquith's reputation plummeted, Lloyd George's rose in esteem accordingly. He has been extolled not only for the dynamism of his war-time premiership, but also for his far-reaching proposals, which went cruelly unheeded, to contend with the social problems of the inter-war period. He has been recognised as a force for conciliation at the Paris Peace Conference, and as a successful negotiator with the leaders of the Indian National Congress and Sinn Fein. The Liberal content of his Coalition Liberalism is no longer dismissed as a sham. In the age of Harold Wilson, his 'presidential style' appeared less unconventional. In the light of the Poulson and Watergate scandals, his financial transactions—including the sale of honours over which he presided—have assumed an element of respectability.[4] In a more permissive climate, his personal morality has seemed a good deal less shocking, perhaps even oddly endearing. Described with candour by his widow, his extramarital relationship has raised fewer eyebrows than Asquith's indiscretions, which had long been shrouded in a hagiographical fog. In 1967, the election of Jeremy Thorpe to the leadership of the parliamentary Liberal Party as successor to Jo Grimond, an Asquithian by marriage as well as by inclination, made possible the restoration of Lloyd George to his rightful place in the party pantheon.

Nothing less than an historiographical revolution has been accomplished, and the individual most responsible for it was A. J. P. Taylor. As he would be the first to admit, the ground had been well prepared by Lord Beaverbrook, who modestly disclaimed professional status, but whose *Men and Power*[5] had a tremendous influence and, parenthetically, initiated the close friendship between its author and his future biographer. Five years later, Taylor stimulated the Lloyd George revival by his Leslie Stephen Lecture, a *tour de force* that captured Lloyd George's incandescent sparkle, his restlessness, and, not least of all, his predicament as a perpetual outsider in British politics.[6] Here was a succinct and, for the first time, an incisive analysis of Lloyd George's 'unique assets' and the part they played in his 'rise and fall'. In his magisterial survey, *English History 1914–1945*,[7] Taylor went on to illuminate Lloyd George's genius and, in no small measure, Asquith's ineptitude: Lloyd George was acclaimed as 'the most inspired and creative British statesman of the twentieth century'; Asquith, on the other hand, was portrayed as 'a strong character, unshakeable as a rock and, like a rock, incapable of movement. His initiative, if he ever had any, was sapped by years of good living in high society.'[8] Taylor's edition of the Frances Stevenson diaries,[9] admittedly a partisan source, nevertheless served as an indispensable corrective to earlier misrepresentations. A prolific flow of book reviews in the *Observer,* the *New Statesman,* and other journals has given him the opportunity to propagate his views.

It would be mistaken, however, to assume that Alan Taylor, like a modern-day Samson, has brought down the Asquithian edifice singlehandedly. As honorary director of the Beaverbrook Library in London, where he officiated from 1967 to 1975, he encouraged a younger generation of historians to make extensive and unrestricted use of the voluminous Lloyd George Papers and other manuscript collections which Lord Beaverbrook had amassed. A dozen revisionist essays, inspired by research materials on deposit at the Library (and since transferred to less commodious quarters at the House of Lords Record Office), were collected by Taylor and published under his editorship.[10] Covering a wide range of topics, these pieces testified not only to the many facets of Lloyd George's career and character, but also to the immense influence of the editor, who has done so much to assist as well as to enliven scholarship. 'The man who likes to stir things up', as he was affectionately described by Beaverbrook, Taylor was never more gratified than when he could point to the fact (which readers of the volume might otherwise overlook) that two of the essays contain evidence that contradicts his own previous pronouncements.

Just as Taylor built on the foundations laid by the historical writings of Lord Beaverbrook,[11] whose participation in the events he chronicled tended ineluctably to compromise the authority of his narrative, other scholars have followed on Taylor's heels, sometimes proceeding far beyond the limits he scrupulously set for himself. He, after all, asked only to have Lloyd George released from perdition, not to have him canonised. The last decade has witnessed a veritable outpouring of books and articles in which Lloyd George's motives and achievements have received more sympathetic treatment, Asquith's usually less so. The cumulative effect has been to substitute one orthodoxy for another.

Among the earliest and most objective of these works were A. M. Gollin's study of Lord Milner, *Proconsul in Politics*,[12] and his essay, 'Asquith: A New View', in Martin Gilbert's *Festschrift* for Taylor's sixtieth birthday, *A Century of Conflict 1850–1950*.[13] Gilbert has made his own contribution in the third volume of the official life of Churchill, and its companion volumes of documents.[14] Lloyd George has also figured prominently in Stephen Roskill's triple-decker biography of *Hankey, Man of Secrets*,[15] and in recent monographs by P. F. Clarke, Bentley B. Gilbert, Neal Blewett, Paul Barton Johnson, Cameron Hazlehurst, Maurice Cowling, and Robert Skidelsky.[16] John Grigg has produced an attractive portrait of *The Young Lloyd George*,[17] and at least two other full-scale biographies have been projected.

In his investigation of *The Downfall of the Liberal Party 1914–1935*,[18] Trevor Wilson has judiciously struck a balance between Lloyd George's vaulting ambition and his capacity for service, his penchant for intrigue and his gift for improvisation, his craftiness and his redoubtable ability. 'The great error in trying to understand him, made by his contemporaries as well as his biographers', Wilson has concluded, 'is to imagine that there was always some purpose, some carefully-laid plan, underlying his every action. Too often he acted without purpose or plan.'[19] An eminently reasonable hypothesis, it has failed to satisfy Lloyd George's more militant apologists, who would have him cleared of any charge of misconduct.[20] Roy Douglas, whose *History of the Liberal Party*[21] spans the wider period from 1895 to 1970, cautiously inclines in that direction: diffusing blame, he finds accidents where others have seen betrayals, and blunders where others have seen moral defects. It is Asquith who emerges from Douglas's account as the arch-blunderer: in 1924, he held back and allowed Ramsay MacDonald to form the first Labour Government ('Why he did so must remain a mystery'), thereby committing 'the most disastrous single action ever performed by a Liberal towards his Party'.[22]

Lloyd George's reputation has been further rehabilitated and, to a lesser degree, Asquith's impaired, by the recent appearance in print of their contemporaries' private journals and correspondence. In addition to the Frances Stevenson diaries, we have been promised a volume of her letters from Lloyd George. Meanwhile, Morgan has skilfully assembled Lloyd George's *Family Letters 1885–1936*,[23] which are mainly addressed to his first wife. Likewise, Wilson has edited *The Political Diaries of C. P. Scott 1911–1928*,[24] which reveal the abiding devotion that Lloyd George could command from a steadfast Liberal, who was also a man of unimpeachable integrity. In *A Good Innings*,[25] Alan Lee has made available a selection from the private papers of Viscount Lee of Fareham, one of Lloyd George's enthusiasts on the Tory side. Several of Asquith's supporters were known to have kept diaries, but possibly not of the type that lends itself to publication. The published diaries of his daughter-in-law, Lady Cynthia Asquith,[26] do not show him in the most favourable light. Nor, for that matter, does the two-volume set of his letters 'to a Friend' (Mrs Hilda Harrisson) which Desmond MacCarthy produced in 1933. 'The editing of these letters has been of course a blow to us and I fear to many others,' Lady Violet Bonham Carter confided at the time.[27] Notwithstanding this experience, the Asquith family have commissioned an edition of Asquith's letters to another confidante, Venetia Stanley (later Mrs Edwin Montagu), extracts of which have been quoted extensively in Jenkins's biography.

The situation, as it has developed, is not without a touch of irony. Lloyd George, as his controversial relations with newspaper editors and proprietors would indicate, was obsessed with the cultivation of his image. 'No public man has made more use of the press', Taylor has stated.[28] Yet the flattery and titles which Lloyd George dispensed so lavishly failed to serve their ultimate purpose, and he had to wait a generation or more to obtain posthumous vindication. Although it is difficult to believe that Asquith paid no mind to the press, as his apologists have sometimes maintained, it is safe to say that he had little use for journalists as such, and that he was surprisingly indifferent to what they wrote about him. Confirmed in the belief of his inherent superiority, he grew to consider himself invulnerable. The events of December 1916 must have shaken him, but—from all appearances—only temporarily. The story circulated among members of the Reform Club, where he often came during the twenties to browse or doze after lunch, that he had put down a novel by his younger daughter, Elizabeth (Princess) Bibesco, and sighed: 'Another nail in the Asquith coffin.' Frank Swinnerton, an *habitué* of the Club, asked Vivian Phillipps, Asquith's private secretary, whether the story was true. Phillipps, Swinnerton has recalled, 'laughed and replied "Mr A. doesn't know there *is* an Asquith coffin"'.[29] So it must have seemed to many who worked faithfully to salvage Asquith's political fortunes, while he, blissfully unaware, allowed them to slip irretrievably.

In outward manner, then, Lloyd George and Asquith could not have been more dissimilar. And, during the post-war years when each was considered the nemesis of the other, the dissimilarity constantly emphasised itself. In retrospect, however, it is more remarkable how much the two of them had in common. Both were products of a Nonconformist background. Both had been orphaned at an early age, and educated at the generosity of uncles. Lloyd George later found reason to exaggerate his humble origins, Asquith to discount his; but both had known genteel deprivation. Both were lawyers by training, who had entered Parliament young, and perhaps audaciously, without the benefit of social connections, family influence, or financial security. Dazzled by the attractions of late-Victorian London, they sent home glowing reports of the sermons they heard and the theatrical performances they attended. Both devotees of Gilbert and Sullivan, it is not inconceivable that they applauded 'The Mikado' at the Savoy on the same night. As time passed, they also shared an addiction to golf.

In the precincts of Westminster, the resemblance paled, but did not entirely disappear. Lloyd George, who carried the banner of his native Wales, and Asquith, who bore the indelible stamp of Jowett's Balliol, were alike regarded as keenly ambitious young men, whose oratorical gifts—though different—were equally undeniable. Both were staunch Home Rulers, who designated themselves Radicals and took a lively interest in questions of social reform. Asquith, who arrived in the House four years earlier, was the first to advance to the front bench. As Home Secretary in Lord Rosebery's Government, he took charge of the 1895 Welsh Disestablishment Bill, and encountered resistance from Lloyd George, 'a natural *frondeur*' who, he hastened to add, was 'already an acute and accomplished debater'.[30] Lloyd George, in turn, paid tribute to Asquith as 'intellectually one of the greatest men in the House of Commons', and 'an abler man intellectually' than Joseph Chamberlain.[31] For him, that was no mean compliment. There was a degree of tension in their relationship during the stormy days of the Boer War and again during the agitation over the 1902 Education Act. But the two men recognised each other's qualities, which, through the outbreak of war in 1914, proved distinctly complementary.

That is not to suggest that they were ever close friends. Asquith superciliously made fun of Lloyd George's untrained mind and mis-spelled memoranda; Lloyd George took a dim view of the social circles in which Asquith moved, and recounted—more in sorrow than in anger—the occasions when Asquith was the worse for drink. Each, in his way, was devoted to his wife, yet passionately attracted to younger women. As kindred spirits, neither could afford to point an accusing finger at the other and, on this score, neither did. 'You say I have my weaknesses', Lloyd George wrote defensively to his wife on 24 July 1924. 'So has anyone that ever lived & the greater the man the greater his weaknesses. It is only insipid, wishy washy fellows that have no weaknesses.'[32] By Lloyd George's own yardstick, Asquith was a very great man indeed. He has been frequently—and justly—rebuked for having communicated Cabinet and military secrets to Miss Stanley; but Miss Stevenson, as Lloyd George's private secretary, enjoyed similar confidences.

Temperamentally, they were poles apart. Nevertheless, they sustained each other in moments of crisis, personal as well as political. Asquith valued Lloyd George for his creative spark and boundless energy; Lloyd George reciprocated with a high regard for Asquith's parliamentary authority, even after it had begun to wane. As the 'honoured

grey-haired old Premier', Asquith had the aura of Anthony Trollope's
Mr Mildmay; and Lloyd George was comparable to Mr Gresham,

> on whose shoulders it was thought that the mantle of Mr Mildmay
> would fall,—to be worn, however, quite otherwise than Mr Mildmay
> had worn it. For Mr Gresham is a man with no feelings for the past,
> void of historical association, hardly with memories,—living alto-
> gether for the future which he is anxious to fashion anew out of the
> vigour of his own brain. Whereas, with Mr Mildmay, even his love of
> reform is an inherited passion from an old-world Liberalism.

Although different, their talents were not disjunctive. Although distant,
their personal relations were not discordant.

At what point did their mutual confidence begin to dwindle, and their
partnership to deteriorate? One cannot say for certain, and any assertion
must be an impressionistic one. According to one historian, their formal
split in 1916 was foreshadowed during the winter of 1909–10.[33] Yet there
is ample evidence that they continued long beyond that time to collab-
orate in such areas as welfare legislation, the land campaign, the formulation of Irish policy, the struggle for the People's Budget, and the
constitutional conflict with the House of Lords. Admittedly, their relationship during the immediate pre-war years had its sticky moments.
Cabinet colleagues since 1905, it is only natural that they should have occasionally lost patience with each other. But Asquith also had profound
disagreements with Reginald McKenna, on whom he came to lean; and
Lloyd George had some of his most rancorous disputes with Churchill,
who was his principal Liberal ally after August 1914. Their ultimate
break, therefore, was no more inevitable than that which occurred between Britain and Germany. One must not mistake the symptoms,
diagnosed retroactively, for the disease.

It was only under the impact of war that their paths gradually
diverged. In their respective responses to inter- and intra-party pressures
and, most obviously, to the imperatives of the military situation, they
clashed not so much in principle as in style, which was not a factor to be
discounted. Asquith may have been heard to allude wistfully to a tradition of Liberal individualism, but he was not by any means the doctrinaire exponent of *laissez-faire* whom the Harmsworth press depicted. All
the same, he appeared to be lackadaisical, slow-moving, and fettered by
conventional methods of organisation and administration. Lloyd
George, whose previous deficiencies now counted as virtues, stood
opposed to Asquith—perhaps involuntarily—as the more vigorous pro-
secutor of the war effort. Harold Macmillan, recalling his own youthful
sentiments at the time of Asquith's displacement, has pointed to the essential contrast: 'For me—much as I admired Asquith's intellectual
sincerity and moral nobility—Lloyd George was the rebel, the

revolutionary; and, above all, the man who would get things done. Asquith represented, as it seemed to me, the qualities but also the faults of the old world.'[34] Haldane, who had observed the antagonists at closer range, put it even more neatly: Asquith, he told Lord Buckmaster, was 'a first class head of a deliberative council, . . . [who] is versed in precedents, acts on principles, and knows how and when to compromise'; Lloyd George 'cares nothing for precedents and knows no principles, but he has fire in his belly and that is what we want'.[35]

This is not the appropriate place to reconstruct the steps that led to the rupture in December 1916 which has been alternately described as a villainous conspiracy and a shining act of patriotism. Various theories and counter-theories have been advanced, some more tentatively than others, to account for the rise of Lloyd George and the fall of Asquith.[36] Without seeking to rekindle an historiographical debate which has been left to smoulder, one may ask whether contemporary opinion can be clearly distinguished from fact (what people thought may have been at least as important as what occurred), and whether anyone can render an authoritative version of these chaotic developments for which the surviving documentation is fragmentary and, worse, contradictory. 'It is inevitable, I suppose', Sir Austen Chamberlain wrote to Lord Beaverbrook, with whom he compared recollections of the 1916 Cabinet crisis, 'that no two accounts of these events will exactly coincide, even though everyone concerned was acting in good faith and tells the truth to the best of his ability.'[37]

Instead, the present essay will address itself to the extended period that followed the war, when Asquith and Lloyd George may be more effectively juxtaposed. Neglected by most historians, who have focused on the heroic themes of pre-war co-operation and war-time confrontation, it is a dénouement to a longer story that qualifies as a drama in its own right. With the assistance of the published works and archival sources surveyed in the foregoing pages, it is now possible to offer a detailed analysis of Liberal politics in these crucial years.

From the time of his stinging defeat in the 1918 general election until his death in 1928, Asquith nursed a burning resentment of Lloyd George, whom he blamed as the instigator of his personal humiliation and, still more, as the perpetrator of their party's misfortune. Lloyd George, in turn, regarded Asquith as a spent force who nonetheless retained a considerable capacity for mischief and who posed an insurmountable obstacle to Liberal reunification. The flames of mutual recrimination, which might have been expected to die down, were assiduously fanned by the men and especially by the women who were devoted to one or the other. 'He never saw a belt without hitting below it', was Margot Asquith's familiar dictum on the man who had deposed her husband from the premiership. The ladies in Lloyd George's entourage retaliated less wittily, but no less venomously.

Their estrangement, although temporarily papered over from 1923 to 1926, was never overcome. It goes far to explain not only the paralysis that fatally afflicted the Liberal Party, but also the kaleidoscopic light in which successive historians have portrayed the two personalities. Asquith's last decade, which his biographers have invariably given short shrift (Jenkins, for example, has allotted it only a few dozen of his 519 pages), was one in which we may perceive the predicament which he shared with Lloyd George, and which Lloyd George continued to face afterwards. Two of the many disparate types who had previously found common shelter beneath the proverbial Liberal umbrella, they now stood exposed to the wind and rain of political adversity. And, looking back, it can be argued that they did not stand in opposition to each other, so much as in apposition. To whatever extent either may have suffered from the other's opportunism or conceit, both were pre-eminently the victims of social and electoral forces that had overtaken them.

In the spring of 1918, Bernard Shaw began work on his 'metabiological pentateuch', *Back to Methuselah*, which had its first public performance in 1921. Written in five sprawling acts, each self-contained, its action (or what there was of it) spanned the centuries from the Creation to the remote future, 'as far as thought can reach'. The second sequence, which was the most conventional in dramatic form, created the greatest stir: it was a 'serious farce', set in the Hampstead study of the Brothers Barnabas, two scientific gentlemen who had discovered the secret by which human life expectancy might be extended to three hundred years or beyond. Word of their revolutionary 'programme' had reached the ears of the two feuding leaders of the Liberal Party, who arrived separately and uninvited one afternoon in order to determine how they might exploit it to their respective political advantage.

The playwright had given a private reading of this segment of his marathon work to Asquith, on whom it had had a 'jarring' effect.[38] Small wonder. The older of the stage politicians, named Henry Hopkins Lubin, was described in the stage directions as 'a man at the end of his sixties, a Yorkshireman with the last traces of Scandinavian flax still in his white hair, undistinguished in stature, unassuming in his manner, and taking his simple dignity for granted, but wonderfully comfortable and quite self-assured . . .'

Reference was made in the text to his obtrusive wife ('Mimi') and to the 'young people' with whom he consorted, to his need on a particular Sunday 'to play as many as sixty-six games of bridge to keep my mind off the news from the front', and, in still more questionable taste, to the son he had sacrificed to the war.

The Barnabases' other caller was Joyce Burge, the mirror image of

Lloyd George: 'He is a well-fed man turned fifty, with a broad forehead, and grey hair which, his neck being short, falls almost to his collar.' Unconvincingly professing a disinterest in politics ('I haven't a scrap of ambition . . . I want to serve my country . . . I want to save my country from the Tories'), he is variously identified as someone who plays golf on Walton Heath, who has a penchant for hymn-singing and a 'reputation as a profligate'. (Significantly, however, it is Lubin who flirts with Franklyn Barnabas's young daughter.) More specifically, it was Burge who 'found the shells' when 'the Hun was at the gate', and 'who— unworthily perhaps, but not quite unsuccessfully—held the helm when the ship of State weathered the mightiest hurricane that has ever burst with earth-shaking violence on the land of our fathers'.

In the 'Socratic dialogue' in which they engage, Lubin pays tribute to the immortal poetry of Horace, and Burge to the indispensability of the Nonconformist vote, to which he hopes to appeal by the Biblical fundamentalism of the Barnabases' teaching. 'I have the privilege of my age and my transparent innocence', Lubin tells his rival. 'I have not to struggle with your volcanic energy.' Both listen inattentively to their hosts' 'gospel', which Lubin agrees to adopt for the party platform if they obtain the requisite approval of the National Liberal Federation. Burge, typically more receptive to innovation, incorrigibly promises the Order of Merit 'if we win'. Together, the two veterans depart, and the younger characters are left to ask whether Lubin is more 'a priceless humbug' than Burge is 'a flaming fraud'. But Franklyn Barnabas, richly endowed with Shavian vision, is inclined to bracket them as two specimens of a breed of European statesmen who had survived into a new age to which they did not properly belong. In the next act, set in the year A.D. 2170, Burge and Lubin reappear, with a hyphen between their names, as a single character.

Two and a half centuries before their facsimiles were impudently united, Asquith and Lloyd George made fitful attempts to achieve a *modus vivendi*. But neither was prepared to accept the other's terms, until it was clear that neither had terms to offer. In anticipation of the 1918 election, Lloyd George renewed his offer to appoint Asquith to the Lord Chancellorship. It was conveyed by Lord Murray of Elibank, a former Liberal chief whip, who reported back that Asquith would 'in no circumstances whatever' serve under Lloyd George. Murray, refusing to 'despair of the arrangement I had in view', had further conversations with Asquith, whom he hoped to bring round. 'I can assure you, with all the sincerity that I possess', he wrote to Lloyd George,

> that there are a great number of people, including those who for the moment pass as yours and his, who wish to see a re-constructed National Government, with you at the head, for the handling of the

immense domestic and imperial problems that immediately face us, but in order to ensure this beneficial result, there must be some give and take, as well as the suppression of personal feelings.

Lord Reading and, at his own initiative, C. P. Scott also tried to mend the breach, but to no avail.[39]

Various people, including the King and Churchill, urged Lloyd George to mollify Asquith by naming him a delegate to the Paris Peace Conference.[40] Summoned to the Prime Minister's room at the House of Commons (where, according to Margot, he was 'received with a friendliness which amounted to enthusiasm'), Asquith expressed keen interest in such an assignment. In his mind, it was an alternative to his taking office; in Lloyd George's, one was evidently contingent on the other. The latter's intentions, always difficult to divine, remain open to question. A year later, he complained to Sir Donald Maclean that 'Asquith and three or four of his colleagues had refused to join the Cabinet', but Asquith flatly contradicted this account. 'All that had passed', he assured Maclean, 'was that Ll. G. had said to him . . . "I suppose you would not care to take office", and Asquith replied that was true, he did not wish to take office but was not at all averse to going to Paris as a British representative.'[41] Nothing more was heard on either score.

Within hours of the armistice, the Prime Minister called a general election which his opponents had good reason to dread. Asquith, who dismissed as 'a tissue of absurdities' suggestions in the London press that his campaign at East Fife was going badly,[42] lost his seat. Consequently, he posed no immediate threat to Lloyd George who, had he forced the issue, might have got himself elected to the leadership of the parliamentary Liberal Party. But he held back, fearful of compromising his position among the Conservatives.[43] Asquith's status was even more anomalous. McKenna, another casualty at the polls, thought that the time had come to

> find a name, a formula and a man to unite Liberal and Labour. . . . I hope Asquith will call an early meeting of the National Liberal Federation. If I were he I should place my resignation in their hands, ask for the appointment of a special emergency committee to consider the whole position, and promise assistance in carrying out such recommendations as they might make.[44]

Like many people, McKenna underestimated Asquith's tenacity. Instead of abdicating, Asquith handpicked Maclean to deputise for him as leader of the depleted band of non-Coalition Liberals in the new Parliament. A holding action, the arrangement was intended to last only until he could negotiate his safe return to Westminster. Maclean, who understood this perfectly, responded stiffly on 13 November 1919, when

Andrew Bonar Law chaffed that Asquith would never 'come back to this House'. A godfearing Presbyterian, Maclean put aside his scruples and bet sixpence that his chief would obtain a new seat 'before February'.[45] He lost the wager, but only by a few weeks.

Others among the 'Wee Frees', as the Opposition Liberals called themselves, would have preferred Maclean to continue on a more regular basis. Sir T. A. Bramsdon, elected at Portsmouth Central without benefit of the Coalition 'coupon', explained that, had he proclaimed himself an Asquithian, 'I should not have attained the unique victory I did. Mr Asquith has not been returned', he argued, 'and it is inconsistent therefore for him to guide the independent Liberals from outside.' J. M. Hogge, who sat for East Edinburgh and was veering towards Lloyd George, threatened to become 'very restive'. 'What is Asquith going to do?' he asked Maclean in September 1919. 'It is now in all conscience long enough since he was defeated and we can't have another meeting of the "Wee Frees" without a decision of some kind.' One of the possibilities, frequently mooted, was a realignment under the joint leadership of Lord (formerly Sir Edward) Grey and Lord Robert Cecil, but Asquith was the stumbling block. 'If the latter were a Gladstone, and glowed with sympathy and indignation and creative genius', Walter Runciman told Maclean, 'I believe R. C. would cooperate with him, but . . . his own interests are more profoundly or (perhaps it would be fairer to say) more *obviously* human, & stirred by sentiment than Asquith's.'[46]

Asquith, biding his time, never doubted that a Liberal revival was in the offing, and that he was destined to lead it. The next government, he was confident, would be a coalition of independent Liberals and moderate Labour.[47] Lloyd George took a markedly different view. Lunching at Downing Street with Sir George Riddell and Sir William Robertson Nicoll, two of his press supporters, he said 'that Labour had completely supplanted the old Liberalism, that the "Wee Frees" were hopeless in every way. George Riddell said there were two parties—one semi-Democratic, semi-Conservative, the other Labour. "Yes", said L. G., "that is it. That is what it will be."'[48] In the long run, his cynicism proved fully justified.

Deterred from standing in a December by-election at Spen Valley, where 'the Labour people' had vowed to oppose him 'hotly', Asquith waited until the early weeks of 1920 to offer himself at Paisley, where a vacancy had meanwhile occurred. A three-cornered contest, it commanded national attention. 'Asquith is making a gallant fight—but on the old lines', Haldane ruefully observed. 'If he gets in it will be on account of respect for him personally.' The Webbs, although 'not sure about Paisley at all', were inclined to predict a Labour victory.[49] Frances Stevenson, who prayed for Asquith's defeat, confided to her diary that Lloyd George was more or less accustomed to the prospect of Asquith's return. On 25 February, when the news came of Asquith's success, 'he was quite resigned and cheerful. . . . Personally', Miss Stevenson consoled herself, 'I think when the *fact* of Asquith's having got in is over, it will be all the better for D. As D. himself says, he will be able to get at him in the House & they will come to grips & I will back D. any time.'[50]

Restored to Parliament and to the leadership of the Independent Liberals, Asquith had conspicuously little to offer by way of energy or ideas. To all appearances, there was no fundamental difference between his brand of Liberalism and Lloyd George's. Privately, as well as publicly, he seemed incapable of taking an effective stand against his successor. Maclean, who accompanied him to a meeting in the Prime Minister's room on 10 August 1920, marvelled at the sight of Asquith and Lloyd George together: 'There was no constraint of any kind, they chatted freely and L. G. was not only courteous but deferential in his manner, and I could see them slipping back, sub-consciously, to the old days when Mr "A" was P.M. and L. G. his Chancellor.'[51]

But, if 'Mr A' had mellowed, 'Mrs A' had lost none of her pugnacity. She took issue with Maclean's statement that political conflict ought not to degenerate into 'a personal affair': 'How can it be otherwise?' she demanded to know. 'Two men who were for 9 years together: one mean & a fighter—the other magnanimous, not young & not a fighter—are now opposed to each other. Can you keep kid gloves on in behaving like great gentlemen & hope to win anything? NO. Every glove must be off & every weapon used & every string pulled.'[52]

Margot Asquith had her chance to gloat in October 1922, when the Conservatives withdrew their support from Lloyd George, who tumbled from power. In the election that followed, the two Liberal factions fought separately and, however each might have tried to disguise the result, fared poorly. The drift to reunion, which Mrs Asquith had hoped to arrest, continued at an accelerated pace. The question remained: on what—or whose—terms was it to be achieved? Lloyd George had the funds, Asquith the titular position and the control of the party machinery. Who was to capitalise on whose assets?

Asquith's lieutenants did not trust him to withstand Lloyd George's blandishments and to strike the best bargain. 'H. H. A. is not Ll. G.-proof by any means', Maclean advised Lord (formerly Herbert) Gladstone, who took charge of the Liberal Central Office. 'We must not let L. G. alone with H. H. A. more than we can help.' Gladstone concurred, and cited the total of 159 Liberal seats in the December 1923 general election as 'a triumph for H. H. A.' that augured well for the party's recovery. 'L. G. knows that apart from the Election costs', put by some sources as high as £160,000, 'he cannot claim any material share in our success', Gladstone oddly asserted. In his view, it was 'not only a question of merging funds. L. G. seems unable to carry on without his . . . saloon, his attendants, his horrible publicity arrangements.' For that reason, control over finance had to be wrested from him, so as to save the party from his image no less than from his whims.[53]

Still 'completely divided on policy', Lloyd George and Asquith had less room for manoeuvre in the aftermath of the 1923 election than either they or many historians have assumed.[54] For different reasons, each of them was prepared to allow Ramsay MacDonald to form a minority Labour Government. It was a miscalculation, which they promptly recognised as such. Throughout 1924, negotiations continued for a complete amalgamation of Liberal resources. 'It seems very clear to me', Maclean told Gladstone, 'that if we submit to the periodic contribution, with no Election Fund in hand, we shall be completely at the mercy of Ll. G., who is, it would seem, all-powerful in financial as well as other matters.' Lloyd George, not surprisingly, held tightly to his purse-strings, determined to obtain value for his money. Regarding a Liberal victory in the next election, which could not be long postponed, as 'impossible', he argued that the party should field fewer candidates 'and save money for a better opportunity'. Accused by the Asquithians of maintaining a 'dole' system, he retorted that the 'rottenness' of the party organisation made him loath to throw good money after bad. On 4 July, Sir Robert Hudson, honorary secretary of the Liberal Central Association since 1893, begged leave to second Gladstone's resolution: 'D— L. G.' He and Maclean had had '40 minutes talk with him [that] was so poisonous that I took to my bed with a temperature the next afternoon, & the Dr has kept me until this morning'.[55]

Lloyd George was obviously stalling and, under the circumstances, who can blame him? 'He thought that for the first time Asquith's "Wait and see" was the only thing to do, or rather "Watch and see",' he admitted in February to Lady Scott, who had switched her allegiance from Asquith to him. Four months later, she enquired: '"Isn't the Liberal Party ready for real leadership?" He said he thought it was; and I asked "Isn't it ready for *your* leadership?" to which he replied, "Oh, no, no. I couldn't do that. I mustn't think of usurping Asquith's position. I must try, if it's possible, to carry him along."'[56]

On 14 September, he conferred at The Wharf with Asquith, Maclean and Sir Alfred Mond, and pointedly mentioned the probability that Asquith would lose Paisley. Secure in his own constituency, he could expect the parliamentary leadership to devolve upon him. For that eventuality, he would have to keep a free hand and as much money as possible.

But Lloyd George's differences with Asquith were not exclusively financial. Asquith held to the nineteenth-century view that politicians, out of office, ought not to be too specific about the policies they intended to pursue. There was no harm in having 'policy . . . expounded in generalities', but any precise statement ran the dual risk of opening party wounds and alienating potential support in the country. Lloyd George disagreed, and wished to launch a detailed programme with as much fanfare as possible. Denied the subsidies which they considered their due, the Asquithians resented the money which Lloyd George lavished on his pet projects, including a new land campaign for which he was laying the groundwork. On 10 October, a 'meeting of leaders' was hastily called to prepare a party manifesto for the election which was to take place on the twenty-ninth of that month. It was particularly urgent to incorporate some measure of Lloyd George's land policy, but how much? Here, Lloyd George met his most strenuous opposition not from any of the Asquithians, but from Mond, who insisted 'that he was not really so much against the policy as against the difficulty of explaining it in the limited time available'. Lloyd George was permitted to add a brief preface to the preamble, drawn up by C. F. G. Masterman, and it was further agreed that, 'on the land question, paragraphs not inconsistent with Mr Lloyd George's policy should be inserted'. But the primary purpose of the document, reflecting the sense of panic that inspired it, 'was to show why the Liberals put the Labour Government out rather than to explain why they ever put it in'.[57]

As MacDonald had intended, the Liberal Party was smashed. Only forty of its 340 candidates survived the débâcle, and Asquith was not among them. On the morning of 31 October, Hudson 'went up to Bedford Square . . . & had a longish talk with H. H. A. while he consumed his breakfast'. Maclean was present, 'no one else'. Asquith, who appeared 'fit enough & unabashedly cheerful', surveyed the wreckage. He 'pictured with some sarcasm our contingent on the Front Bench of the new House: "L. G. flanked by Simon & Runciman. I have no particular desire to join them—but we can see about that later on."' Hudson and Maclean 'urged that . . . as soon as possible, he should summon his colleagues, including L. G. of course, for consultation: he firmly taking the chair, & (after private consultation with L. G.) that *he* should nominate the new chief whip' to replace Vivian Phillipps, who had lost his seat. They proposed the names of William Wedgwood Benn and Sir Godfrey Collins, both of whom Lloyd George was believed to dislike.[58]

Another, more formal session was held at Bedford Square on the morning of 5 November, the day before Asquith left on a seven-week visit to Egypt. The party's elder statesmen attended, and the outcome, according to Hudson, was 'thoroughly unsatisfactory'. Lloyd George stood firm against the proposal to call a Liberal convention 'of M.P.s *plus* defeated candidates, clearly fearing that such a joint meeting wd. turn into a pro-Asquith Demonstration'. With some misgiving, he accepted a compromise by which Asquith would address Liberal M.P.s over lunch at the Reform Club, while Lord Beauchamp would host a private reception at which Asquith would deliver 'a second but secondary speech' to Liberal M.P.s, peers and candidates.[59] With that decided, Asquith went on holiday. He carried with him the King's offer of a peerage, which he wished to give 'mature and deliberate consideration'.

Margot, who stayed behind in London, grieved bitterly over the situation. 'In the country our Party is alive but in the H. of C. it is a painful sight, & I am glad Henry is out of it', she wrote to John St Loe Strachey, the editor of the Tory *Spectator*. 'Ll. G. has been the curse of our Party & but for Baldwin wd. have ruined yours.' That she was to become the Countess of Oxford and Asquith offered scant satisfaction. 'It is a hard wrench', she confessed to another journalist.

> I have wept many times at leaving the H. of Commons, but there is *no* safe Liberal seat & he must lead his shattered Party from the Lords. The alternative was retirement from public life wh. wd. have killed him. . . . Nor do I see him happy muddled up with 3 men who detest one another—Ll. G., Simon, & Runciman (of these, Simon has the best brain). Ll. G. will never lead anyone anywhere & has been our curse.[60]

Quite obviously, her husband was not going to lead anyone anywhere either. Elevated to the peerage, he entered the last phase of his struggle with Lloyd George.

On 29 January 1925, the Liberal Party opened a two-day convention to revive its spirit and to launch an appeal for a million pounds to be raised through the constituency associations. Lady Scott, who had expected a display of fireworks, came away disappointed on the second day: 'The debate on the leadership fizzled out', she recorded in her diary, because 'few cared to be rude to Mr Asquith. Oh dear! how I wish he could have died when he should in 1916. What a great name my beautiful friend would then have left.'[61] Raised to the peerage, Asquith had acquired a cumbersome new name, but a more incongruous position. His presence alongside Lloyd George on the convention platform could not disguise the fact that the parliamentary party, in its shrunken state, remained deeply divided: some Liberal M.P.s, like Sir John Simon, swore fealty to him; others were devoted to Lloyd George (who had been elected, twenty-six votes to seven, to lead the party in the Commons); and a third bloc, under Runciman, had constituted itself a Radical Group.

Behind the scenes, there was a frenetic effort to devise a common policy. Various committees and commissions were set up, and Asquith (as we shall continue to call him) and Lloyd George vied to pack them with their own nominees. The Asquithians, still entrenched at party headquarters and in the executive of the National Liberal Federation, wanted Lloyd George's money, preferably in a lump sum. Lloyd George, for his part, sought party approval and facilities for his scheme of land nationalisation soon spelled out in his 'green book', *The Land and the Nation*. Mond and Runciman were hostile to Lloyd George's land proposals, and Asquith 'was not enthusiastic'. In particular, he resented the costliness of the land inquiry, and the self-glorification that Lloyd George got out of it. 'All this Press pushing of Ll. G. & his "policies" is "Pretty Fanny's way"', he wrote with acerbity to Maclean:

> He has got poor Francis Acland well into the net. He (F. A.) wrote to me a week or two ago to ask me to give a good 'Kick-off' to the much boomed demonstration which is to be held at Killerton shortly— regardless of expense & with infinite touting, as I am informed in an angry sputtering letter from C. Hobhouse. I replied to Acland that there was no greater adept in the art of 'Kicking-off' than his present hero, and that I observed that all the sackbuts & psalteries were being turned up for the advertised descent of Moses from the Mount.

The National Liberal Federation, having played no part in the formulation of Lloyd George's policy, declined to put its organisation at his disposal. Lloyd George thereupon set up his independent Land and Nation League, with himself as president. By autumn, there was the serious threat of an open split. Deputations shuttled back and forth between Lloyd George's house at Churt in Surrey and Asquith's residences in Bedford Square and Berkshire. W. M. Eager, who served as secretary to Lloyd George's land inquiry and subsequently to his industrial inquiry, recalled how he 'went through the flirtations and engagements and disengagements of Ll. G. and the Asquithians, even to the extent of being Ll. G.'s emissary to Asquith, which gave Margot the chance of being rude to me at her own lunch table, and some priceless cracks from Oxford himself.'

Finally, at a parley on 2 December, an agreement was reached: Asquith, to the discomfort of his associates, acceded to Lloyd George's land proposals in principle, if not necessarily in detail.[62]

His subordinates, *plus royaliste que le roi*, had tried their best to stiffen their leader's backbone between the rounds. On 25 November, they held a war council in Carlton House Terrace at the house of Lord Cowdray, one of their most generous benefactors. Those present included Asquith, Grey, Maclean, Gladstone, Simon, Runciman, Collins and Sir William Plender. It was 'the general view to break with Ll. G. on the financial opening', but Asquith 'said he could not "rush" it & wanted time to think it over'. The next thing they knew, Asquith—true to form—had backed down. Maclean protested that he had been betrayed, and recounted that Phillipps, as chairman of the Liberal Organising Committee, 'felt that . . . his head had been handed on a charger to Ll. G.'

The situation might have been saved when the National Liberal Federation met in executive session in December, but Asquith 'knocked the affair endways' by leaving before the topic came up for discussion. Cowdray, Maclean recapitulated, 'is roused to rage . . . & vows that if a clear issue between Ll. G. & Headquarters is not defined by *Asquith*, he will close his support & allow things to take their course as far as he is concerned'. Shortly thereafter, Maclean had heard 'that Asquith says he is going on with the financial severance. I place no reliance on that', he concluded. Others shared his despondency. Early in 1926, Mond defected to the Conservatives, ostensibly out of opposition to Lloyd George's land policy. 'So the Little Welsher has cost us (or lost us) Alfred Mond', Hudson lamented. 'Nor are the entries on the debit side of that particular a/c *yet ended*. I still hold to my gloomy view that our poor old Party will never have a chance until we have had a sequence of notable public Funerals.'[63]

The showdown came in May 1926, at the time of the General Strike. The Liberal Shadow Cabinet—to which both Asquith and Lloyd George belonged—unequivocally backed the Baldwin Government against the insurgent trade unions. Asquith spoke to this effect in the House of Lords, and he and Grey contributed articles to the *British Gazette*, the official anti-strike daily. Lloyd George, however, writing for the Hearst syndicate in America, took what his colleagues regarded as 'a much too pro Labour line. . . . But I did it deliberately', he told his wife, '& I mean to stick to it.' Furthermore, he declined to attend a second meeting of the Shadow Cabinet, scheduled for 10 May, and sent word via the chief whip that he would not endorse any party statement that did not condemn in equal measure the Government's intransigence. His meaning, like his strategy, was unclear. Maclean, 'in high hopes', initially presumed that Lloyd George 'was in full cry to join Labour'; but the next day, Maclean informed Gladstone, Lloyd George 'sent a message to H. H. A. asking whether he would speak with him at Carnarvon on July 3rd!' Asquith reportedly replied 'that he could not consider matters of that kind just now'. There was, as yet, no indication that he attached any great importance to the episode.[64] On 18 May, there was 'a very private confabulation' at his house in Bedford Square, where he was joined by Simon, Runciman, Maclean, Collins, Phillipps, Hudson, W. M. R. Pringle, and Lords Buxton, Buckmaster and Beauchamp. The last, who was the only Lloyd Georgite among them, 'left early', and the 'talk became more free after his departure'. Hudson was pleased to report that their host was '*far more* indignant at L. G.'s behaviour than I have ever seen. Runciman Simon & Buckmaster all declared with emphasis position to be intolerable. Others murmured assent.' It was 'agreed unanimously that H. H. A. should write to L. G. & say flatly that his patience was exhausted'. Asquith concurred, but pointed out 'that any letter he wrote must be so framed as to put L. G. in the wrong if it had to be published'. Hudson, although impressed by 'H. H. A.'s indignation', refused to take anything for granted: 'we shall see *what we shall see!*' But, this time, Asquith did not waver. On the evening of the twentieth, he dispatched by hand a letter of rebuke to Lloyd George. 'At last I really think the break has come', Maclean crowed with incredulous delight. 'I never thought he would come right up to it, but he has.' Phillipps, too, confessed his relief: 'I did not expect such a deliverance'.[65]

With the editorial assistance of C. P. Scott, Lloyd George replied in a lengthy document that 'effectively countered' the suggestion that his absence from the Shadow Cabinet was tantamount to an act of resignation.[66] Drummed out of the Shadow Cabinet, he was sustained in the Commons by a majority of the Liberal M.P.s. Where did this leave matters?

In the closing days of May, the executive of the National Liberal Federation convened to plan the agenda for its annual session, slated for 17 June at Weston-super-Mare. Of the twenty-four members present, sixteen were identified as Asquithians, eight as followers of Lloyd George. Maclean moved (and Hudson seconded) a resolution of 'unabated confidence in Lord Oxford as Leader of the Liberal Party'. There followed 'a good deal of discussion as to the terms of this resolution', and Walter Layton delivered the minority opinion that the executive ought not to adopt 'any motion which would imply a vote of censure on Mr Lloyd George'. Various amendments were proposed, and Maclean and Hudson consented to append to their original resolution an expression of 'hope that as speedily as possible a united Liberal Party may be able to discharge its vital functions in the interests of the community'. It was logically asked 'whether this meant with or without Mr Lloyd George, and Sir Robert Hudson made it quite plain that it was without Mr Lloyd George'. It being 'obvious there could be no agreement', Layton moved (and Ernest Brown seconded) that a decision should be postponed until a deputation had seen Asquith to 'ascertain his views upon the form of words suggested'. Except for 'the absolute "die-hard" element' (Maclean, Hudson, Phillipps, R. D. Holt, Layland Barratt, and Lady Violet Bonham Carter), there was substantial sympathy among the majority for 'the plea that individual members of the Committee and the rank and file of the Party as a whole ought not to have been put in the position of having made an apparent choice between Lord Oxford and Mr Lloyd George'.[67]

Five days before the National Liberal Federation was due to meet, Asquith was incapacitated by a stroke. 'The Lord alone knows where we stand as regards W super M now that H. H. A. is ill!' Hudson wrote in distress to Gladstone. Although the assembled delegates, with only one dissentient vote, passed the resolution of 'unabated confidence' in his leadership, it was devoid of any real significance. Lloyd George, in robust health, was accorded a rapturous welcome. More seriously, the Liberal Candidates' Association, repudiating its Asquithian officers, implored the ailing leader to receive Lloyd George back into the fold. He adamantly refused and, in the face of mounting opposition within the party, tendered his own resignation the following October. Before taking that momentous step, he was said to have repented of his action the previous May. On 29 September, his wife motored over from North Berwick to visit Lord Balfour at Whittingehame. There, she found one of her relatives, to whom she admitted that she and Asquith 'had made a dreadful mistake over the whole business' of the General Strike. 'We were entirely misled', she averred. 'Certain prominent rich Liberals came to Herbert & said "we shall not give a shilling to the Liberal Fund until you have got rid of Lloyd George".' Assured that 'people in the party overwhelmingly agreed', Asquith had seized 'the opportunity' fortuitously offered by the Strike, and 'wrote the disastrous letter'. He was now, by his wife's description, 'miserable over the whole business'.[68] Aside from the incidental fact that Margot would not have referred to her husband as 'Herbert', the story rings true.

Asquith had moved too late, and on the wrong issue, to make good his rejection of Lloyd George. By the same token, Lloyd George acquired control of the party too late either to revive its fortunes or to satisfy his lingering ambitions. Preoccupied with their rivalry, the two veteran leaders had no comprehension of how peripheral to national life they had become. As they have receded into history, their images have blurred—like those of Burge and Lubin—into a composite, and the differences between them have seemed increasingly attenuated. Had either Asquith or Lloyd George not existed in the post-war decade, the other would have had to invent him as a political foil. Perhaps, to all intents and purposes, that is what each of them did.

# Notes

1　Haldane to ?, 26 Sep 1924 (copy), Haldane Papers, Vol. 5915, fol. 154 (National Library of Scotland, Edinburgh).

2　*Lloyd George* (London, 1974) p. 200. Morgan has usefully surveyed the vast field of Lloyd George literature in 'Lloyd George and the Historians', in *The Transactions of the Honourable Society of Cymmrodorion* (Session 1971, Part I) 65–85.

3　See, for example, the lectures given at Heidelburg University in 1936 by Thomas Magnay, Liberal National M.P. for Gateshead (1931–45), *English Political Institutions and Public Opinion* (London, 1939) p. 64.

4　The present writer, having referred in a *New Statesman* review (17 May 1974) to the 'wholesale debasement of public life' under Lloyd George, was reproved by an American reader, who compared the harmlessness of the Lloyd George system to the corrupt practices of the Nixon administration.

5　London, 1956.

6 Reprinted as 'Lloyd George: Rise and Fall', in Taylor, *Politics in Wartime* (London, 1964) pp. 123–49.

7 Oxford, 1965.

8 pp. 70, 192, 14–15.

9 *Lloyd George: A Diary* (London, 1971).

10 *Lloyd George: Twelve Essays* (London, 1971).

11 *Politicians and the War*, 2 vols (London, 1928); *Men and Power* (London, 1956); *Decline and Fall of Lloyd George* (London, 1963).

12 London, 1964.

13 London, 1966.

14 London, 1971; 1972.

15 London, 1970–4.

16 Clarke, *Lancashire and the New Liberalism* (Cambridge, 1971); Gilbert, *The Evolution of National Insurance in Great Britain* (London, 1966); Blewett, *The Peers, The Parties and The People* (London, 1972); Johnson, *Land Fit for Heroes* (Chicago, 1968); Hazlehurst, *Politicians at War* (London, 1971); Cowling, *The Impact of Labour* (Cambridge, 1971); Skidelsky, *Politicians and the Slump* (London, 1967).

17 London, 1973.

18 London, 1966.

19 p. 384.

20 Cf. Hazlehurst, pp. 299–300, on Wilson's 'deductive gymnastics'.

21 London, 1971.

22 p. 175.

23 Cardiff and London, 1973.

24 London, 1970.

25 London, 1974.

26 London, 1968.

27 Lady Violet Bonham Carter to A. G. Gardiner, 4 Dec 1933, Gardiner Papers (British Library of Political and Economic Science, London).

28 'Lloyd George: Rise and Fall', in *Politics in Wartime*, p. 130.

29 Swinnerton to the author, 8 Aug 1973.

30 Asquith, *Fifty Years of Parliament* (London, 1926) I, 230.

31 *Cambria Daily Leader*, 15 Dec 1898; *North Wales Observer*, 28 Sep 1900.

32 Morgan (ed.), *Family Letters*, p. 203.

33 Robert J. Scally, *The Origins of the Lloyd George Coalition* (Princeton, N.J., 1975).

34 Macmillan, *Winds of Change* (New York, 1966) pp. 96–7.

35 Buckmaster to Maurice, n.d., quoted in Major-General Sir Frederick Maurice, *Haldane* (London, 1939) Vol. II, p. 45.

36 See, for example, Beaverbrook, *Politicians and the War*; Lady Violet Bonham Carter, *Winston Churchill as I Knew Him* (London, 1965) ch. xxiv; Barry McGill, 'Asquith's Predicament, 1914–1918', *Journal of Modern History*, xxxix (1967) 283–303; Stephen Koss, *Lord Haldane, Scapegoat for Liberalism* (New York, 1969) ch. vii; Hazlehurst, *Politicians at War*, Part III; Peter Lowe, 'The Rise to the Premiership', in Taylor (ed.), *Lloyd George: Twelve Essays*, pp. 95–133; A. M. Gollin, 'The Unmaking of a Prime Minister', *Spectator*, 28 May 1965, and the ensuing correspondence between Gollin and Robert Rhodes James.

37 Chamberlain to Beaverbrook, 30 June 1931, Beaverbrook Papers (consulted at the Beaverbrook Library, London).

38 Shaw to H. Granville Barker, 18 Dec 1918, in Bernard Shaw, *Letters to Granville Barker*, ed. C. B. Purdom (New York, 1957) pp. 198–9.

39 Memorandum by Murray, 2 Oct 1918, and Murray to Sir William Wiseman, 8 Oct 1918, Elibank Papers (National Library of Scotland, Edinburgh); Murray to Lloyd George, 30 Oct 1918, Lloyd George Papers F/41/5/26 (consulted at the Beaverbrook Library, London); diary entry, 25–26 Oct 1918, *The Political Diaries of C. P. Scott*, pp. 258–60; Lloyd George to Scott, 5 Jan 1919, Lloyd George Papers, F/45/2/14.

40  George V to Lloyd George, 19 Nov 1918, Lloyd George Papers, F/29/263; Churchill to Lloyd George, 26 Dec 1918, ibid., F/8/2/49.

41  Margot Asquith, *Autobiography*, ii (London, 1922) pp. 302–3; memorandum of 7 Nov 1919, Maclean Papers (Bodleian Library, Oxford).

42  Asquith to A. G. Gardiner, 16 Dec 1918, Gardiner Papers.

43  Wilson, *Downfall of the Liberal Party*, pp. 187–8.

44  McKenna to A. G. Gardiner, 29 Dec 1918, Gardiner Papers.

45  Memorandum of 17 Nov 1919, Maclean Papers.

46  Bramsdon to Maclean, 31 Jan 1919; Hogge to Maclean, received 8 Sep 1919; Runciman to Maclean, 30 Dec 1919, Maclean Papers; on the attempt to establish a 'centre party' under Grey and Cecil, see Douglas, *History of the Liberal Party*, pp. 157–9.

47  Memorandum by Maclean of a conversation with Henry Cadbury, 16 Jan 1920, Asquith Papers, Vol. 148, fols 92 ff. (Bodleian Library, Oxford).

48  Memorandum dated Tuesday, Dec 1919, Nicoll Papers (courtesy of Mrs Mildred Kirkcaldy).

49  Haldane to his sister, 17 Nov 1919, 12 Feb 1920, Haldane Papers, Vol. 6013, fols 72, 84; Haldane to his mother, 28 Jan 1920, ibid., Vol. 60003, fol. 26 (National Library of Scotland, Edinburgh).

50  Entries for 10, 19 and 25 Feb 1920, *Lloyd George: A Diary by Frances Stevenson*, pp. 200–4.

51  Memorandum 'A day in the House—Aug. 10, 1920', typed 13 Aug 1920, Maclean Papers.

52  Margot Asquith to Maclean, 6 Feb 1921, Maclean Papers.

53  Maclean to Gladstone, 29 Dec 1923; Gladstone to Maclean, 30 Dec 1923, Viscount Gladstone Papers, British Museum Add. MSS. 46, 474, fols 52, 54.

54  Chris Cook, 'A Stranger Death of Liberal England', in Taylor (ed.), *Lloyd George: Twelve Essays*, pp. 311–13.

55  Maclean to Gladstone, 10 Jan 1924 (copy), Maclean Papers; Gladstone's memorandum of 1923–4, dated 11 July 1925, ibid.; Hudson to Gladstone, 4 July 1924, Viscount Gladstone Papers, Add. MSS. 46, 475, fol. 125.

56  Diary entries for 5 Feb and 1 June 1924, in Kathleen, Lady Kennet (formerly Lady Scott), *Self-Portrait of an Artist* (London, 1949) pp. 224, 226.

57  Memorandum by W. McG. Eager of a conference on 10 Oct 1924, Eager Papers (Reform Club Library, London).

58  Hudson to Gladstone, 1 Nov 1924, Viscount Gladstone Papers, Add. MSS. 46, 475, fols 141 ff.

59  Hudson to Gladstone, 5 Nov 1924, ibid., fols 145–7.

60  Margot Asquith to Strachey, 'Xmas Day, 1924', Strachey Papers S/11/7/75 (consulted at the Beaverbrook Library, London); Margot Asquith to Gardiner, 23 Jan 1925, Gardiner Papers.

61  Kathleen, Lady Kennet, *Self-Portrait*, p. 231.

62  Eager's memoranda dated 13 Feb, 7 July, 27 Aug, 28 Nov and 2 Dec 1925, Eager Papers; A. J. Sylvester to Lloyd George, 18 Nov 1925 (copy), Eager Papers; Phillipps to Maclean, 1 May 1925, Maclean Papers; Oxford to Maclean, 12 Sep 1925, Maclean Papers; Eager to Thomas Jones, 1 May 1945 (copy), Eager Papers.

63  Maclean to Gladstone, 21 Nov and 24 Dec 1925, Viscount Gladstone Papers, Add. MSS. 46, 474, fols 181, 183; Hudson to Robert Donald, 27 Jan 1926, ibid., Add. MSS. 46, 475, fol. 183.

64  Lloyd George to his wife, 18 May 1926, in *Family Letters*, p. 206; Maclean to Gladstone, [11] May 1926, Viscount Gladstone Papers, Add. MSS. 46, 474, fol. 45.

65  Hudson to Gladstone, 18 May 1926, ibid., Add. MSS. 46, 475, fol. 194; Maclean to Gladstone, 20 May 1926, ibid., Add. MSS. 46, 474, fol. 189; Phillipps to Gladstone, 20 May 1926, ibid., Add. MSS. 46, 475, fol. 280.

66  'Diary note, referring to the events of 21 May 1926 but written some time subse-

quently', *Political Diaries of C. P. Scott*, pp. 486–7.

67 Copy of a memorandum, 'private and confidential', sent to members of Lloyd George's staff [May 1926], Eager Papers.

68 Hudson to Gladstone, 14 June 1926, Viscount Gladstone Papers, Add. MSS. 46, 475, fol. 198; Mrs W. Coombe Tennant to Lloyd George, 30 Sep 1926, Lloyd George Papers G/31/1/39; on the events of June-October 1926, see Wilson, *Downfall of the Liberal Party*, pp. 332–6.

# 5 Myth and Reality: Britain in the 1930s

## JOHN STEVENSON

The nineteen-thirties have been called the black years, the devil's decade. Its popular image can be expressed in two phrases: mass unemployment and 'appeasement'. No set of political leaders have been judged so contemptuously since the days of Lord North. Yet, at the same time, most English people were enjoying a richer life than any previously known in the history of the world: longer holidays, shorter hours, higher real wages. They had motor cars, cinemas, radio sets, electrical appliances. The two sides of life did not join up.[1]

A. J. P. Taylor

The thirties have had a bad press. Though the decade can now only be remembered by the middle-aged and the elderly, it retains the all-pervasive image of the 'wasted years' and the 'long weekend' even for those who did not live through it, haunted by the spectres of mass unemployment, hunger marches, appeasement, and the rise of fascism at home and abroad. By the outbreak of the Second World War, the thirties had already been condemned by self-confessed critics as a period of missed opportunities and wasted time; a judgement which the disasters of the early part of the war seemed only to vindicate. In a sense the intervention of the war years served to perpetuate the more depressing image of the 'low dishonest decade' and the 'hungry thirties', partly at least because the politics of the immediate post-war era were fought out on the record of the pre-war years. As late as 1951 the Labour Party campaigned with the election slogan of 'Ask your Dad!' an illustration of the way in which the emotive image of the 'hungry thirties' had become part of the standard repertoire of political cliché. The popular image of the thirties as a 'low dishonest decade' was undoubtedly hardened and reinforced in the years after the war; an image which became sharpened against the background of full employment and the affluence of the fifties and sixties. Thus even today the ghost of the thirties stalks political platforms as an emotive symbol of economic disaster, social deprivation, and political discontent. Indeed, though the appeasers have found their apologists in post-war historical writing, much of the domestic history of Britain in the thirties is still dominated by the issue of mass unemployment. But the very pervasiveness of the image of the 'hungry thirties' has done much to distort our view of the period and its more constructive and substantial achievements. A concentration upon unemployment and social distress has also led to a diversion of writing into certain themes and away from others. Hence there have been few attempts to take up the challenge offered by A. J. P. Taylor in a review of a recent book on the thirties, when he asked 'Which was more significant for the future—over a million unemployed or over a million private cars?'[2]

It would, of course, be fatuous to suggest that the thirties were not for many thousands of people a time of great hardship and personal suffering. The constant problem of mass unemployment meant that there were never less than a million people out of work in Britain during the decade. From 1931 to 1935 there were an average of over two million people out of work and the peak figure for unemployment was reached in the winter of 1932–3 when there were almost three million unemployed, representing almost a quarter of the insured population. Even these figures may well have been underestimates for the official statistics did not include many important groups, such as agricultural workers, domestic servants, the self-employed, and married women who had not bothered to sign on for unemployment relief when they became unemployed. Thus the peak total of unemployed in Britain was almost certainly well over three million people. But beside the picture of the unemployed must be put the other side of the case. There was never less than about 75 per cent of the population in work and for most of the period considerably more. Beside the pictures of the dole queues and the hunger marches must also be placed those of another Britain, of new industries, prosperous suburbs, and a rising standard of living. Any attempt to do justice to the condition of Britain in the thirties must give full weight to what J. B. Priestley described as the England of 'arterial and by-pass roads, filling stations and factories that look like exhibition buildings, of giant cinemas and dancehalls and cafes, bungalows with tiny garages, cocktail bars, Woolworths, motor coaches, wireless, hiking, factory girls looking like actresses, greyhound racing and dirt tracks, swimming pools, and everything given away for cigarette coupons.'[3]

Above all else, for those in work, the thirties were a period of rising living standards and new levels of consumption, upon which a considerable degree of the new industrial activity was concentrated. This was the paradox which lay at the heart of Britain in the thirties, where new levels of prosperity contrasted with the intractable problem of the distressed areas.

C. L. Mowat claimed that it was the problem of the distressed areas which 'tarnished the picture of recovery and was the basis for the myth

of the "hungry thirties".'[4] The concentration of Britain's staple industries created conditions in which whole areas were in industrial decay as
a result of the depression in world trade. The disastrous downturn in demand for British textiles, coal, iron and steel, and ships posed the most
acute economic and social problems for the older industrial areas. The
depressed regions were well defined: Northern Ireland, industrial Scotland, the North East, South Wales and Lancashire. Their experience in
the thirties has been well described in the literature of the period, particularly in George Orwell's *The Road to Wigan Pier* and Ellen Wilkinson's
*The Town that was Murdered*. But the problem of the unemployed and the
distressed areas was only a part of the total picture of Britain in the thirties. Economic historians have long recognised that as well as being a
period of prolonged depression in the old staple industries, these years
can also be seen as the time when a new industrial structure was being established which provided the real basis for the export boom and the
rising prosperity of the second half of the twentieth century. The picture
of depression was not evenly spread, but was concentrated in the old industrial areas. Unemployment rates in 1932 varied for the different regions of the country between 36 per cent in Wales and only 13 per cent in
London and the South East. By the mid-thirties the disparity was even
more striking, with unemployment rates in some towns in the depressed
areas revealing tragic stories of the decay and impoverishment of whole
communities; places such as Brynmawr, Dowlais, Jarrow, Gateshead,
Greenock, and Motherwell had almost three-quarters of the insured
population out of work in 1934, whereas a social survey of the Oxford
area in 1938 could dismiss the problem of unemployment as being
'almost negligible'.[5] When in 1936 the town of Jarrow sent a deputation
of its unemployed on the famous Jarrow 'Crusade' to petition parliament
for work to be brought to the area, the marchers passed through parts of
the country which were experiencing almost boom conditions. A hunger-
marcher from South Wales on his way to demonstrate in the capital in
1936, found Slough thronged with Welshmen who had come to seek
work in its new light industries. 'Thousands lined the streets', he wrote,
'the accents were so thick I thought we were in Rhondda, with this difference, instead of silent pits, massive factories all lit up were in full go'.[6] By
the mid-thirties the recovery of the economy could be seen in the mush-
rooming suburbs of London, in the new industrial estates, and the light
engineering towns of the Midlands and the South East. Thus any assessment of Britain's economic performance depends entirely upon the focus
of the enquiry: as one economic historian has remarked, 'whether the
spotlight is turned upon Jarrow or Slough; on Merthyr Tydfil or on
Oxford; on Greenock and Birkenhead or on Coventry, Weston-super-
Mare and the environs of London'.[7]

Economic revival began to reduce the number of unemployed by 1933.

It was concentrated in a range of new industries, such as electricity supply, construction, vehicle-building, engineering, chemicals and consumer durables. The thirties saw a boom in electricity supply, output rising fourfold between 1925 and 1939. From 1929 to 1939 the number of electricity consumers rose from just under three to over nine million. It meant not only an enormous industrial transformation, freeing industry from the coalfields, but a major social advance as well. In 1930 only one house in three was wired up for electricity, but by 1939 the figure was two houses out of three. Electricity brought a host of new electrical appliances into people's homes, such as 'mains' radio, the gramophone, electric irons, vacuum cleaners, and above all electric lighting. By 1939 Britain was producing over half a million motor vehicles of all kinds each year and there were already over two million private cars. Mass production by assembly-line methods had concentrated production in a few centres mainly in the Midlands, at Birmingham, Coventry, Luton and Oxford. Motor cars, aircraft, motor-cycles, electrical equipment and consumer durables contributed to a great expansion of the engineering industry, in which output was 60 per cent higher in 1937 than in 1924. Another expanding sector of the economy was the construction and building industry, based upon a boom in house-building, plus a large amount of public and industrial construction. Even the depressed areas shared in a certain amount of slum clearance, municipal building and relief schemes. Though there remained terrible black-spots of bad housing, the thirties saw a major effort at slum clearance in which a quarter of a million unfit dwellings were demolished and several large new housing estates established, such as Kirkby near Liverpool and Wythenshawe near Manchester. House-building for private sale added to the pace of activity, creating acres of semi-detached houses on the fringe of almost every town and city. By the end of the decade over two and a half million houses had been added to the housing stock, two-thirds of them built for private purchase. In the five years before the outbreak of war, over 350,000 houses were being completed each year, a figure exceeded only once between 1945 and 1964.

These were also years of important changes in the patterns of production and marketing. Rationalisation by merger of small firms into a number of giant concerns continued during the thirties, creating household names such as I.C.I., E.M.I., Unilever, Shell, and Courtaulds. The 'retailing revolution' concentrated distribution on a few centres and created chains of retail outlets. A number of major chains of retailers continued to expand in the thirties with the building of several hundred new stores. There was a great expansion in advertising which absorbed £100 million by 1938, mainly spent on newspapers. Alongside the growth in outlets and advertising went the growth of credit, especially the expansion of hire-purchase, which accounted for two-thirds of all larger purchases by 1938. Patterns of employment reflected this growth of new industries and a shift towards consumption and services. The heavy industries experienced a net loss of workers in the thirties, whilst the distributive trades, services, and light industries took a greater share of the employed population. Many of these new types of employment were filled by women and girls, so that the total number of working women rose sharply. Thus the pattern of employment which is normally associated with 'affluence', that is a transference of workers from producing goods to supplying services, was well under way by the end of the decade.

A powerful contributor to this recovery was a growth of consumption. It has been calculated that average real living standards for those in work rose during the thirties by between 15 and 18 per cent. It is this aspect of the period which is most easily forgotten amidst the images of the 'hungry thirties'. With a majority of the population in work, even in the worst years of the depression, most people in Britain were better off by 1939 than they had been ten years earlier. This was less because of substantial improvements in wages, though there were some, than the large fall in the cost of living by almost a third during the inter-war period; a fall which the thirties experienced as much as the twenties and which especially affected the price of food. Sugar, for example, was halved in price over the period, so was flour; meat was substantially cheaper too. There was also a wider variety of cheap processed foods available, adding some semi-luxury items to the diets of all but the poorest sections of the community. As well as food, there were also cheaper clothes, furniture and household goods. Moreover, families were becoming smaller and less income was needed for food and rent, so that more could be consumed or saved. Whereas in 1914 the average working-class family had spent three-quarters of its total income upon rent and food, by 1937–8 these items had fallen to under half the total expenditure. The result was a significant increase in living standards for the majority of families in regular employment.[8] A quite perceptible improvement in the standard of comfort was witnessed by many people, as for example, electricity replaced gas and candles for lighting and gas or electric cookers supplanted coal and coke ranges. An increasing number of families could afford a 'three-piece suite', carpets and a radio bought on H.P. Some contemporary writers noticed another important sign of improvements in living standards in the growth of small savings, for example in building societies. G. D. H. Cole thought the latter one of the most important obstacles to serious political upheaval in Britain, as substantial sections of the middle and working classes acquired savings and property.[9]

For many of the middle classes, this was definitely a period of raised living standards. Though people in government service saw their wages cut in the trough of the depression from 1931 to 1934, they also benefited from the fall in prices and a greater disposable income because of smaller families. For many salaried people 'affluence' began, not in the 1950s but in the thirties when it became possible for an average salaried person to buy his own house, usually on a mortgage, run a car, and begin to afford a range of consumer durables and household goods hitherto considered quite out of reach. These, by and large, were the people who fuelled the private house-building boom of the thirties. A typical 'semi' could be obtained for between £450 and £600, only two or three times the annual average salaried income. Interest rates were around $4\frac{1}{2}$ per cent and deposits were as low as £25 in some cases. By the early thirties a small family car could be bought for about £100, a price which an increasing number of people could afford. Car ownership and the work and leisure patterns it created were already well established in Britain by the outbreak of the Second World War. The burgeoning suburbs, arterial roads and sprawling 'ribbon development' provided evidence of the growth of middle-class commuter suburbs around the major cities. The south east of England absorbed almost two-thirds of the total population increase of the whole country during the inter-war years and the London conurbation increased from $7\frac{1}{2}$ million people in 1921 to $8\frac{1}{4}$ million by 1939. Much of this increase took place in the outer suburbs of a 'semi-detached London' with the development of arterial roads, the spread of the London Underground into the home counties, and the electrification of the Southern Region.

This is the perspective in which we can come to terms with one of the most intriguing questions in the political history of Britain in the thirties: not why the swing to political extremism was so great, but why it was, in fact, so small. As W. G. Runciman wrote some years ago, 'The various accounts of the Depression all make one wonder, at first sight, why discontent was not much more vehement'.[10] The problem was that the accounts of the depressed areas, whilst often a true reflection of their condition, were not representative of the state of the country as a whole. Britain, fortunately, was not wholly represented by the Wigan of Orwell's *The Road to Wigan Pier* and the Jarrow of *The Town that was Murdered*. For many people the depression was at worst only a brief period of belt-tightening before prosperity returned in the middle and late thirties. The political repercussions were most obvious in the case of Fascism. Two recent historians have written of the situation in Britain in the early thirties:

> When Sir Oswald Mosley formed his British Union of Fascists in the autumn of 1932 it seemed that many of the ingredients which were shortly to bring Hitler to power existed also in Britain. Here also there was mass unemployment and a paralysing economic depression; here also the middle class was insecure and could be presumed to be

searching for a 'saviour' . . .[11]

But in almost every respect Fascism in Britain was a non-starter. In Germany the recipe for a successful Nazi movement had not depended to a major extent upon the unemployed. Almost all the detailed studies which have been made of the growth of the Nazis show clearly that their ranks were filled primarily by the lower-middle classes. The representation of workers, both employed and unemployed, was much less than other groups. On the contrary the voting strength of the S.P.D. and the membership of the German trade union movement held up very well during the depression. As Allen has shown in his study of a small German town during the Weimar and Nazi eras, the effect of the depression was not so much to drive the unemployed and working class into the ranks of the Nazis, but rather to polarise the middle class into supporting the Nazis in fear of a left-ward swing which never took place. Thus the success of the Nazi Party, at least in terms of attracting votes and support, lay in the insecurity of the German middle class.[12] But the British middle classes were anything but insecure after 1931, with the return of a National Government with a five-hundred seat majority, the rout of the Labour Party, and the maintenance of a reasonably stable, if not actually improving, standard of living.

Although the B.U.F. was founded in October 1932, the widespread mass rallies and marches which seemed to give Mosley's blackshirts their most threatening air only got under way on a large scale after 1933, when the worst of the depression was ending. The violence and militancy with which the movement became associated, whether intrinsic to it or provoked, meant that the Fascists were regarded with great suspicion by the majority of the British electorate. The loss of Rothermere's backing after the Olympia meeting of 7 June 1934 and the alienation of a wide section of the community which had hitherto been neutral towards the movement was very significant. In the context of returning prosperity in the mid-thirties, the violent and militant methods of extra-parliamentary groups of all kinds were unlikely to appeal to a wide audience. Most respectable people were shocked by the disturbances surrounding Fascist meetings, whoever was to blame for them, just as they were alienated by the violence surrounding the hunger-marches and demonstrations organised by the National Unemployed Workers' Movement in the early thirties. There was no obvious reason to vote Fascist in a Britain securely governed by the National Government and which did nothing to perturb the growing prosperity of the middle classes. Thus at its peak the B.U.F. could claim only 40,000 active and non-active members, a total reached in 1934, after which the movement declined. Although contemporaries and other more recent commentators have argued that Britain escaped the presence of a larger and more successful

Fascist movement because the depression was neither more prolonged nor deeper than it was, this view is based upon a number of misconceptions about the mechanism for such a movement's growth. The primary reaction in Britain to the depression was to support the Conservative-dominated National Government. There is no evidence to suggest that a deeper slump after 1931 or a renewed depression in 1938–9 would have provoked a different reaction. Germany's situation was quite different: without a strong conservative party to guarantee the security of a middle class which had experienced the inflation of the early twenties, the Nazis were able to make their claim as the party of order. Even then, Hitler had to be jobbed into power by others. But in Britain there was a powerful Conservative government already in control of the situation. Mosley himself envisaged his movement coming to power in a situation of crisis. Hence he organised the movement on military lines 'in case we are called upon to save the nation in a condition of anarchy when the normal measures of government have broken down'.[13] Thus Mosley awaited his opportunity in the form of an attempted Communist revolution which never materialised. Without it, and with a strong National Government in firm control, the movement never stood a chance.

The Communist Party also fared poorly in the thirties. At the onset of the depression, the C.P.G.B. had just undergone a process of 'Stalinisation' in which control of the movement was dictated from Moscow and power within the British party was concentrated upon a narrow clique. In pursuit of a sectarian 'Class against Class' policy under instructions from Moscow, the party severed connections with sympathetic left-wing organisations, such as the I.L.P. and 'liquidated' or 'Bolshevised' organisations which contained a mixture of Communist and non-Communist members. The effect was to drive many people from the party and into the ranks of other organisations. By November 1930 the British Communist Party was effectively shut off from official contact with the Labour Party, the T.U.C. and the I.L.P.; and its membership had dwindled to just over two and a half thousand members, virtually extinguishing the party's influence beyond a hard core of activists. Moreover, as the 'Class against Class' policy involved attacks upon the 'social-fascists' of the Labour Party and the T.U.C., there was little chance that the Communist Party could expect any sympathy from the leaders of the official Labour movement, many of whose leaders spent a considerable part of their efforts attacking and inhibiting Communist influence in their respective organisations. Thus the Communist Party was unable to capitalise upon weaknesses of the Labour Party in 1931; its following was too small and it was regarded with deep suspicion by the majority of working people. As a result the twenty-six Communist candidates in the General Election of 1931 were able to poll only 75,000 votes against the 6,500,000 of the Labour Party. When the Communist

Party attempted to build up a rival organisation of industrial workers, known as the Minority Movement, they were also unable to wrest power from the existing representatives of organised labour. The Minority Movement set up two independent unions, the United Mineworkers of Scotland, based upon the miners of Fife, and the United Clothing Workers in the East End of London. But in spite of some bitter industrial conflicts in South Wales and Lancashire in 1931, the Minority Movement failed to rival the official trade union movement. When the T.U.C. at its lowest point in 1933 had four and a half million members, the Communist membership of the Minority Movement stood at a mere seven hundred. So obvious were the failures of the organisation that the Communist Party decided to wind it up in 1933, after an attempt to set up a Communist union of seamen had to be called off for lack of support.[14]

From 1933 the Communist Party changed its policy line and moved towards a 'United Front' of all socialist parties against Fascism. This change in line was precipitated as much by the failures of earlier policies, as by the demands of Russian foreign policy. The change was gradual, through a 'United Front from Below' phase, to attempts to re-establish formal relations with the Labour Party, the T.U.C. and the I.L.P. Attacks upon the leaders of these bodies were suspended and attempts were made to enlist their support for joint activity. The Communist Party was still, however, a dwarf amongst giants, for its membership was only 6000 in 1931, swollen to some extent by the depression, but much less than had been expected. Although these approaches failed to allay the distaste felt by the organs of the official labour movement in dealing with the Communist Party, from the mid-thirties the party began to find favour with a new section of the community. Whereas formerly it had attracted the majority of its adherents from industrial workers, with also a strong Celtic and colonial component, the Communist Party now began to recruit a younger generation of writers, intellectuals and scientists who became attracted to the party as the most vocal opponent of Fascism at home and abroad. The Spanish Civil War, in which the Communist Party took a leading part in aiding the Republic, provided a considerable boost to membership in the late thirties. Thus on the eve of the Second World War, in 1939, the Communist Party achieved its greatest membership with 17,756 members.[15]

Significantly this growth came after the worst of the depression was over. In the trough of the depression, when it might have been expected that the Communist Party would do well, membership hovered around the 6000 mark. As was often the case in the trade unions, Communists gained support as good unionists or organisers of the unemployed, but were unable to maintain it on a purely political level. For example, in South Wales there were seventeen Communist Party members as district or local councillors by the mid-thirties and there was considerable

Communist influence in the South Wales Miners Federation. Communists were active in the fight against 'Company Unionism' which the S.W.M.F. undertook in the mid-thirties when there was some revival in the coal industry. Local Communists also organised 'hunger marches' of the unemployed in 1932, 1934 and 1936.[16] Even so, the majority of South Wales miners continued to support the Labour Party, though there was a tendency in some areas for men to vote Communist in local or lodge elections, whilst voting Labour nationally. At the parliamentary level the Communist Party was as unsuccessful in South Wales as elsewhere, though Harry Pollitt achieved a near miss at East Rhondda in 1935. After 1939 many Communists who had been active in the thirties turned their efforts to trade union activity, rather than carrying on campaigning on behalf of the C.P. Even in South Wales, where Communism was stronger than in almost any other industrial area in the thirties, the C.P. claimed the allegiance of only a fraction of the working population. It was more readily accepted and influential than in other areas, but it was a minority allegiance in an area which was at variance with the experience of the rest of the country anyway. That the Communist Party could not muster a membership of more than nearly 18,000 after the worst depression in British history and could obtain the election of only one M.P. was a testament to the fundamental stability of British politics.

The history of the National Unemployed Workers' Movement in the thirties in attempting to mobilise the unemployed is also evidence of the failure of the country to take a lurch to the left under the impact of the depression. In some ways the N.U.W.M. was an impressive organisation. Founded in 1921, under the leadership of Wal Hannington, the movement was from the outset a Communist-dominated organisation founded to campaign for better conditions for the unemployed. By 1929 the movement was brought into step with the political line from Moscow for 'Class against Class' activity, consisting of a militant campaign of mass demonstrations, hunger marches and propaganda on behalf of the unemployed. This phase of activity reached a climax in the demonstrations, disturbances and the 'National Hunger March' of 1931–2.[17] During this phase membership rose rapidly. The N.U.W.M. grew from 20,000 to 37,000 strong in 1931 and by December 1932, Harry Pollitt could report to the Twelfth Plenum of the E.C.C.I. that the movement had 50,000 members organised in 387 branches. It is possible that the organisation may have expanded further in the early months of 1933, but there are no reliable membership figures on which to work. Certainly by the end of 1933 the organisation was beginning to run out of steam with the first stirring of recovery and a fall in the total of unemployed. Thereafter the movement went into decline, though still mounting a number of demonstrations and hunger marches. But even Wal Hannington confessed himself disappointed with the number of unemployed recruited to the movement, claiming that they never captured more than a tenth of the unemployed at any one time. Similarly Profintern complained of the N.U.W.M.'s failure to broaden out into a really powerful mass movement. Hannington primarily blamed the lack of co-operation shown by the T.U.C. and the Labour Party for the failure to mobilise more than a fraction of those who were out of work. He also blamed the 'apathy' of the unemployed and their tendency to regard unemployment as a natural catastrophe which could not be helped. He found too, that some remained optimistic about getting a job and hence regarded joining the N.U.W.M. as inappropriate. Thus the movement which had been created to rouse the unemployed to militant action and which the Communists urged between 1929 and 1933 to take to the streets in order to create a mass working-class movement, failed to do so, even in the eyes of its own organisers. Instead, after 1933, the N.U.W.M. became bogged down in individual case-work and attempted to follow the new Moscow line of a 'United Front' in co-operation with the T.U.C. and the Labour Party against Fascism. The N.U.W.M. had been unable to break the dominance of traditional labour organisations in the depressed areas. The hostility and suspicion with which it was regarded as a Communist-dominated organisation meant the N.U.W.M. was fighting an uphill struggle against entrenched attitudes and influence which the depression had not destroyed.

It was to the unemployed that most people looked for a source of political discontent in the thirties, whether mobilised by the right or left. Yet the over-all record of extra-parliamentary agitation by the unemployed was very limited, mainly confined to marches and demonstrations organised by the N.U.W.M. Just as the N.U.W.M. as an organisation failed to mobilise anything like a majority of the unemployed, its hunger marches attracted only a small number of people. The 'hunger marches' of 1932, 1934 and 1936 each involved only between one and two thousand participants. Although impressive rallies were mounted in support of them in London, even these fell far short of the numbers claimed by the organisers. By far and away the largest demonstrations mounted by the N.U.W.M. were organised in London in October and November 1932, when 25–30,000 people attended rallies in Hyde Park and Trafalgar Square. The peak attendance at any later demonstration was 12000, in 1936. These figures appear reliable, coming from police records intended solely for internal circulation. Much larger figures are still quoted by historians because they have uncritically accepted the totals given by Wal Hannington. In fact the majority of N.U.W.M. demonstrations were small affairs. The N.U.W.M. did not mobilise the tens or hundreds of thousands of supporters which might have turned their movement into an effective extra-parliamentary force and had to be content with a fraction of the numbers they might have commanded with the support of the mass of organised labour. Instead the N.U.W.M. marched and demonstrated as a rather suspect minority organisation, especially in the militant phase of its campaign from 1929 to 1933, cut off from the support of the official labour movement, and constantly under the shadow of police surveillance and interference.[18] The sum of disorder that arose out of mass unemployment was small compared to the expectations of many observers in the thirties. If the most militant phase of N.U.W.M. agitation is examined, between 1929 and 1933, the total number of disturbances totalled about fifty, most of them small-scale affairs of a few scuffles and minor injuries. The most serious disturbances in terms of casualties, were the riots in Belfast in October 1932 when two people were killed. On the mainland of Britain, there were no fatal casualties arising directly out of demonstrations of the unemployed. During the most serious disturbances in London in October and November 1932, at the conclusion of the N.U.W.M.'s 'National Hunger March' there were at most a handful of serious injuries, and a number of minor ones. The total cost of damage compiled by the police came to just over £200, mainly consisting of broken windows, one of which alone cost £120—scarcely violence on a revolutionary scale.[19]

The famous Jarrow March of 1936, almost the synonym for all the 'hunger marches' of the thirties, was actually the smallest, the least disorderly and the only march not organised by the National Unemployed Workers' Movement. It consisted of two hundred men, was quite deliberately non-political, and was organised with the full co-operation of the police. Because they accepted the stringent conditions laid down by the authorities that they were not to undertake a mass lobby of Parliament but attend in small groups to named M.P.s, the Jarrow 'Crusaders' were allowed to have tea in the House of Commons, in the words of the Special Branch, 'since the Marchers show every sign of being orderly, it would be a good way of encouraging and placating them'. The Special Branch was further encouraged by the news that one man had been expelled from the march because he was a Communist and that when the marchers reached London they refused to allow any Communist speakers to share their platform. The Special Branch noted with approval that they showed their enthusiasm for the monarchy by 'cheering lustily' when the King passed them in the Mall. The Jarrow marchers peacefully attended the House of Commons, were entertained to tea by sympathetic M.P.s, and taken on a sight-seeing trip down the Thames. When they returned they found that their petition had been presented in their absence. The marchers were naturally rather disgruntled at being deprived of what was supposed to be the crowning episode of the march. They were, however, 'prevailed upon not to create a scene' and returned to their billets.[20] On the following day they left London by train for Jarrow. Though the march had obtained considerable public sympathy, particularly because of the orderly way in which it was conducted, it achieved little practical result. A councillor who heard the replies of Walter Runciman and the Prime Minister to the presentation of the petition was reported to have said to his fellow marchers when they returned to the House of Commons, 'It means you have drawn a blank.' He was proved right, but the stolid dignity of the Jarrow marchers did help them to become the symbol of the depressed areas. Followed up by Ellen Wilkinson's book, *The Town that was Murdered*, Jarrow and its march became imprinted on the national memory. But it would be wrong to conclude that the Jarrow march was either the biggest or the most intimidating protest movement by the unemployed. A week after the Jarrow marchers left London, the N.U.W.M. staged its last major hunger march of the thirties. Almost 2000 marchers converged on London in a number of different contingents. A rally was held in Hyde Park attended by London Labour Party and Trades Council representatives at which about 12,000 people attended. It was a larger and more significant demonstration than the Jarrow march because it brought together the N.U.W.M., Labour Party and T.U.C. on the same platform for the first time in the thirties.[21] Yet this march and demonstration received far less attention in the press than the Jarrow 'Crusade'. Even the Labour Party which had spoken against the Jarrow march at its annual conference at Edinburgh in 1936 was to fall under Jarrow's spell, so that by 1947, a history of the Labour Party could describe it as the 'most spectacular perhaps' of the hunger marches.[22]

Yet hunger marches and demonstrations occupied only a fraction of the unemployed. Harry Pollitt, General Secretary of the C.P.G.B., was forced to report to Moscow in 1933: 'the Communist Parties and the revolutionary trade unions have not sufficiently liberated the masses of the workers from the influence of the Social-Democratic parties and of the trade union bureaucrats.' 'Masses of workers', he claimed, 'were throwing themselves into the arms of the social-fascists.' Municipal election results, he said, showed that the mass of the workers had failed to come over to the Communist Party, the N.U.W.M., or the Minority Movement.[23] At the local level George Orwell summed up his experiences at a N.U.W.M. social in Wigan:

> Admission and refreshments (cup of tea and meat pie) 6d. About 200 people, preponderantly women, largely members of the Co-op, in one of whose rooms it was held, and I suppose for the most part living directly or indirectly on the dole. Round the back a few aged miners sitting looking on benevolently, a lot of very young girls in front. Some dancing to the concertina . . . and some excruciating singing. I suppose these people represent a fair cross-section of the more revolutionary element in Wigan. If so, God help us . . . There is no *turbulence*

left in England.[24]

It is clear from electoral and other evidence that the unemployed as a whole were not disposed to become revolutionary. Many general explanations have been put forward for this. W. G. Runciman has suggested that the overriding characteristic of the unemployed was a fatalism derived from a sense of powerlessness in the face of a crisis which seemed almost beyond human control. Much of the literature of the depression expressed this view; the titles speak for themselves: 'The Riddle of Unemployment', 'What is Unemployment', 'Is Unemployment Inevitable', and so on. Moreover these were views which were largely shared by the traditional leaders of working-class communities, the Labour Party and the trade unions. Runciman also suggests that because whole communities suffered in common, there was less of the ill-feeling and resentment which might have been evident had the unemployed felt themselves to be 'starving in the midst of plenty'.[25] Thus the very concentration of unemployment in the old industrial areas acted as a check upon the expression of violent discontent. A. J. P. Taylor, on the other hand, has stressed the point that such discontent as there was concentrated upon the issue of relief scales rather than anything more fundamental and that the presence of basic relief at all, however minimal, prevented the erection of barricades in Britain between the wars.[26] Orwell had his own ideas—he recorded the general tendency amongst the unemployed to 'sit it out', living normal lives in reduced circumstances: 'They have neither turned revolutionary nor lost their self-respect; merely they have kept their tempers and settled down to make the best of things on a fish-and-chip standard.' He saw the plethora of cheap luxuries which were available as an effective palliative to discontent. 'It is quite likely', he wrote, 'that fish-and-chips, art-silk stockings, tinned salmon, cut-price chocolate (five two-ounce bars for sixpence), the movies, the radio, strong tea, and the Football Pools have between them averted revolution.'[27]

An additional handicap to the unemployed becoming an effective political force was their geographical concentration, hidden away in the mining communities of the Welsh valleys or the villages of County Durham. Once the trough of the depression was past by 1933–4, the problem of long-term mass unemployment was, as it had been prior to 1929, a regional problem. As we have seen earlier, many communities remained little affected by the depression, while others were beginning to obtain their first taste of prosperity. For a long time the unemployed were cut off from the mainstream of public opinion during the thirties. The unemployment problem was not new, it had been present since the early twenties in the staple industries, and there was a tendency to regard it as a natural catastrophe to which there was no obvious answer. The N.U.W.M. hunger marches were an attempt to break out of this position and at least to draw the attention of a wider public to the plight of the unemployed. Whatever the motives of the N.U.W.M., they did in part succeed in this, but initially their efforts were diffused by the threat which, as a Communist-dominated organisation, they seemed to pose to public order. Cole and Postgate wrote in *The Common People*: 'What was the use of rioting in South Wales, or of making orderly demonstrations? Who would take notice of them? And when the unemployed of the distressed districts tried "hunger marching" on London the leaders of Trade Unionism and of the Labour Party, disavowed them, and the police stood ready, at the government's orders, to prevent them making "scenes".'[28] In the worst phase of the depression, unemployment seemed to many an act of God, while as conditions improved it became a regional and provincial problem, which impinged only intermittently upon the public in general. Newspapers of the thirties only rarely had items about unemployment, usually connected with demonstrations or hunger marches. Even these were rarely given major prominence; thus the bigger N.U.W.M. marches obtained only a few paragraphs in the national newspapers. The most prominent features were the advertisements. Side by side with reports of demonstrations in local newspapers were pages of advertisements for clothes, furniture and all manner of consumer goods. In this context the unemployed became in Ernest Bevin's phrase a 'third nation', generally forgotten by those in work. At least the hunger marches brought the problem of the unemployed back into view, and many contemporaries testified to their impact in bringing home the reality of mass unemployment. Nonetheless, the depressed regions were beyond the experience of many people and it is easy in an age accustomed to 'instant' news coverage and intensive documentary journalism to assume that the problem of mass unemployment was constantly in people's minds. Even the unemployed tended not to make direct comparison of their own experiences with the growing prosperity elsewhere. Though contemporary writers could make outraged comparisons between a Lancashire where people were reduced to putting blank discs in gas meters and the building in Blackpool of the biggest and most luxurious hotel in Britain, complete with 2500 bedrooms, each with telephone and wireless, 3000 telephones, and a garage for 500 cars, or with Orwell reflect upon the 'queer spectacle of modern electrical science showering miracles upon people with empty bellies', the unemployed on the whole did not react to these ironies.[29] Their comparisons were made amongst each other.

As a corollary to this, one of the most interesting things about the social literature of the thirties was that so much of it appeared so late in the decade or even after the war started. Orwell's classic, *The Road to Wigan Pier*, appeared in 1937 and Ellen Wilkinson's *The Town that was Murdered* only in 1939. The more academic studies of the problems of mass unemployment were also slow to appear. The Pilgrim Trust's study of the long-unemployed, *Men Without Work*, came out in 1938. The Carnegie Trust's report on unemployed youth in South Wales, *Disinherited Youth*, had to wait until 1941. Unemployment and the 'condition of Britain' only really became a major political issue after the worst of the slump was over and unemployment was beginning to decline. The spate of literature on unemployment and social issues reflected a timely recognition that the problems of unemployment would require something more than the slow workings of the policies of 'natural recovery'. As a result the problem of unemployment was rather slow to find effective political voice in the thirties. It was only after 1933 that the T.U.C. took steps to organise the unemployed, and then not very successfully. Similarly it was only in the mid-thirties that the Labour Party took active steps to support the unemployed with its opposition to the new Unemployment Assistance Board regulations in 1934–5.

This made the absence of a major swing to either political extreme all the more significant. For most of the thirties the Labour Party was unable to offer a constructive alternative to the unemployed, so that the party largely confined itself to a sympathetic attitude towards unemployment benefit, criticising the operation of the means test, and questioning the conduct of Government and police towards demonstrations by the unemployed. In the much-weakened Parliamentary condition of the party and its inability to formulate a practical solution to the economic policies of the National Government, the Labour Party could give very little hope or encouragement to its supporters, whether employed or unemployed. It was not until the National Executive began to develop policies for a 'planned economy' that the party could begin to make a concerted attack upon the National Government. By the time it did so, the attention of the party and of parliament as a whole was increasingly focused upon developments overseas. Conference after conference in the thirties displayed the party's primary concern for the issues of foreign policy, which became increasingly urgent from 1935 onwards. Nationally then, the Labour Party gave little lead to its unemployed supporters. The Labour Party organised only one demonstration on behalf of the unemployed in co-operation with the T.U.C., in February 1933. Its attitude towards demonstrative behaviour by the unemployed remained suspicious, leading to criticism from Labour leaders even of the Jarrow march. At most, in the worst years of the depression, the party counselled a more humane treatment of the unemployed, but offered neither a militant policy of achieving it, nor for much of the period a clear alternative economic policy to that being pursued by the National Government.

The response of the trade union movement to the unemployed was also extremely limited. Trade unions were traditionally organisations of workers in employment, and they found that prolonged mass unemployment presented them with new problems of organisation and policy. Although some unions had branches for unemployed members, there was no major effort by the unions to stem the loss of members. By 1933 trade union membership had fallen to four and a half million, compared with a peak of eight million in the aftermath of the First World War. It was only with the improvement in the economy in the mid-thirties that union membership began to rise again. The difficulties of the trade unions in the early thirties were a combination of falling membership, weak finances, and having to operate in the 'back to the wall' conditions of mass unemployment. Many unions had suffered a steady drain upon their financial resources as a result of strikes during the twenties; heavy unemployment now forced them to pay out a high level of benefit. Even militant unions such as the A.E.U. were forced to sacrifice some of their concessionary contributions for unemployed workers and operate upon the principle of members either paying a full union contribution or losing their membership. It was not surprising then that many unemployed workers saw the union contribution as an unnecessary luxury when living on the tight budget imposed by the dole. Therefore unions often tended to lose touch with their unemployed members. In South Wales, where unemployment had been a problem throughout the twenties and the organisational difficulties it created should have been familiar, it was not until the S.W.M.F. began the struggle against company unionism in earnest from 1935 that a belated effort was made to organise unemployed miners in an attempt to reduce the supply of 'blackleg labour' available for strike-breaking.[30] The result was that during the depression, particularly up to 1933, many unions suffered a loss of members and also lost touch with the unemployed. Any efforts to create organisations of unemployed workers as a whole, however, were regarded with suspicion both by the T.U.C. and by individual unions, who no matter how incapable of maintaining links with their own unemployed still regarded them as the responsibility of the union to which they belonged when employed. In addition the activities of the N.U.W.M. inhibited the T.U.C. from taking a militant line which might have played into the hands of the Communists. Thus they refused to mount more than one national demonstration, that of February 1933, and took a very cautious attitude towards its organisation. By 1932, however, the success of the N.U.W.M. forced the trade unions to reconsider their position. They refused to have anything to do with the N.U.W.M., having severed formal ties within it in 1927, and refused a N.U.W.M. deputation permission to speak at the T.U.C. Congress in 1932 in Newcastle. When the expansion of the N.U.W.M. in 1931–2 threatened to fill the vacuum left by the lack of provision for unemployed workers by trade unions, the General Council in 1932 proposed creating Unemployed Associations under the auspices of local trades councils. These had been proposed in 1927, but had met with little enthusiasm amongst affiliated unions. This time the movement did get under way and fifty-eight associations were in being by 1932, reaching a peak in 1934–6 when there were over one hundred and thirty associations with over a hundred centres. The associations, however, could hardly be considered a great success, never having more than about 50,000 members in the whole country. Though they provided a recreational focus for a small minority of the unemployed, the T.U.C. was too anxious to define their functions and control their actions for them to have much appeal. Recreation and a certain amount of legal case-work were their most important activities, but members were discouraged from undertaking any kind of sponsored employment for fear of creating competition with the employed. Members were also expected to make a pledge that they would join a union once they found employment. As recent historians of the T.U.C. have concluded: 'It is difficult to escape the conclusion that the reasons for their formation were essentially negative, reflecting the narrow self-interest of individual unions, and the ideological antagonism of the T.U.C. leadership to Communist militancy.'[31]

The Unemployed Associations were the only major effort by the T.U.C. to organise the unemployed, but their relatively marginal influence illustrates to what extent the absence of a swing to the left in Britain during the thirties owed less to the positive efforts of the T.U.C. and the Labour Party than is often accepted.

It is easy to forget the importance which must be attached to the rise in living standards which had taken place in the majority of households in the thirties. Indeed, it is an analysis based upon rising expectations which may well explain the increasing militancy of the middle and late thirties, compared with the worst years of the depression. But above all else, raised living standards explain the single most important political feature of the thirties, the dominance of the National Government and the Conservative Party. There is a strong tendency amongst some historians to wish the National Government away and pretend it did not exist, to argue that people voted for it out of base or mistaken motives. It is, however, worth quoting the evidence of one or two contemporaries before dismissing the support for the National Government. Perhaps some historians have become analogous to the foreigner who, George Orwell wrote, 'sees only the huge inequality of wealth, the unfair electoral system, the governing-class control over the press, the radio and education, and concludes that democracy is simply a polite name for dictatorship.' Orwell, however, continued: 'But this ignores the considerable agreement that does unfortunately exist between the leaders and the led. However much one may hate to admit it, it is almost certain that between 1931 and 1940 the National Government represented the will of the mass of the people.'[32] This was not a solitary opinion. Writing in 1938 G. D. H. Cole recorded:

> I do not at all like the way Great Britain is governed. But the very slow-
> ness of the Labour Party's electoral progress is a sign that, in the mat-
> ters which most closely touch the everyday lives of the electorate, it is
> not governed without a good deal of skill. Tory spokesmen are not talk-
> ing sheer nonsense when they claim that the National Government has
> pulled Great Britain successfully through the greatest depression in
> history.[33]

It is appropriate now to return to the issues raised at the beginning of
this essay. Any assessment of the thirties must essentially rest upon a
value judgement about whether the undoubted sufferings of the unemployed were outweighed by the rise in living standards for the majority of
the population. This does not, however, exonerate historians from
attempting to come to terms with the thirties as they were in reality,
rather than with their myth. The question of why Britain did not suffer a
major political upheaval in the thirties demands that we turn our attention to the central features of the political history of the period, the tendency of the majority of the population to support middle-of-the-road,
conservative government. No matter how interesting the hypothetical
possibilities of a Britain dominated by Mosley, Lloyd George, or any
other 'saviour', the primary question that has to be answered is why the
majority of the British people reacted to the depression by voting for the
National Government. If this was an expression of a fundamental conservatism, then the most pressing question to consider is what were the
sources of this conservatism in the politics of the early decades of the
twentieth century and earlier. Equally, we need to come to terms with
the major characteristics of working-class politics in the thirties, the
overwhelming tendency of both employed and unemployed to vote
Labour in the face of the depression rather than for either extreme. We
need a much more detailed account of the electoral features of the period,
rather than still more attempts to say something new about unemployment—particularly when the enquiries of the period were so good
anyway. We need to look beyond the critics of the 'Devil's decade', both
then and now, with their concentration upon its failings, and recognise
the significance of a decade which saw for many the beginnings of
'affluence', the evolution of the welfare state, and a confirmation of the
stability of British politics.

## Notes

1  A. J. P. Taylor, *English History, 1914–1945* (Oxford, 1965) p. 317.
2  *Observer*, 21 Mar 1971.
3  J. B. Priestley, *English Journey* (London, 1934) p. 401.

4  C. L. Mowat, *Britain Between the Wars, 1918–1940* (London, 1968) p. 463.

5  Survey Committee of Barnett House, *A Survey of the Social Services in the Oxford Area* (Oxford, 1938) p. 97.

6  Claude Stamfield MSS, University of Swansea Library.

7  P. Mathias, *The First Industrial Nation* (London, 1971) p. 431.

8  S. Pollard, *The Development of the British Economy, 1914–1950* (London, 1962) pp. 289–96; D. H. Aldcroft, *The Inter-War Economy; Britain, 1919–1939* (London, 1970) ch. 10.

9  G. D. H. Cole and R. Postgate, *The Common People, 1746–1946*, 6th ed. (London, 1961) pp. 638–9.

10  W. G. Runciman, *Relative Deprivation and Social Justice* (London, 1966) p. 63.

11  N. Branson and M. Heinemann, *Britain in the Nineteen Thirties* (London, 1971) p. 281.

12  See W. S. Allen, *The Nazi Siezure of Power* (London, 1965); and also D. Schoenbaum, *Hitler's Social Revolution* (London, 1967) ch. 1.

13  R. Skidelsky, *Oswald Mosley* (London, 1975) pp. 358–9.

14  H. Pelling, *The British Communist Party* (London, 1958) chs 3 and 4.

15  Ibid., ch. 5.

16  See H. Francis, 'Welsh Miners in the Spanish Civil War', *Journal of Contemporary History*, Vol. 5, no. 3 (1970); D. Smith, 'The Struggle against Company Unionism in the South Wales Coalfield, 1926–39', *Welsh History Review*, Vol. 6, no. 4 (1973).

17  See J. Stevenson, 'The Politics of Violence', in G. Peele and C. Cook (eds.), *The Politics of Reappraisal* (London, 1975).

18  Ibid.; on the police, see R. Hayburn, 'The Police and the Hunger Marchers', *The International Review of Social History* (1973).

19  Stevenson, 'Politics of Violence'.

20  Public Record Office, Metropolitan Police Records (Mepol), Ser. 2, Vol. 3097, Special Branch report on the Jarrow march, 6 Nov. 1936.

21  Mepol 2, 3053, reports on Means Test demonstration on 8 November 1936.

22  W. Glenvil Hall, *The Labour Party* (London, 1947) p. 45.

23  *Report of the Thirteenth Plenum of the E.C.C.I.* (London, 1933) p. 14.

24  S. Orwell and G. Angus (eds), *The Collected Essays, Journalism, and Letters of George Orwell* (London, 1971) pp. 206–7.

25  Runciman, *Relative Deprivation*, pp. 63–5.

26  Taylor, *English History*, p. 149.

27  G. Orwell, *The Road to Wigan Pier* (London, 1972) pp. 80–1.

28  pp. 627–8.

29  A. Hutt, *The Condition of the Working Class in Britain* (London, 1933) p. 69; Orwell, *Road to Wigan Pier*, p. 81.

30  See Smith, 'The Struggle against Company Unionism'.

31  J. Lovell and B. C. Roberts, *A Short History of the T.U.C.* (London, 1968) p. 129.

32  G. Orwell, 'England Your England', *Inside the Whale and Other Essays* (London, 1968) p. 76.

33  G. D. H. Cole, *Economic Prospects: 1938 and After* (London, 1938) p. 81.

# 6 The Historiography of Appeasement

## DONALD WATT

In an essay published in 1965,[1] and originally read as a paper to the Anglo-American historical conference in London the previous summer, I expressed something of the iconoclastic effect A. J. P. Taylor's publication in 1961 of *The Origins of the Second World War* had upon the accepted view of the role of the British Government in the events leading up to the outbreak of the Second World War—iconoclastic and liberating. Before Mr Taylor's publication, historical work on the subject had been the province of two generations of historians, those who had played a major role in the war guilt controversies of the 1920s[2] (and had to a man, more or less, opposed the policy of appeasement in the 1930s) and those, often their pupils, who had come of age in the days of the Popular Front when Tory Right, liberals, radicals, social democrats, and fellow travellers had been united in their opposition to Fascism and to the public policies of the Conservative Government, so very much less than whole-heartedly obstructive towards Hitler and Mussolini as these appeared.

These generations of historians echoed, were echoed by and conferred respectability upon a much larger public view for which 'appeasement' and 'Munich' had become pejorative words and 'anti-appeasement', in the words of a younger British historian, Professor Keith Robbins, had 'become a general law of foreign policy'.[3] This public view, reinforced and self-reinforcing during the late 1940s and 1950s, was that as the state of relations between the United States and her West European allies and the Soviet Union and its enforced East European satellites seemed to have petrified into frigid and repetitive verbal conflict, foreign relations were concerned almost entirely with the restraint of aggression. States, like characters in a detective thriller, could be classified into criminals and victims, aggressors and objects of aggression. Concessions to an aggressor, in this view, were and are always wrong. Foreign relations thus became the province of the political puritan; to understand the problems of foreign policy it was enough to diagnose the underlying sins of those who conducted that policy. Once the sinner was identified the remedy became clear. Isolate, disown, expel, cast out, denounce, rebuke the sinner—President Bhutto, Fidel Castro, the (eponymous) colonels, the Reds, the C.I.A., President Nixon, the Soviets, the British, the Americans, the Chinese—and all would be well again.

The sin theory of international relations has sunk very deep into the public consciousness of the free world these last thirty years. And it dominates both politics and history on the Soviet side of the great European divide. It dominated the thinking of Lord Avon's last year in office, the year of the Suez disaster, when one was treated to the tragic and ludicrous spectacle of a major issue in British foreign policy being argued on both sides on the basis of a bad historical analogy. For Lord Avon, as his speeches at the time and his later memoirs[4] make clear, Nasser was Adolf Hitler in Egyptian. Action against him once he had nationalised the Suez Canal would have stopped his career before his potential grew too great just as, so it was argued then, action against Hitler in March 1936 on the occasion of the remilitarisation of the Rhineland could have brought about his overthrow and prevented the Second World War. Inaction would, by contrast, merely have encouraged him still further until a major war would have been necessary to dislodge him.

The effects of the Suez disaster rather discredited argument by historical analogy in Britain. It had no such effect in the United States. The thinking of the late Mr John Foster Dulles was permeated with concern for what he felt to be the lessons of Munich. And when in 1966 Mr Cabot Lodge addressed the Oxford Union in one of the great 'teach-ins' on Vietnam, it was to the lessons of the 1930s, the need to resist aggression, the costs of appeasement and the inevitable progress from Munich to Dunkirk that he appealed. It was perhaps unfortunate that Sovietophil propagandists had convinced much of his audience that North Vietnam rather than South Vietnam was the Czechoslovakia in the case.

Professor Ernest R. May has recently called our attention to the disastrous role played in recent American policy by misleading appeals to the rather simplistically conceived lessons of the past.[5] His remedy was a more active participation in the policy-making process by properly informed historians. In the case of 'appeasement' such men would still be difficult to find in America. The majority of American political analysts and historians remain uncritically convinced of the dogmas of the anti-appeasement school. No major American historian has concerned himself with the re-examination or reinterpretation of the evidence on the origin of the Second World War in Europe. Where those of the First World War engaged the energies without exception of the major American modern historians, W. L. Langer, Bernadotte Schmitt, Sidney Fay, Malcolm Carroll, Raymond Sontag, to name only a few, they have had no successors. Langer produced a demi-official history,[6] Schmitt, Carroll and Sontag were associated as American editors with the tripartite project for the publication of the captured German diplomatic documents (and the last two edited *Nazi-Soviet Relations, 1939–1941*, the first historians' shot of the Cold War); but after their retirement or withdrawal from the field they had no successors.

In their place the field has been left to a small number of minor writers of little-known monographs, distinguished mainly by their unquestioning dedication to part or whole of the anti-appeasement critique. Professor Arthur Furnia,[7] mainly relying on William Bullitt's too ready acceptance of Daladier's rhetoric, would have us believe that it was British pusillanimity which held back a noble and otherwise resolutely anti-Hitlerian France. Mrs Margaret George,[8] who apparently believes that the cabinets of Macdonald, Baldwin and Chamberlain were filled with scions of the British aristocracy, alleges that the sole motive of British policy was to preserve the privileged position of that aristocracy from the threat of Bolshevism and the Soviet Union. Dr William Rock[9] apparently ascribes the British Government's failure to stand up to Hitler to stupidity and malice towards the supporters of Churchill. There are signs of dissatisfaction with these oversimplified views in the recent work of Professor Arnold Ofner[10] and in the useful summaries of the state of the controversy produced by the late Professor John L. Snell,[11] by Professor Donald Lammers[12] and by perhaps the most percipient and original student of the subject in America, Professor Francis L. Loewenheim.[13] But the standard textbooks in European or American diplomatic history still betray no real advance on the views of the 1930s current thirty years ago. For the vast bulk of the historical profession in America, Sir Winston Churchill's view of British policy before 1939 has hardly required a moment's critical examination.

In these last thirty years in Britain, however, things have not remained so still. As a result a vast gap has opened between the views of the professional historians of today and the dogmas still voiced by the laymen interested in the period. Working on an immensely successful British journalistic venture of the late 1960s (recently reissued in the mid-1970s), the part-work *History of the Second World War*, its editor, Mr Barry Pitt, spoke of the flood of letters which poured into the editorial offices protesting at the evidence of rethinking shown by the contributors to the series.[14] All bore, in his words, that 'note of deep indignation and outrage' which is the reaction of honest men to the destruction of long-held and long-cherished beliefs. Any historian who writes or lectures for popular as well as academic audiences can match his experience.

Not that the historical profession presents a united front. British writing in the field of contemporary history has gone through a considerable evolution over the last thirty years. But it is still dominated by an obsession with the causes of the Second World War and of the role and co-responsibility of the British government in this to a degree unmatched by the historiography of any other major power.[15] And in this domination, the release under the Public Records Act of 1967 of the full British archives for the inter-war period has confirmed the increasing insularity of this obsession. Where Sir Lewis Namier and his contemporaries wrote in the late 1940s and early 1950s from a viewpoint too exclusively European and concerned with central Europe rather than the Mediterranean, the most recent works on Baldwin, Munich and Chamberlain have been concerned almost totally with the motives inspiring British policy rather than with the general causes, course, outcome and consequences of the crisis of 1938 for the history of Europe as a whole.[16] (And when one finds a work which does not at first sight conform to this model, the author turns out to be a transatlantic product of a British graduate school,[17] less subject to the political and generational imperatives of his British contemporaries.) It is a curious thought that A. J. P. Taylor's own work has followed the same narrowing (if so value-laden a word can be used) process over the last fifteen years since his *Origins of the Second World War* was followed by his volume in the Oxford History of England, *Britain 1914–1945* and his biography of Lord Beaverbrook, Canada's gift to British nationalism and Taylor's friend, part-time employer and sometime mentor. Mr Taylor's own forthright opposition to the idea of British accession to the European Economic Community is part and parcel of the same development.

It is no part of the purpose of this essay to write an intellectual biography of the dedicatee of this volume, a man the intensity and comprehensiveness of whose historical vision has so often been obscured by his critics' ability to find flaws in the individual brickwork out of which that vision is constructed. But no discussion of the historiography of appeasement over the last thirty years can neglect the links with the development of Britain's own internal political debate or the changes in Britain's external relations with Europe and with the world.

The original critics of British appeasement came from the generation of British historians that had come of age before the 1914–18 war. Some of them had served in the Political Intelligence division of the Foreign Office during the war. A number were members of the British delegation to the Paris Peace Conference and subsequently associated with the establishment of what was to become the Royal Institute of International Affairs. They shared the common assumption of their generation that Britain was a world power one of whose major and abiding concerns was the balance of power in Europe. In culture, education, knowledge of countries abroad and orientation they were Europeans. They had friends and colleagues in the universities of the Commonwealth and of the east coast of the United States. But their major preoccupation was inevitably Europe. Few were enamoured of Wilsonianism or of the territorial clauses of the Treaty of Versailles. Still fewer could have been described as Germanophiles. Their resistance to the policies of the British Government in the 1930s stemmed as much from a failure to reconcile themselves to the realities of British weakness and from injured national pride. There were those such as Sir Lewis Namier, whose Zionism[18] and whose Austro-Polish origins had added extra impetus to their hostility to Nazism. Many however, it should be noted, had been alienated from any great degree of sympathy with German nationalism by the necessity of defending British pre-war policy from the assaults of German and American historians upon the War Guilt clause of the Treaty of Versailles.

This generation, among whom one might mention Sir Charles Webster, G. P. Gooch, R. W. Seton-Watson, was followed, or rather augmented, in the inter-war years by a very different group of historians, men and women who tended to share their historical views of German nationalism since they had in many areas done their research in the mass of published British, French, German, Russian and Italian documentation covering the years 1870–1914. Three groups of pupils, those of Sir Lewis Namier, of H. V. Temperley, and of R. W. Seton-Watson, imbibed their basic approach to the question of the expansionist form taken by German nationalism in the 1890s and during the years of German victory in the 1914–18 war. In their more general attitude to international politics and mores they tended to share the generally radical progressive views which made them sympathetically disposed towards the European governments of the centre and the non-totalitarian left, at whose expense and over whose dead Hitler was to establish his New Order. And whether they came to scholarship through writing on current affairs, as did Sir John Wheeler-Bennett and the late Miss Elisabeth Wiskemann, or by appointment to academic posts, as did Sir Llewellyn Woodward, Mr Rohan Butler, Sir Alan Bullock, Professor Max Beloff and Professor Hugh Trevor-Roper, to name only a few, they were as unsympathetically disposed towards the idea of conciliating Nazi Germany as their predecessors, once the initial years of adjustment (that is, roughly 1933–5) were over.

In this group there were two distinguished exceptions to this rule, E. H. Carr and W. N. Medlicott. Carr was to desert the field after 1945 for his great, if controversial, work on the Bolshevist revolution and its subsequent history. But in the years of the 1930s his experience in the Foreign Office in the 1920s gave him a realistic assessment of the relationship of power and a detestation of the more unreal sides of both the imperial and the collectivist rhetoric in which much of the debate on British foreign policy was conducted, which made his advocacy of an adjustment to a world in which Fascism and Nazism might coexist with liberal democracy difficult to oppose at its own level.[19]

Professor W. N. Medlicott however, was in the long run to exert the greater influence. Although he was and is a conservative by instinct, his defence of British foreign policy in the inter-war years[20] stemmed less from any particular idealism or identification with the politics of the Conservative Governments of the inter-war years than from a degree of professionalism as a historian of diplomacy which made him concerned not to condemn but to understand and expound the real rationale of British foreign policy. His major work was done on Bismarck and the Bismarckian system.[21] And, unlike the vast bulk of his contemporaries, he did not abandon his devotion to historical method when he approached contemporary history. Contemporary history was for him simply the continuous unrolling of the past, to be studied from the past to the present not as a kind of back projection from the present. From the London historians of the early 1920s he had imbibed the attitudes of historical positivism. But if he can in any way be described as a positivist it is a positivism of method not of conclusions.

It is interesting to note that Professor Max Beloff also parted early company with the dominant school of writers on appeasement, possibly as a result of his move from the seventeenth century to the foreign policy of the Soviet Union in the inter-war years. His subsequent move into contemporary political studies however delayed the impact of his criticism and it is only with his work on the decline of British imperial power that he has returned to the field.[22]

It is often said that the war of 1939–45 was much more of a dividing line between generations now alive than any other experience. As a statement it is accurate as far as it goes. What it fails to recognise is that the years 1939–45 gave rise to two age groups, the second of which was as isolated from subsequent generations by its experience as it was from its predecessors. The first of these groups reached maturity just before or during the years of the war. Call-up took them into the forces on their eighteenth birthday. They served as soldiers, airmen, sailors or marines all over the globe. Those that survived, acquired on demobilisation the chance of a free university education, provided they had or could quickly acquire the necessary qualifications. A whole age group of those who had left grammar school at eighteen for clerkships or the like for reasons of economic necessity now had the chance of a university education. Amongst them were many whose interests turned to contemporary history, and a few who became academic historians interested in the 1930s. In their approach they were to be as heavily influenced by the Popular Front version of 'anti-appeasement' as their predecessors;[23] they were, however, to move in their views away from this approach as the experience of the 1950s developed. And they were also to be very much subject to the concentration upon British foreign policy as an extension of British developments through which their successors, as noted below, were to pass.

The second age group spent the years of the Second World War as children or adolescents; if military service claimed them as it very largely did, they served their countries in a Europe ruined and divided by the onset of the Cold War, or in one of a dozen trouble spots from Palestine to Hong Kong where fighting could erupt at any moment. They entered universities at the tails of or in the company of the younger veterans of the war and stayed during the years in which the first flush of post-war idealism in national and international politics was to give way to the hard realities of the 1949 devaluation, the Korean War, the division of Germany into two states and of Europe into two alliance systems balanced on a nuclear knife-edge. They were to see their elders blunder into the Suez disaster, to live with a map which in their childhood had been painted red but from which the red now seemed to ebb continuously away. Nor did the new members of the Commonwealth long retain the trappings of British political democracy inherited with their achievement of full independence.

As a whole the members of this age group spent their formative years incarcerated in Britain by war or currency shortage. Travel abroad was an adventure won only through military service or undergraduate initiative. Paradoxically the members of this age group were to prove themselves far more conscious of their links with Europe's cultural heritage than any other in contemporary Britain.[24] Politically they tended to produce more liberals and social democrats than conservatives.

As a generation this group produced few contemporary historians. When they entered employment the immediate post-war university expansion had come to an end, not to be resumed until the 1960s. Nor was research in the field particularly encouraged. The elder statesmen had spoken. The facts were clear. The documents were published, the official histories all written or being written. British historical journals were on the whole uninterested in articles written about the very recent past. Apart from the Nuremberg documentation, no actual archives were open (even the German archives were only opened to general research in 1960). Meanwhile the flood of officially published evidence continued unabated. To the German and British official publications and the few Soviet crumbs were added the Italian series edited by Professor Toscano. Professor W. V. Wallace of the New University of Ulster had a brief sight of the Czech archives.[25] But would-be diplomatic historians seeking for research degrees were directed rather to the British records of the turn of the century;[26] before the 1958 Public Record Act even a 50-Year Rule was an act of administrative grace by the individual keepers of departmental records. And systematic investigation of private papers for the closed period was only just beginning.

In the meantime the younger generations of Britain were going through three new sets of experiences. The first was the reopening of foreign travel both to the United States and to Europe. The second was the rapid decline of British power and expansion of British commitments embarked on by the Labour Government in 1947–50 and continued by its Conservative successors. The third was the debate on Britain's programme of developing its own hydrogen bomb and nuclear deterrent. Together it amounted to an experience of the gap between resources and commitments and between poverty and rhetoric. Curiously its effect on a considerable group of the young was to incline them against the development of resources and in favour of radical rhetoric. These were the years of C.N.D. and of the *New Left Review*. Its historical fruit was the appearance in 1962 of *The Appeasers*.[27]

The authors of *The Appeasers* were both members of C.N.D. and prominent in its Oxford activities as undergraduates.[28] Both came from solidly wealthy upper-middle-class backgrounds against which they were in revolt. In this, and not only in this, they resembled the young radicals of the 1930s; although for their generation which had grown up past the Soviet suppression of the Hungarian revolution of 1956 there could be no romantic refuge in Soviet Communism, bureaucratic, repressive and power-conscious as it was. Israeli kibbutzim, Indian village socialism, Polish and Jugoslav variants on the road to socialism, all had their moment. But the real romantic heroes of this generation were Fidel Castro and Che Guevara, especially after the abortive C.I.A.-backed invasion at the Bay of Pigs. Prior to this however, there was a curious cult of the 1930s, a nostalgia for the years of the Spanish Civil War,[29] the Jarrow hunger marches and so on which would have been obscene had it not been so innocent.

*The Appeasers* reflected this nostalgia very strongly. In theme it echoed the indictment of the Conservative Government of 1937–9 produced by the pamphleteers of the Left Book Club in the years 1938–43, especially the enormously successful books, *Guilty Men* and *Tory M.P.*[30] The failure to conclude an alliance with the Soviet Union in 1938 and 1939, the efforts to break a way into German autarchy via talks on industrial cartels, the 'offer' of a condominium for the exploitation of Central Africa contained in Herr Wohltat's talks of July 1939 with Sir Horace Wilson and Mr Robert Hudson, loomed very large in their pages as did the egregious buttering-up of the Nazis by the unhappy Sir Nevile Henderson, perhaps the most striking example of that *déformation professionelle* of diplomacy that puts the maintenance of friendly relations with the government to which he is accredited before all else in an ambassador's duties.

What was so striking about *The Appeasers* was its reception. Commercially it was an enormous success, widely translated and serialised in Europe and in the United States. Its reception by professional historians was much less happy. Where A. J. P. Taylor's book had achieved only condemnation as a heresy by the apostles of orthodoxy,[31] Messrs Gilbert and Gott were received with a sense of *déjà vu*. Mr Taylor's review of the work of his former pupils was particularly severe. Collectively, it was clear, professional historians were no longer content to accept what had been so widely accepted by the public of the 1940s.

Mr Gilbert was subsequently to modify his views considerably, until he finally emerged as the official biographer of Winston Churchill, succeeding Randolph Churchill on the latter's death. His later work made it clear that he was only one of a number of historians of his generation whose main interest in the 1930s had developed from a study of and a sympathy with radical cùrrents in British foreign policy. Their knowledge of European history and the European sources for the period was only a partially acquired gloss on their basic interest in and knowledge of British history. And where they took Mr Taylor as their mentor it was not his extraordinary and thorough grounding in the printed and archival sources for nineteenth- and twentieth-century European history[32] that they sought to emulate but his work on English radicalism. The seminal work for them was his *The Trouble Makers*.[33] And their driving-force was the discovery that the policy of appeasement came not from the political right in Britain (as it did in France, for example) but from the centre and the left, or as Mr Martin Gilbert put it, appeasement was not 'a silly or treacherous idea in the minds of stubborn and gullible men, but a noble idea, rooted in Christianity, courage and common-sense'.[34]

The examination of this group, to which we will return, has taken us a little past the 1950s when seemingly so little was being directly contributed to the study of the period, and when the only new entrants to the field were a scattering of those who came of age in the late 1940s, of whom only the author of this paper, Mr Esmonde Robertson,[35] Professor John Erickson[36] and Dr L. Kochan[37] achieved academic appointments in the 1950s.[38] Apart from Mr Taylor the main influences in this field came from a very different political direction, and one with which Mr Taylor himself had very little sympathy. Two of them stemmed from London where Professor W. N. Medlicott succeeded to the Stevenson Chair of International History at the London School of Economics in 1953. There his influence coincided with that exerted by the late Professor Reginald Bassett, lecturing on recent British politics to specialists in the study of British government. The L.S.E. already contained, albeit uneasily, Sir Karl Popper, whose *Open Society and its Enemies*[39] was perhaps the most important single philosophical influence on the generation of the 1940s.[40] It was also to acquire from Cambridge in 1953 the redoubtable figure of Michael Oakeshott, the most powerful political philosopher of the post-war years, who in his years at Cambridge had fostered a generation of political commentators, whose capture of the intellectual side of the Conservative movement was to act as the vehicle for publishing his neo-traditionalist approach to politics. His emphasis on the past as the master of the present was to continue at Cambridge long after his removal to London.

The influence of this quartet was as diffuse and indirect as it was pervasive. Its most immediate effect was to make conservatism intellectually respectable among the young at a time when whatever was happening to Britain's world position the standard of living and general level of welfare of the British people was rising enormously and recruitment to the governing élites in parliament, press, business and the universities was drawing from a much wider social circle than before. And all the time the flood of new evidence on the 1930s was pouring out and the perspectives of the 1930s and 1940s were changing.

In the process by which conservatism was to re-establish its respectability among contemporary historians Professor Bassett was to exert a considerable influence. In age and background he belonged to the 1930s, of lower class origin, a supporter of Ramsay Macdonald up to and beyond the latter's desertion by the rump of the parliamentary Labour party and the bulk of the Labour movement in 1931. Bassett had fought on the opposite side to the pamphleteers of the Left Book Club. He had watched the cementing of the alliance between Tory Right and radical Left with increasing anger. And he was to devote much of the remainder of his academic career to refighting the battles of the 1930s, using both contemporary evidence and what became available later to 'demythologise' the period of all that he felt to be myths and misrepresentations of the propagandists of the anti-appeasement alliance.

His first and most devastating shot was a direct challenge to Winston Churchill's damnatory dismissal of Stanley Baldwin in the index to *The Gathering Storm*, 'Baldwin, Stanley, confesses to putting party before country'.[41] This was followed by examinations of British policy in the Manchurian Crisis of 1931–2[42] and of the governmental crisis of 1931,[43] the main theme of which was the contrast between the later pronouncements of those participants who had established the radical orthodox interpretation with what they had said and done at the time.

Professor Medlicott's influence lay in a rather different direction. He was never a polemicist like Bassett. He dealt steadily and consistently as a reviewer with the continuing flood of volumes of documents and memoirs. But his main influence was exerted through the establishment of an undergraduate and graduate school of international history from which the concept of the subject was to spread by means of his former students through the British provincial universities. Only Oxford, where the study of the subject at a graduate level tended to concentrate at St Anthony's, and Cambridge, where undergraduate studies in history continued throughout the 1960s to end at 1914, remained largely outside this influence. In these universities the study of the 1930s continued to be somewhat compartmentalised into studies of British, French, German or Russian history and foreign policy, unreflective of the more ecumenical approach embodied in the concept of international history as studied at London; the concepts of European history and of international relations practised at Oxford made it perhaps less open to these strictures. But the one left its students shielded from the need to consider American, Middle Eastern or Far Eastern influences; the other was only available to specialists in the School of Social Studies.

During the 1950s also the strategists of the Conservative Party had put a great deal of effort into wooing the new educated youth produced by the 1944 Education Act. So it was from this background that there were to emerge new groups of historians, convinced by their instincts and their politics of the injustice done by the Tory critics of the Conservatives of the 1930s, concerned to look again at the record of the Chamberlain cabinet, and sympathetically disposed, from their observation of the difficulties faced by the Conservative cabinets of the 1950s, towards the evidence, amply produced in the official histories produced by the Cabinet Office, of the disparities between British strength and British commitments which underlay, or so it was assumed, the weaknesses and hesitations of British foreign policy towards the tripartite challenge to British interests produced by Germany, Italy and Japan.

The impact of these younger Conservative and Tory historians has still to be completely felt; since their work has been cut across by two developments, both the result of the efforts begun in 1963 by a group of senior historians, many of whom were connected with the Cabinet Office historical branch or the Foreign Office Research Department (responsible for the publication of the two sets of series, *Documents on German Foreign Policy, 1915–1945* and *Documents on British Foreign Policy, 1919–1939*), to obtain a revision of the 1958 Public Records Act so as to lower the limits of the closed period for public archives from fifty years to thirty. Their campaign was fired by the apparent ease with which ex-ministers could obtain access to the papers dealing with their period in office to produce what were widely believed to be partial, if not partisan, defences of their record while in office: their individual protests were so abruptly rejected by Mr Macmillan before his retirement from office in 1963 that they were driven to lobby the Cabinet Office collectively.[44] The subsequent debate within the government and Cabinet Office took place against a background of two general elections (1964 and 1966) and was dependent upon the agreement of a committee of Privy Councillors drawn from all three parties. The debate lasted for four years until the Public Records Act of 1967 lowered the closed period to thirty years, and began, with each New Year's Day, a rush of journalists and historians to skim the cream off each fresh release of papers. They were to be followed by a new group of professional cream-skimmers, 'instant historians', the urgency of whose publishers' dead-lines made any collation with other sources, let alone any possibility of serious digestion and rethinking of the *idées reçues*, virtually impossible. Some of these had been participants in the events they now re-examined, as, for example, the late Ian Colvin who as the *News Chronicle* correspondent expelled from Berlin at the end of March 1939 had brought back false information as to the imminence of a German attack on Poland which had helped the British cabinet to reach its hurried decision to guarantee Poland.[45] Some had already shown in their biographical studies of the past[46] that new evidence did little to change minds already set in their views. The majority, however, had no excuse other than the willingness of their publishers to issue and of the public to absorb works, the novelty of whose source materials did nothing to upset the received ideas of the past.[47]

From this, to a historian distasteful, aspect of the continuing public interest in the period, one can now return to the historical writing of the later 1960s. One effect of the knowledge that the papers of the 1920s and 1930s were soon to be released was to speed the production of biographies based on private archives even while it delayed the production of more general histories whose authors now saw their volumes, like much of British military aircraft manufactured in the 1930s, rendered obsolete at the moment of production. Thus the enormous re-evaluation of Baldwin based on the massive Baldwin archive which constitutes perhaps the major work so far of the young Conservatives of the Macmillan era, was only to appear in 1969.[48] The publication of Professor Dilks' considerable narrative study of British foreign policy has been repeatedly postponed, now until after the appearance of his forthcoming biography of Neville Chamberlain.[49] For his published views the reader has to turn to his inaugural,[50] to the careful and painstaking introduction to his edition of Sir Alexander Cadogan's diaries,[51] and to his often expressed admiration for Anthony Eden, Lord Avon, whom he served as a research assistant during the preparation of Lord Avon's memoirs of the 1930s.[52]

With Professor Dilks' work this review of the historiography of appeasement is brought full cycle to the influence of Professor Medlicott[53] and to the 'positivism of method' which he inculcated so much by his own example. His own work in the 1960s, proceeding from his Historical Association pamphlet,[54] his final volume in the Longman's History of England series,[55] his reissue, enormously revised, of his first volume of 1940,[56] his Creighton lecture of 1968,[57] and finally his guest lecture at the University of Oulu, Finland, in 1972[58] (which it is to be hoped he will sometime collect together with other occasional pieces), now constitutes a very considerable *oeuvre* in the whole body of writings on appeasement.

Medlicott's insistence on the military and economic factors in the thinking of the cabinets of the 1930s has been followed fairly thoroughly by the military historians of the inter-war generation and their successors. Professor Michael Howard's Ford lectures, delivered at Oxford in 1970,[59] and Captain Stephen Roskill's massive biography of Lord Hankey,[60] have been augmented by Peter Dennis's study of the conscription issue,[61] F. Coghlan's study of armaments,[62] Brian Bond's edition of the diaries of Sir Henry Pownall[63] (head of the War Office's plans division in the 1930s) and a number of Ph.D. theses still awaiting publication (probably in vain in these days of massively increasing costs of publication). Apart from Dr Coghlan's article already referred to, little work has been done on the economic side in English; though one important aspect of it has been examined by Dr C. A. Macdonald in his study of British illusions about the strength of the so-called German 'moderates'.[64] It has been left to the German historian, Bernd-Jürgen Wendt, to produce the first full-length study of economic appeasement,[65] one far too massive, unfortunately, for it to be economically feasible for an English translation to be produced.

Another aspect of the neo-Conservative case, the resistance of public opinion to rearmament and its support for the policy of appeasement, has also attracted attention. Apart from Mr Watkins' book, already noticed,[66] the three main full-length studies so far produced have come, characteristically, from non-English pens. Brigitte Granzow's study of British opinion in the period before Hitler's appointment as Chancellor[67] was the offshoot of a German university doctorate in the field of political science. Franklin Reid Gannon's well-documented study of the British press in the late 1930s[68] was the product of a London M.A. and an Oxford B.Litt. by an American who began as a fervent admirer of Robert Kennedy and is currently (1975) aiding ex-President Nixon in the preparation of his memoirs. Dr Lawrence Thompson's study of the parliamentary opposition to appeasement[69] is again the product of an Oxford research degree by an American now returned to the United States. A much vaster work is promised on the same subject by one of the Cambridge neo-Tories, Maurice Cowling.[70] Other published work by English historians has mainly come from historians of populist or radical views in the Taylorian tradition concerned to show that British public opinion was much less opposed to rearmament than supposed by Conservative politicians at the time and their apologists later,[71] or to illustrate Mr Taylor's contention that the swing—in his words 'an underground explosion of public opinion such as the historian cannot trace in precise terms'[72]—of public opinion against Germany in the winter of 1938–9 antedated or was not appreciated by official opinion at the time.[73] An exception to this rule, again a student of Professor Medlicott, is David Carlton, whose work *began* with an interest in radical politics and has developed, *inter alia*, towards the demythologisation of the 1930s, a notable instance of development in a direction exactly counter to that of many of his contemporaries.[74]

It would not be altogether fair when reviewing the work of the younger British historians in the 1930s not to mention that small group which has transferred its familiarity with the issues roused by the historical debate on British appeasement to the study of its French equivalent. Here the field has been less cluttered with ideas formed in the political debate in Britain, though not of the myths produced by this process. Of the generation to reach economic maturity in the 1940s even fewer turned towards contemporary French history than towards Europe, Britain or Germany. Dr Alastair Parker[75] was the only prominent figure at first, though he was to be joined later by Professor Douglas Johnson whose work in the 1950s focused on nineteenth-century France. The most distinguished work is possibly that of Professor Geoffrey Warner.[76] But one should add to this Dr Neville Waites,[77] Dr Anthony Adamthwaite,[78] Mr P. M. Bell[79] and yet another Canadian graduate of London, Professor Robert J. Young.[80] Of these Professor Warner and Mr Bell are from Oxbridge and of the generation of the 1950s. Dr Adamthwaite and Dr Waites like Professor Young are of the generation of the 1960s and hold first degrees from provincial universities where Mr Taylor's influence is probably at its weakest. Significantly Mr Bell's work at Oxford lay in recent British history.

It is at this moment perhaps that a few criticisms might be ventured of the way in which the current studies of the 'age of appeasement' are now moving. The first is that the essential ambiguities of the term 'appeasement' have rarely been properly appreciated.[81] In its usages in the political vocabulary of the 1930s it has usually been applied to mean the alleviation of international tension, or the relaxed state of international tranquillity it was supposed would follow such an alleviation. Lord Avon wrote in his memoirs that the term could have two meanings, 'to bring to peace, settle strife etc.' or to 'pacify by satisfying demands', and that his use of the word was limited to the first of the two meanings. Its embracement as a term of opprobrium began with Chamberlain's opponents on left and right and spread from them into the demonology of aroused American populist nationalism as early as 1939 after the reaction to the Munich settlement had set in on both sides of the Atlantic. The transition of the term from one of high persuasive value to one of opprobrium ('appeasement never pays') deserves a study in itself.

The second is that the polemical element still present in much historical discussion of the period needs to be recognised and accepted. It need not and should not lead historians to suppose that historical objectivity implies total moral indeterminacy. To write that the lesson of Munich is that there are no lessons is easy; but it comes perilously close to an abdication of the historian's responsibilities for the approach of the chronicler or the antiquarian. If the historian is engaged in the task of reinterpreting the past, to and in the light of the present in which he lives and works, he owes it to each to do the job properly.

A third point to be made is that such reinterpretation needs to preserve the flavour of the time, how it looked and felt to the participants. To dismiss the ideological divisions is as misleading as to ignore the important common ground to which the Scottish historian, Professor Marwick, has so perceptively called our attention.[82] The degree to which the participants felt that Britain either was or need not feel herself to be part of a European power system; the degree to which what most outraged them was behaviour such as we now take in our stride, hostile and abusive propaganda, unilateral action rather than international agreement, the arbitrary use of state power against political opponents or racial and cultural minorities, the total Humpty-Dumptyish misuse of a political vocabulary; these, to give only two examples, are factors of enormous importance in considering the debate over appeasement. Other factors which need to be examined are the intellectual content of the debate on foreign policy, a difficult task in view of the uncritical acceptance so many of the concepts employed in that debate still enjoy; naive economic theories of the origin of war in conflicts of trade and capital; the belief that all conflict is the result of a 'failure of communication' between the participants, that there is no such thing as national selfishness or unresolvable conflict; the continuing belief that if only Britain would make the right decisions the international system would rearrange itself in accordance with British desires.[83]

Then there are the questions of honour and fear. Rightly or wrongly these questions bulked much larger in the minds of the politically active in the period than comment today would allow. Fear of annihilation by aerial bombardment and the use of poison gas carrying bombers hit the electorate, especially in the South East, that part closest to the continent. Their fear was fed by the exaggerations of that section of the popular press which was campaigning for a larger air force, as by the newsreel pictures of the bombardment from the air of Shanghai and Barcelona. Military advisers and strategic planners feared a new 'bolt from the blue', an unheralded air strike on London which would leave a quarter of a million dead, cause panic flight from the cities, paralyse government and destroy law and order. The public feared extinction.

For others what was far worse was the purchase of release from this fear by the desertion of those who had relied upon British support to withstand the spread of Nazi hegemony. This was dishonour, such as to cause those who felt it sleepless nights and acute physical nausea and vomiting.[84] Their sense of dishonour was rendered the more unbearable by the knowledge of what Nazi hegemony implied, in allowing the entry of the Gestapo and the SS. into a democratic country, the terror, the arrests, the beatings, the tortures, the imprisonment in camps, the killings, the destruction of families, the expulsion of women and children, repeated over and over again. In the end it was perhaps this memory, more than anything else, that tarnished Chamberlain's name and made of 'Munich' a pejorative.

The increasing professionalism of the historians engaged in studying the period should not blind them to the notions of error, misjudgement, incompetence and the possible inefficiencies in the British machinery of government. To understand is an essential preliminary even to condemnation, but it should not be a substitute for judgement. The methods of government currently practised in Britain did not function very well. They made it easy both to spread responsibility until it altogether disappeared or to concentrate it in the hands of those very few who were not afraid to exercise it. The British cabinet moreover was prone to alternate between undignified attacks of panic and ludicrous outbursts of overconfidence. For long terms of government the British system was unequalled. In the short run, in an immediate crisis, it could on occasion function very badly. Its representatives abroad were moreover of as weak a range of quality as was the judgement of those who appointed them; and the internal security of the administration was disastrously compromised by social myopia.

Perhaps the largest field for regret is the continuing, if not increasing, parochialism of the historical debate. So many of the historians who engage on it seem to lack even the basic familiarity with the archives and historical literature of the countries with whom Britain had active political relations. German documents and memoirs are cited only from their, often inadequate, English translations. The question of foreign influences, not merely by clandestine subversion but by the extension into Britain of the intellectual and ideological debates which convulsed Europe, is hardly mentioned, although at certain levels of the foreign policy making process it could be of significant importance. Much more attention needs to be devoted to the overseas networks of social relationships, into America, South Africa, Australia and Canada on the one hand, into Europe on the other, in which the members of the foreign policy making élites were involved. There have been outstanding studies of these under frameworks, as in Christopher Thorne's study of the Manchurian Crisis[85] or Dr Peter Ludlow's investigations of the end of appeasement[86] and its connections with European Christian conservatism (though it is not altogether pointless to remark that he felt obliged to publish them outside Britain).

Mr Taylor has confessed himself increasingly disinterested in Europe, increasingly conscious of the uniqueness of the British democratic experience and of the steps that have been taken in Britain since 1914 towards a genuine democracy of equals, a levelling of social barriers, a placing of the wealth and culture of the ages in the reach of the many rather than their preservation as the jealously guarded culture of the few. His sympathies have always been populist and radical rather than élitist, and the ties between the countries of Europe have always been at the level of whatever were the current rating élites, whether aristocratic, *grand bourgeois*, or as today, meritocratic-managerial. For the younger historians of today however, who owe to Mr Taylor their freedom from received stereotypes and the example of one of the strongest and most creative historical visions in twentieth-century Britain, a vision to put alongside those of Froude or Tawney, it is the reach and grasp of the Taylor of the *Habsburg Monarchy, The Struggle for Mastery in Europe* and the *Origins of the Second World War* that should be most celebrated as a model and a challenge.

# Notes

1  D. C. Watt, 'Appeasement: the Rise of a Revisionist School?', *Political Quarterly* (1965).

2  As percipiently noted by my colleague, Esmonde M. Robertson, in the introduction to the collection of reprinted papers by various hands which he edited, *The Origins of the Second World War* (London, 1971).

3  Keith Robbins, *Munich 1938* (London, 1968).

4  Sir Anthony Eden, *Full Circle* (London, 1960).

5  Ernest R. May, '*Lessons' of the Past: the Use and Misuse of History in American Foreign Policy* (New York, 1973).

6  W. L. Langer and S. E. Gleason, *The End of Isolation* (New York, 1952).

7  Arthur H. Furnia, *The Diplomacy of Appeasement* (Georgetown, 1959).

8  Margaret George, *The Warped Vision: British Foreign Policy 1933–1939* (Pittsburgh, 1965).

9  William Rock, *Appeasement on Trial: British Foreign Policy and its Critics* (London, 1960).

10  Arnold Ofner, *American Appeasement: United States Foreign Policy and Germany 1933–1938* (Cambridge, Mass., 1969).

11  John L. Snell, *The Outbreak of the Second World War: Design or Blunder?* (Boston, 1962).

12  Donald H. Lammers, *Explaining Munich: the Search for a Motive in British Policy* (Stanford, 1966); see also his 'Britain, Russia and the Revival of Entente Diplomacy, 1934', *Journal of British Studies*, 6 (1967); 'Fascism, Communism and the Foreign Office, 1937–1939', *Journal of Contemporary History*, 6 (1971).

13  Francis L. Loewenheim, *Peace or Appeasement? Hitler, Chamberlain and the Munich Crisis* (Boston, 1965). See also his masterly exercise in investigative historiography, 'An Illusion that Changed History: New Light on the History and Historiography of American Peace Moves before Munich', in Daniel R. Beaver (ed.), *Some Pathways in Twentieth Century History* (Detroit, 1969).

14  Barry Pitt, 'The War: an Overview', *History of the Second World War*, Vol. VI, p. 2676.

15  The only true parallel is in the mushroom growth of the radical American left revisionist school of historiography of the origins of the Cold War, a movement of much more obvious and overt political inspiration.

16  See for example Robbins, *Munich*; Keith Middlemas, *Diplomacy of Illusion: the British Government and Germany, 1927–1939* (London, 1972).

17  As for example, Sidney Aster, 'Ivan Maisky and Parliamentary Anti-appeasement 1938–1939', in A. J. P. Taylor (ed.), *Lloyd George: Twelve Essays* (London, 1971); *1939: The Making of the Second World War* (London, 1974). See also the forthcoming books of Professor

Lawrence Pratt, *East of Malta, West of Suez* (Cambridge, 1975) and T. R. Emmerson, *The Reoccupation of the Rhineland* (London and Iowa, 1976). Dr Aster and Professor Pratt are Canadians. Professor Emmerson is American. All are graduates of the University of London.

18  It should be noted that sympathy with Zionism was not uncommon among non-Jewish British establishment figures of conservative political views in the inter-war years. See Norman Rose, *The Gentile Zionists* (London, 1973); 'The Seventh Dominion', *Historical Journal*, xiv (1971).

19  See, for example, his *International Relations since the Peace Treaties* (London, 1938); *Britain: a Study of Foreign Policy from the Versailles Treaty to the Outbreak of War* (London, 1939); *Ambassadors at Large* (London, 1940); *Conditions of Peace* (London, 1942); *The Twenty Years Crisis, 1919–1939* (London, 1942).

20  *British Foreign Policy since Versailles* (London, 1940).

21  *The Congress of Berlin and After: a Diplomatic History of the Near Eastern Settlement of 1878–80* (London, 1938); *Bismarck, Gladstone and the Concert of Europe* (London, 1956).

22  See his 'Professor Namier and the Prelude to War', *Fortnightly* (Apr 1950); 'Historians in a Revolutionary Age', *Foreign Affairs*, 29 (1957); see also *The Foreign Policy of Soviet Russia*, 2 vols (London, 1947, 1949); *Imperial Sunset*, 2 vols, (London, 1969).

23  Typical of this group are Professor F. S. Northedge (*The Troubled Giant*, London, 1966); the late Mr Frank Spencer, a pupil of Sir Lewis Namier's (*A History of the World in the Twentieth Century, Part II, 1918–1945*, London, 1967); and K: G. Watkins (*Britain Divided: the Effect of the Spanish Civil War on British Political Opinion*, London, 1963). Dr R. A. C. Parker (footnote 75 below) also shared this viewpoint in his earliest work.

24  This age group is particularly prominent among Labour M.P.s supporting British association with Germany and the European Economic Community. See D. C. Watt, 'die Labour Partei und Deutschland', *Europa-Archiv*, 19 (1964) 855–60.

25  See for example his 'New Documents on the History of Munich', *International Affairs* (1959); also 'The Foreign Policy of President Benes in the Approach to Munich', *Slavonic and East European Review*, xxxix (1960); 'The Making of the May Crisis of 1938', ibid., xli (1963).

26  As for example Professor J. A. G. Grenville (*Lord Salisbury and Foreign Policy*, London, 1964) and Professor C. J. Bartlett (*Great Britain and Sea Power 1815–1953*, London, 1963) both of whom were subsequently to work in the contemporary field, Professor Grenville in producing documentary films on Munich and the 1938–40 period, Professor Bartlett with his book on British defence policy, 1945–70 (*The Long Retreat*, London, 1971).

27  Martin Gilbert and Richard Gott, *The Appeasers* (London, 1962).

28  Mr Gott was to stand against the official Labour candidate in the Hull by-election of 1966 on a platform confined to nuclear disarmament and to lose his deposit.

29  Professor Hugh Thomas's *The Spanish Civil War* (London, 1961), though the product of the 1940s generation, is very much a prototype of this kind of interest.

30  Simon Haxey, *Tory M.P.* (London, 1939); Frank Owen *et al.*, *Guilty Men* (London, 1940); 'Cassius' (alias Michael Foot), *The Trial of Mussolini* (London, 1943).

31  For a useful summary see C. Robert Cole, 'Critics of the Taylor View of History', in Robertson (ed.), *Origins of the Second World War*.

32  As displayed, for example, in *The Struggle for Mastery in Europe, 1848–1918* (Oxford, 1954).

33  *The Trouble Makers. Dissent over Foreign Policy, 1792–1939* (London, 1957).

34  Martin Gilbert, *The Roots of Appeasement* (London, 1966) p. xi.

35  *Hitler's Pre-War Policy and Military Plans* (London, 1963).

36  *The Soviet High Command, 1918–1941* (London, 1962).

37  *The Struggle for Germany* (Edinburgh, 1963).

38  Professor Hugh Thomas and Mr Christopher Thorne, two of the most distinguished historians of this generation now holding academic posts, only gravitated to the universities during the expansion of the 1960s.

39  London, 1945.

40  See Bryan Edgar Magee, *Popper* (London, 1973).

41  'Telling the Truth to the People: the Myth of "Baldwin's Confession"', *Cambridge Journal*, II (1948). It should be noticed that the *Cambridge Journal* was edited by Michael Oakeshott.

42  *Democracy and Foreign Policy* (London, 1952).

43  *1931 Political Crisis* (London, 1958).

44  For an account of these controversies and representations see my 'Foreign Affairs, the Public Interest and the Right to Know', *Political Quarterly* (1963); 'Contemporary History in Britain, Problems and Perspectives', *Journal of the Society of Archivists* (1969).

45  *Vansittart in Office* (London, 1965); *The Chamberlain Cabinet* (London, 1971).

46  As, for example, G. M. Young, *Stanley Baldwin* (London, 1952); Lord Birkenhead, *Halifax* (London, 1965).

47  By far the most successful, and most monstrous, case of such instant history had taken place over the German archives with the American William Shirer's *Rise and Fall of the Third Reich* (New York, 1963). His British imitators include Leonard Mosley, *On Borrowed Time* (London, 1969); Roger Parkinson, *Peace for Our Time. Munich to Dunkirk, the Inside Story* (London, 1971); George Scott, *The Rise and Fall of the League of Nations* (London, 1974); and Frank Hardy, *The Abyssinian Crisis* (London, 1974).

48  R. K. Middlemas and A. J. L. Barnes, *Baldwin* (London, 1969).

49  Written in partnership with Mr A. J. Beattie.

50  D. N. Dilks, 'Appeasement Revisited', *The University of Leeds Review*, 15 (1972).

51  D. N. Dilks (ed.), *The Diaries of Sir Alexander Cadogan, 1938–1945* (London, 1971).

52  *Facing the Dictators* (London, 1962).

53  Generously acknowledged in Professor Dilks' inaugural.

54  *The Coming of War in 1939* (1963).

55  *Contemporary England, 1914–1964* (London, 1967).

56  *British Foreign Policy since Versailles, 1919–1963* (London, 1968).

57  *Britain and Germany: the Search for Agreement 1930–1937* (London, 1969).

58  *Appeasers and Warmongers*, collected papers of the guest lecturers in the Department of History, University of Oulu, Finland, NR 6 (Oulu, 1972).

59  *The Continental Commitment: the Dilemma of British Foreign Policy in the Era of the Two World Wars* (London, 1972).

60  *Hankey, Man of Secrets*, 3 vols (London, 1970, 1972, 1974).

61  *Decision by Default: Peacetime Conscription and British Defence 1919–1939* (London, 1972).

62  'Armaments, Economic Policy and Appeasement', *History*, 57 (1972).

63  B. Bond (ed.), *Chief of Staff: the Diaries of Lieutenant General Sir Henry Pownall*, Vol. I *1933–1940* (London, 1972).

64  'Economic Appeasement and the German "Moderates"', 1937–1939: an Introductory Essay', *Past and Present*, 56 (Aug 1972). Professor Medlicott's emphasis on economic factors has borne more fruit on the German side in A. Milward, *The German War Economy* (London, 1965) and in the work of Mr T. W. Mason. See his 'Some Origins of the Second World War', *Past and Present* (Dec 1964) reprinted in Robertson (ed.), *Origins of the Second World War*.

65  *Economic Appeasement. Handel und Finanz in der britischen Deutschland-Politik 1933–1939* (Düsseldorf, 1971).

66  See note 22 above.

67  *A Mirror of Nazism: British Opinion and the Emergence of Nazism, 1929–1933* (London, 1964).

68  *The British Press and Nazi Germany, 1936–1939* (Oxford, 1971).

69  *The Anti-Appeasers* (Oxford, 1972).

70  *The Impact of Hitler: British Politics and British Policy, 1933–1940* (Cambridge, 1975).

71  Richard Heller, 'East Fulham Revisited', *Journal of Contemporary History*, 6 (1971).

72  Cited in Robertson (ed.), *Origins of the Second World War*, p. 101.

73  Roger Eatwell, 'Munich, Public Opinion and Popular Front', *Journal of Contemporary History*, 6 (1971).

74  *Macdonald versus Henderson* (London and New York, 1970); 'Eden, Blum and the Origins of non-Intervention', *Journal of Contemporary History*, 6 (1971); 'The Dominions and British Policy in the Abyssinian Crisis', *Journal of Imperial and Commonwealth History*, 1 (1972–3).

75  R. A. C. Parker, 'The First Capitulation: France and the Rhineland Crisis', *World Politics* (1955–6); 'Great Britain, France and the Ethiopian Crisis, 1935–1936', *English Historical Review*, LXXXIX (1974). Another Oxford contributor on the French side was W. F. Knapp, 'The Rhineland Crisis of March 1936', *St. Antony's Papers No. 5. The Decline of the Third Republic.*

76  *Pierre Laval and the Eclipse of France* (London, 1968); 'La Politique d'Italie à l'égard de la Grèce et de la Yougoslavie', *La Guerre en Méditerranée 1939–1945, Actes du Colloque International tenu à Paris, Avril 1969* (Paris, 1971). Professor Warner has now moved entirely into the field of post-Second World War history. See for example his two important review articles, 'Truman Doctrine and Marshall Plan', *International Affairs*, 50 (1974); 'The Division of Germany, 1946–1948', ibid., 51 (1975).

77  Waites (ed.), *Troubled Neighbours. Franco-British Relations in the Twentieth Century* (London, 1971).

78  'Bonnet, Daladier and French Appeasement, April–September 1938', *International Relations*, III (1967); 'Reactions to the Munich Crisis', Waites (ed.), *Troubled Neighbours.*

79  'The Breakdown of the Alliance in 1940', Waites (ed.), *Troubled Neighbours; A Certain Eventuality* (Farnborough, 1974).

80  'French Policy and the Munich Crisis of 1938', Canadian Historical Association, *Historical Papers 1970*; 'Preparations for Defeat: French War Doctrine in the Inter-War Period', *Journal of European Studies*, 2 (1972); 'The Aftermath of Munich: the Course of French Diplomacy, October 1938 to March 1939', *French Historical Studies*, VIII (1973).

81  A point made with some force by Professor Medlicott in his Finnish lecture (see note 57 above).

82  'Middle Opinion in the Thirties', *English Historical Review* (1964); *Britain in the Century of Total War: War, Peace and Social Change, 1900–1967* (London, 1968) pp. 241–8.

83  A belief which is now more frequently heard in and about the United States.

84  See the graphic account of Mrs Dugdale's sufferings in N. Nicolson (ed.), *Harold Nicolson, Diaries and Letters, 1936–1939* (London, 1969) entry of 22 September 1938; Norman Rose (ed.), *Baffy. The Diaries of Mrs. Blanche Dugdale, 1936–1947* (London, 1973) entries of 20 September–10 October 1938. Mrs Dugdale was the daughter, and biographer, of Arthur Balfour, Conservative Premier, Foreign Secretary and elder statesman, and very much a member of the political élite, a close friend of several Cabinet ministers of the 1930s.

85  Christopher Thorne, *The Limits of Foreign Policy* (London, 1973). Mr Thorne is also the author of a short but invaluable study of the events of 1937–9, *The Approach of War, 1938–1939* (London, 1967).

86  P. W. Ludlow, 'Scandinavia between the Great Powers', *Historisk Tidscrift* (1974); 'Papst Pius XII, die Britische Regierung und die deutsche Opposition im Winter 1939/40', *Vierteljahresheft für Zeitgeschichte* (1974).

# 7 Japan and the Outbreak of War in 1941

## IAN NISH

Every schoolboy knows that the origins of wars are 'easy meat'. It is, I understand, an international phenomenon that candidates for examinations in modern European history cannot resist 'having a go' at questions dealing with the causes of the wars of 1914 and 1939, which have the merit, so one is told, of being easy to memorise and easy to reproduce in a schematic form at the moment of trial. Every historian knows that the study of the origins of wars presents special difficulties over evidence, special controversies and special sensitivities. But, as he casts his eye over a sheaf of scripts, muttering 'not another on Sarajevo', he realises that the tide of 'historical writing' is flowing against him.

The war on which Japan embarked on 7 December 1941 must surely rate as one of the most complex of all the wars of history. Most wars are many-sided; and Japan's war was no exception. Japanese at the time generally described it as the 'Greater East Asia war' (Dai To-A senso); but this title, which had distinct propaganda overtones, has subsequently fallen into disuse and been replaced by the now universal description of 'Pacific war' (Taiheiyo senso). This essay endeavours to unravel the various threads of this many-sided and multi-coloured war of 1941 from the Japanese point of view.

The rescript issued by the Japanese emperor on his country's entry into the war does not assist an enquiry into its terminology. The rescript which contains a statement of Japan's motives, remarkably frank by the standards of such documents, does not employ the terms 'Pacific war' or 'Greater East Asia war'. It does, however, insist that Japan's prime war aim was 'to insure the stability of East Asia and to contribute to world peace'. By dwelling on the 'stability of East Asia', Japan was reiterating her long-standing complaint about the unstable situation in China and her own claim that Japan was the only stable force in East Asia. By extension, this concern for stability was enlarged in 1941 into the Greater East Asia zone by her campaigns in the colonial territories in South-East Asia. It was primarily to China and South-East Asia that the Japanese applied their phrase 'Greater East Asia war'. By contrast, the term 'Pacific war' seems in origin to have been an American one and is traceable to the creation of the Pacific War Council in Washington on 30 March 1942. It aptly describes the naval warfare between the Pacific fleets of Japan and the United States. It can be applied to the campaigns of island conquest in the Pacific area, starting with Japan's capture of the Philippines and the south Pacific islands and merging with the American island-hopping campaign of retrieval. It would be unreal to present these campaigns as unrelated wars. But they do have distinct characteristics: the Greater East Asia war being more economic and ideological, while the Pacific war was more strategic in conception. It is appropriate to consider these characteristics separately to start with.

*The China War*
The rescript says of the China imbroglio of 1941:

> More than four years have passed since China ... compelled Our Empire to take up arms. Although there has been re-established the National Government of China with which Japan has effected neighbourly intercourse and cooperation, the regime which has survived at Chungking, relying upon American and British protection, still continues its fratricidal opposition.'

The complicated China war was a disturbing backcloth to Japanese life in the thirties. Many Japanese scholars consider that Japan was really involved in a Fifteen Years' war with China which started with the Mukden affair of 18 September 1931 and did not end until 1945. This is true in the broad sense that Japan with her conscript armies was mobilised for war from the Manchurian affair (Manshu jihen) onwards; and it goes far to explain why Japan's Kwantung army was not content with its acquisitions in southern Manchuria and began making inroads into north China. But it is also untrue in an important sense: whereas Japan held special rights in Manchuria prior to September 1931 which gave her some justification for interference in defence of her own interests, she had no such basis for her actions in China proper. There was, therefore, a qualitative difference between what happened in 1931 and what took place in north China in the middle thirties through the political agencies and special relationships which she created.

This entered a new phase with the small incident at Marco Polo bridge (Lukouchiao) in the neighbourhood of Peking in July 1937. In Japanese terminology this was the North China incident (Hoku-Shin jihen). When, however, fighting commenced also in central China at Shanghai, it began to be described as 'the China incident' (Shina jihen), as indeed it was known to the Japanese during the long period of undeclared war. The central China campaign was enlarged when the capital of Nanking was taken in December. Until the spring of 1938 it was still possible to think in terms of a limited war; but thereafter, with the taking of Suchow (May) and Hankow (September), it could not be other than an extended war for the Japanese. The Kuomintang Government under Marshal Chiang Kai-shek retired to the hinterland to a new capital at Chungking from which it presided—at some distance, to be sure—over a united front of resistance to the Japanese. Such was the position of stalemate which endured until 1945. It developed into a war of attrition, an elaborate guerrilla war which baffled the Japanese military commanders.

What gives rather a strange quality to the China incident is that the Japanese army was divided in its opinion over it. It appears that within the War Ministry, the military affairs section was anti-expansionist and the administration section expansionist, while in the general staff, the anti-expansionists dominated the war guidance section and the expansionists the operations section.[1] Gone were the days when the Manchurian campaign had been steered by the Kwantung army. It still dominated in north, but not in central, China. It would continue to have a voice in affairs through General Tojo Hideki. But the anti-expansionists also had an influential voice during the China incident in General Ishiwara Kanji, one of the army heroes of the Manchurian campaign. Ishiwara now took the view that the real threat to Japan came from Soviet Russia and that Japanese troops should not become over-extended in China in such a way as to leave Manchuria under-defended. That these fears were well founded was soon demonstrated in the serious Russo-Japanese clashes which took place at Changkufeng in the Soviet-Manchurian border in July 1938 and culminated in the Japanese defeat at Nomonhan on the Mongolian border in August of the following year. It was not conceivable after this reverse that many troops could be spared from the north for further advances in China. Until Japan signed the neutrality pact with the Soviet Union in April 1941, Japan conducted a holding operation in the north. It is readily understandable that the stalemate in China, combined with the humiliation of the Kwantung army in Manchuria, should give rise to such frustration in the Japanese army.

The 'China war' was full of ambiguities. One of these ambiguities was the consequence of limited resources. Thus, Japan occupied the city of Canton (October 1938) where her interests and population had never been large, when the exigencies of her campaigns made this desirable. But her troop strength was not large enough to permit her to occupy the surrounding territory but only to 'control' the general area from well-chosen bases such as Hainan Island which she occupied in February 1939. In this way, Japan avoided the headache of 'occupying' a hostile south-east China. Indeed, some describe the Canton area as having been by-passed till 1941.

Another ambiguity of the China war was that the Japanese army was often involved in a gossamer-like web of peace making. Through its various political agencies, it encouraged the setting up of regional autonomous governments, the creation of a new National Government under Wang Ching-wei at Nanking in March 1940 (duly recognised in November) and even the making of overtures to Chiang Kai-shek. While Japan had some success with these devices, she failed in her supreme effort to get Chiang to accept her peace feelers and thus failed to relieve the pressure from her sorely strained armies.

With the failure of her China diplomacy, Japan faced the major problem of winning the loyalty of 'occupied China' by other means. She attempted to find a solution by convincing the Chinese of the advantages of her New Order in East Asia. Within Japan this had its manifestation in calling for a return to the *kokutai* (national polity) which had been lost through undue contact with Western culture. In the international sphere, the New Order was taken to mean that Japan had in the past forgotten her Asian roots in her zeal to imitate the West, and now undertook to jettison the West which had become her implacable rival and cultivate her friends in East Asia. Thus, a new restored Japan would lead the down-trodden peoples of the under-developed world away from their oppression at the hands of the imperialist powers and the mounting menace of Communism, especially in China. This amounted to a call for a sort of pan-Asianism, which like pan-Slavism of yore was open to the accusation that, however much it professed to offer protection to underdeveloped peoples, it was fundamentally imperialist and expansionist. It was doubtful how responsive the Chinese would be to this propaganda message as it was gradually spelled out.

Her first important declaration on the New Order in East Asia was formulated on 3 November 1938 and it was implicit in the statement on China policy issued later that month. The thinking underlying it was laid down, not by the Foreign Ministry but by the Koain (East Asia board) which first met in December. Premier Konoe, in announcing the formation of his second cabinet in July 1940, reiterated these sentiments in a broadcast:

> we must ourselves take the lead in bringing about world change and must resolve to build a new order in the world by our own strength. In the economic field, we must speedily throw off dependence on foreign countries . . . . With this in mind it is necessary increasingly to bind ourselves economically to Manchukuo and China and to proceed to South-East Asia.

Quite apart from the vagueness of the Japanese language, there was a calculated ambiguity here over the scope of the doctrine. Then in the policy statement of 1 August, it was stated that Japan should strive for world peace, based on the great spirit of *Hakko ichiu*—all points of the compass under one roof—and that she should aim for a New Order in Greater East Asia, with Japan as the cornerstone and a firm alliance (ketsugo) between China, Manchukuo and Japan as the foundation.

The cabinet later elaborated this by setting as its object the establishment of a Greater East Asia Co-prosperity Sphere based initially on Japan, China and Manchukuo and depending on the great spirit of the Imperial Way. Foreign Minister Matsuoka went on to tell reporters that the sphere must naturally take in French Indochina and the Netherlands East Indies. This was the first time that the phrase had been explained in this extended way. It was finally adopted as a national objective in November 1940.

Like much theology, these doctrines encountered scepticism from listeners in the pew. That much of them was high-flown theory was confirmed by Japan's actions in China. Among the most glaring examples were the Nanking atrocities which occurred in the last weeks of 1937 and allegedly resulted in the killing of over 100,000 Chinese males and the rape of some 5000 females. After such episodes it was patently obvious to people throughout the world that the Japanese were fighting in China a colonial type of war of conquest and that the much-heralded New Order and Co-prosperity Sphere were highly suspect. They cut little ice then or later and had small attraction except for those who were looking for a nationalist solution under the Japanese umbrella.

It was only in Japan that these doctrines had some credibility. The military and chauvinistic attitudes generated by the education system had bred a generation receptive to this kind of approach. Sir George Sansom, who had resided in Japan for twenty-five years, remarked in 1939: 'All Japanese want a 'new order' in Asia . . . . The difference between the extremists and the moderates is not one of destination, but of the road by which that destination is to be reached and the speed at which it is to be travelled.'[2] There were moderates: these doctrines were not universally accepted in agencies of government like the Foreign Ministry. It is perhaps for this reason that the terminology of the New Order and the Co-prosperity Sphere was not included in the rescript on the declaration of war.

The China war dragged on and formed a depressing backcurtain to Japan's other actions. It was always a drain on Japan's manpower and resources. Although Japan tried desperately to finish the China Incident, her efforts were always abortive.

## Greater East Asia War

In 1941—or some might say 1940—the East Asian war was extended to South-East Asia. The imperial rescript of 1941 throws some light on this transformation from the Japanese angle:

Eager for the realization of their inordinate ambition to dominate the Orient, both America and Britain, giving support to the Chungking regime, have aggravated the disturbances in East Asia. Moreover these two Powers, inducing other countries to follow suit, increased their military preparations on all sides of Our Empire to challenge us. They have obstructed by every means our peaceful commerce and finally resorted to a direct severance of economic relations.

The United States and Britain were by this date linked together as responsible for the 'encirclement' and economic harassment from which Japan was increasingly suffering. To Japan it appeared that the colonial government of the Netherlands East Indies, acting on its own after the capitulation of Holland in May 1940, had been persuaded by the United States to temporise over the negotiations over oil. First, Kobayashi in September 1940 and later Yoshizawa in January 1941 had tried to work out regular supplies but found themselves up against stone-walling tactics. On these counts, the rescript could claim that Japan had been provoked.

The touchstone for Japan's new actions to the south was the war in Europe. By June 1940 hostilities had ended in France. France allowed a Japanese military mission into northern Indochina. As Japan joined the axis in September of that year, she was under increasing pressure from Germany to harry Britain around Singapore. Quite apart from her obligations under her alliance, Japan was aware of certain tasty morsels which naturally tempted her in the south. She invaded north Indochina in September, securing from the French assurances that the border to China would be closed, taking over airports in Tongking, and making inroads to the south similar to those she had made in China.

It was not easy in 1940 for the rulers of South-East Asian countries to understand whether they lay in the path of Japanese expansion, because of the vagueness of Japan's pronouncements and the imprecise nature of the Japanese language. They had to assume they were to come within the New Order. Most difficult of the terms used in the pronouncements was 'Nanyo' (literally 'southern ocean') which applies to the colonial territories of South-East Asia, but not to Australia and New Zealand. In June 1940, Foreign Minister Arita in his policy statement had laid down that

While Japan is proceeding with her New Order in east Asia, she is devoting much thought to developments in the European war and the influence it will have on various territories in east Asia, including the 'Nanyo'. The fate of these territories is of the greatest importance for Japan, considering her mission in east Asia and responsibilities as a power for stability there. The opportunity was created by Germany in Europe.[3]

After the fall of France and the overrunning of the Netherlands, Japan became more and more interested in the 'fate' of these European colonial territories. But her interest was in the main economic until the spring of 1941 when supplies deteriorated and the 'southern thrust' took shape. It was then that Japan defined at the various liaison conferences the likely spheres of operations of her armies and laid down that the areas to be seized by the (Japanese) southern army were the Philippines, British Malaya, Java, Sumatra, Borneo and Timor.[4] This was, of course, a grave extension of the Co-prosperity Sphere which brought Japan's attitude to South-East Asia very much into line with that she had earlier adopted towards China and Manchuria.

One factor which impelled Japan to act towards the south was the centrality of the China issue for her. Just as Napoleon had his Spanish ulcer so Japan had a China ulcer. In both cases, it led the way to more ambitious courses. In the case of Japan, it prodded her to make inroads into South-East Asia. It is, of course, a misnomer to write of South-East Asia at this time since the area had no cohesion and embraced widely differing colonial societies like French Indochina, British Malaya and the Netherlands East Indies. It is not inconceivable that Japan might have made inroads into South-East Asia without her Spanish ulcer. But the continuing resistance of Chiang Kai-shek in his retreat in Chungking was a matter of surprise and frustration. Not unnaturally, Japan's incapacity to handle the situation was blamed on the supplies which Chiang was receiving along routes controlled by European powers, the Burma Road, the Hanoi-Yunnan route, the air route from Indochina to name but a few. One by one she secured the closure of these routes, the Burma road only temporarily. Although China was central to Japan's thinking down to December 1941, I do not believe that the China war automatically led on to the conquest of South-East Asia. The China war was a thing of fits and starts; and it would not be accurate to present a picture of Japanese expansion as a carpet being rolled out from central China through south China and further into Indochina.

Operations against South-East Asia could not have been begun until the Japanese made the decision to pull their forces out of Manchuria. After the Neutrality Pact with the Soviet Union (April) and the German attack on the Soviet Union (June), there was evidence of troop movements to Taiwan. Even then there were many military and political conferences before Japan came down in favour of the southern option in July. This only became certain when the maverick Foreign Minister, Matsuoka Yosuke, who had favoured supporting Germany by attacking the Soviet Union in the rear, was forced into retirement in July 1941. It was then that Japan invaded southern Indochina.

In pursuing the southern option, the Japanese had hoped that they could confine the opposition to Britain, who stood alone among the former colonial rulers, and could avoid a confrontation with the United States. She did not expect American involvement until late in 1941, but the navy felt no campaign in South-East Asia could be mounted until Japan had acquired control of the seas. But these desiderata could not be so easily attained.

Not long after war was declared on 7 December, the Japanese Government announced that: 'Japan's present war against the United States and the British Empire, including the China incident, will henceforth be called the Greater East Asia war. The reason for adopting the name is that the present war is aimed at establishing the New Order in the region of Greater East Asia.'[5]

By this Japan was endeavouring to show that she was carrying on a colonial crusade and that her actions were designed to enter the old colonial regimes. She, of course, condemned the colonial rule of European countries less from altruistic motives than from the hardship caused to Japan from their restrictive trade policies.

Japan applied the Greater East Asian doctrines to South-East Asia in the hope of securing the loyalty, or at least the tacit acceptance, of the colonial peoples. In this the motive was basically the same as in China: to create an atmosphere of trust. This was an uphill task because Japan was recognised in the area as a colonial power of half a century's standing. Her performance as a colonial ruler was, indeed, relatively far-reaching compared to other colonial powers, Japan being geographically closer to her overseas territories. In the 1930s large numbers of her working men sought to emigrate and intended to stay overseas until their dying days. Thus, it was difficult for Japan to cope with the task of employing local people in her colonies. Europeans, by contrast, tended to stay in their colonies for a comparatively short part of their working lives and not to compete for jobs with local labour.

At the same time the extension of the Co-prosperity Sphere to South-East Asia was founded on economic necessity. The extent of this is made clear in the following contemporary commentary: 'With the outbreak of the Greater East Asia War, the natural resources in the South Sea regions have been brought under Japanese control and the responsibility of developing them with our own technical skill to meet the demands of the one billion of East Asiatic races has been vastly increased.' There can be little doubt that Japan took seriously the need to harvest the resources of this area of conquest. Witness the case of oil:

The petroleum produced in Japan Proper is limited to a small per cent of the national demand. This condition had always been an everlasting source of worry to the thinking class of the Japanese and the production of artificial liquid fuel, therefore, had been an important national problem in this country. But since Japan had acquired the vast petroleum resources in Sumatra, Borneo, etc, particularly now the great refineries operated by the Anglo-American interests at Palembang have been restored to their former condition and are operated by certain Japanese concerns, the only remaining problem is how to get the fuel to Japan in great quantity.[6]

As the war lengthened, it became more difficult to harness the riches of these raw materials for her home needs. But that does not alter her desperation for them at the outset of the war.

Thus, the war in South-East Asia was ambiguous. It used the rhetoric—and it used it skilfully and in copious amounts—of anti-imperialism, of Japan's New Order and of her Co-prosperity Sphere. But behind these words Japan was interested in territorial acquisition: it was a war of colonial succession. In economic terms the acquisition of raw materials like tin, rubber, petrol and quinine in which South-East Asia was rich was a matter of great urgency.

## Pearl Harbor and the Pacific War

The attack on Pearl Harbor inaugurated the naval war between Japan and the United States, the so-called Pacific war. It is wrong to describe this as inevitable or to date its coming too early. Of course things had gone wrong between Japan and the United States since 1905 and distrust had been the characteristic of their relationship. Japan's navalists had recognised the American fleet as their major rival in the Pacific from 1921 onwards, if not earlier. But the United States steered clear of taking an active role in the China struggle until late in the 1930s and did not show her hand over South-East Asian problems until long after the fall of France. True, she had abandoned the American–Japanese commercial treaty in 1939 and had imposed an embargo on the export of strategic materials to Japan in July 1940. But these were signs of displeasure rather than sanctions or threats.

Even after the adoption of a forward policy in Indochina in 1940, the Japanese did not conclude that it would involve them inevitably in war with the United States. Indeed, they set about negotiations with Washington which only ended with the declaration of war itself. In these they were feeling out the American position. For long their conclusion was that the American commitment to the South-East Asian colonial territories was suspect and that they might safely move ahead regardless. Things came to a head in August 1941 when the Americans had shown their disapproval in two positive ways; by freezing Japanese funds in the United States; and by imposing a total oil embargo on Japan. Should Japan try to buy off America or contemplate a confrontation with her?

The Tokyo answer appears to have been, both. At the critical meeting of the Imperial Conference on 6 September the findings of liaison committee meetings were sustained: Japan would continue to negotiate with Washington but would make war if after one month its response was inadequate; preparations for war with the United States would proceed. They were contemplating war without enthusiasm but with resignation. There was little confidence in victory except in the short term. It was not unlike the feeling among Japanese leaders in 1904 when they could contemplate a possible defeat at the hands of Russia at the very moment they were preparing to declare war on her.

Behind this epoch-making decision there was a long period of gestation in secret committees. The attack on Pearl Harbor was the navy's *sine qua non* for participation in an expanded war in the south. Scholars have traced the decision back to the navy's First Committee, which in May 1941 endorsed the policy of a southward thrust by force and whose middle-ranking officers undertook to convert their superiors to the wisdom of proceeding in the direction of war. From the strategic drawing-board to the final act took six months, which should have been time enough for rational consideration. Indeed, there was detailed examination at military, political and diplomatic levels.

In this process there was a remarkable degree of miscalculation and risk-taking. There was misjudgement which could have been condoned if there had been broadly-based studies. But, considering the enormity of the problem, the studies undertaken had grave defects. On the question of risk-taking, Japan had made gambles before and got away with them. The nature of decision-taking in pre-war Japan was not usually one where snap decisions were made. It was mainly slow and exhaustive. The compromise result was generally cautious. There is, therefore, an enigma over her decision for war with the United States about which we shall always speculate but never know for sure. Probably the ascendancy of Japanese nationalism from the late thirties onwards had left little room for compromises. Certainly by 1941 many of the voices of caution were smothered. There were plenty of diplomatic 'might-have-beens' in the talks with Washington which occupied the three months before war was declared. But, without saying that all the faults were on the side of the Japanese, the responses in Tokyo were rather taut, inelastic and 'positive', as might well be expected with General Tojo at the head of government. Those Japanese who were able to 'bend' were on the whole out of power.

It is in dealing with the United States that the elements of irrationality in Japanese decision-taking become most obvious. In dealing with China and South-East Asia, it may be said that the Japanese military did not completely err in assessing the capacity of their opponents for resistance. In Japan's dealings with the United States, whose long-term superiority in sea and air power was recognised, her judgements were wide of the mark. Perhaps they relied too much on that other ingredient—a spiritual ingredient—at which Viscount Okabe, Minister of Education in 1943, hints: 'we are quite aware of the difference between our scientists and [America's], in that while the American scientists base their efforts on material gains, ours are burning with patriotic spirit. We can fully expect the difference in the results also.' This was the extra ingredient, the 'tiger in the tank' of Japan. Lieut.-Gen. Tada Reikichi also drew optimistic conclusions:

A high spiritual and intellectual culture has existed in our country ever since its foundation. It was because of this highly developed culture that Japan has been able to assimilate the materialistic culture of the West in such a brief space of time. Not only did she assimilate it; she made further improvements upon it, finally overtaking those countries which introduced it to Japan.[7]

This was a doctrine of intellectual and perhaps racial superiority which was a convenient part of the rhetoric of the time. It was part of the heroics in which the Japanese had indulged since the *samurai* days and which was still known in the modern wars of 1904 and 1914. It gave confidence where caution might have been more suitable. It silenced opposition which lay open to the charge of disloyalty.

The attack on Pearl Harbor, with its high drama and its terrible toll in casualties and destruction, was a step of the greatest daring and cunning. Naturally attention has ever since tended to be focused on it in the outside world. It was such a stunning blow to the Americans that the events leading up to 7 December 1941 have since tended to be summed up as 'the road to Pearl Harbor'. But there is a distortion here. It was certain that Pearl Harbor was the road to the Pacific war and the road to the American–Japanese war. But Pearl Harbor was, in the wider context of the Greater East Asian war, less important. It might be described (without in any way decrying its significance) as a tactical side-show in order to neutralise the American fleet and prevent or postpone its involvement in what was intended to be a short Greater East Asian war.

### Shortcomings of Japanese Society
The hard-pressed examinee, grappling with the origins of the war of 1914 and 1939, would feel bound—indeed, would jump at the chance—to attribute much of 'the blame' to social and economic factors. It is fitting that we should follow in his footsteps and consider some of the aspects of Japanese society which may have pushed her over the brink into war. It is still helpful to discuss some of the shortcomings of Japanese society and government in the 1930s. 'The key thing that went wrong was the usurpation of power by the military rather than a

broader economic-social breakdown.' In these words. Professor Edwin Reischauer, historian and ambassador to Japan, tries to sum up a set of scholarly essays, by asking the question which we have all asked from time to time: what went wrong? It would, of course, be possible to give the answer, nothing. Many popular accounts would take the line that Japan aimed throughout the modern period at the domination of Asia and that 1941 was the year of fulfilment. We do not accept this view and prefer to believe that it was the conditions of the thirties which pushed Japan in the direction of war. According to Reischauer, Japan had attained spectacular economic growth but had not coped well with the economic crises of the twenties, notably a disastrous fall in agricultural prices. This in turn led to a decline in the relative standing of the farming community. Their feeling of grievance passed to the army which, being outraged by the performance of the politicians, sought its own remedies. Japanese society was disunited; the policy-forming élites were divided; and widely divergent policies were followed. Such were, in Reischauer's analysis, some of the things which went wrong.[8]

The central question over which scholars have been poring is that of the role of the military in pre-war Japan. That they were dangerously powerful is not in dispute. The points which are emerging are that some of their power was legitimate: they had rights under the Meiji constitution of direct access to the Emperor as commander-in-chief; they had the right of supreme command which enabled them to take the handling of operations out of the hands of the civilian government, as they had done in Siberia in 1918, in Shantung in 1928 and in Manchuria in 1931; there was no adequate control mechanism to their conduct. This was all the more embarrassing because the army and navy were not a unity in themselves: within each service there were tensions between factions and jealousies between the ministry and general staff. There were antagonisms between the army and navy. The other factors which caused trouble were the place of the junior officers, some of whom achieved notoriety by the assassinations which they manipulated in the thirties, and the role of the middle-echelon officers who were skilful in steering through policies based on the army's conception of Japan's interests. Most notable of these were Colonels Itagaki and Ishiwara, who manipulated the Mukden incident on 18 September 1931 and the consequential takeover of southern Manchuria. But there are some who have expressed doubts about the power of the juniors to manipulate seniors; Bergamini, for example, has said: 'The multiplicity of cover stories would convince western historians that junior officers had acted on their own and later shamed senior officers into sanctioning what had been done.' In reality, he argues, 'every man on the ladder, from the lowest to the highest, conspired to deceive, knowing exactly what was afoot.'[9] Many officers were not apolitical and the degree of control exercised over them was dangerously small, because of lax discipline from above and the intensity of feeling from below. But the exact responsibility of those in the chain of command will always contain an element of mystery.

By contrast, the Japanese navy tends to have been regarded as a technical, non-political service, built on solid British lines and imbued with solid British virtues. By the 1930s—the period of the naval disarmament disputes—this image is shown to have been wide of the mark. The navy is shown in a recent study by Pelz to have been as divided as the army and as prone to expansion and adventure. While the navy was initially opposed to, and always sceptical of, an alliance with Germany, it was its influence which in the end told in favour of war with the United States and the operation against Pearl Harbor. For most of the 1930s, its jealousy of the army prevented the adoption of the army's northern strategy. In 1940 it was the navy which promoted the southward policies.

We come now to the relationship between the services and the civilians. For long the tendency was to blame the soldiers for the war. Needless to say, new studies have uncovered some of the implication of civilians with the services. Some authors like Crowley have argued that Japanese army leaders were concerned with national defence needs—Japan's quest for autonomy, a legitimate aspiration of any state.[10] In some instances, it was civilians who were more expansionist, less ready to take the unpopular course of restraint. Thus, Dr Kurihara has pointed out that the selfsame Colonel Ishiwara who had pushed Japan into Manchukuo, was by 1937 urging against embarking on, and extending, the China adventure, while the civilian cabinet members like Konoe and Hirota were insisting on following a tough-line. But of course Ishiwara was a loner and not representative of army thinking as a whole.[11] Much evidence of civilian co-operation with the military has been uncovered. The civil service was penetrated by the army and by revisionist bureaucrats who had close connections with the military leaders. In some cases power was syphoned from a ministry into a separate agency where the army called the tune. In short, the army seems to have applied the political techniques which it had earlier used to grapple with the administration of Manchukuo to the bureaucratic institutions of Japan herself.

Even the Foreign Ministry, whose record in the 1930s best stands up to scrutiny, was open to this penetration. The long-accepted distinction between a good and enlightened Foreign Ministry and a bad and nationalistic military no longer holds water. The Ministry was an infinitely complex place with many who were opposed to the military, some who concealed their opposition and some who shared the adventurous policies and objectives of the soldiers. It is, of course, arguable that there was a case for some degree of 'collaboration' in order both to prevent the Foreign Ministry being permanently by-passed and to act as a brake on the attainment of military policies. But the Ministry, whose influence was in any case deteriorating, was no longer a consistent force for moderation throughout the 1930s.[12]

While the relation between the army and the bureaucracy was a manysided one, the important link between the army and villages was a very subtle one. Among the recruits to the army, half came from villages where, indeed, the majority of the population lived in the 1930s. The villages and agriculture as a whole suffered greatly as the government concentrated on economic growth, primarily in the industrial sector. The peasant farmers meanwhile continued to pay a large share of the taxes that financed the ever-growing budgets. The younger army officers, who were mainly drawn from the ranks, were greatly concerned about the injustice done to the impoverished farming community; and many of them were tempted to seek a solution for their country by a campaign for regeneration and restoration, for which they were prepared to resort to force. 'Domestic reform' was a popular, if deceptive, slogan by which they hoped to win support for the army. Clearly many senior military men did not go along with this radical doctrine. They were anxious that the army should build up a base of rural support by showing concern for the peasant farmers. But they did precious little for the village communities and, in the final analysis, tended after 1937 to favour continued industrial growth and far-reaching state controls which they assumed were indispensable for the country's war effort.[13] Nonetheless the upper echelons of the army were inclined to 'patronize agriculture for its potential for promoting expansion abroad'. The fact of rural impoverishment convinced many that Japan's prime problem was that of over-population and that this could only be eased by encouraging emigration and 'enlarging the empire'.[14]

The role of the emperor and the court in the approach of war has been explored by foreigners with relentless curiosity. Most scholars would not hold that the Emperor Hirohito ruled, though it was convenient at moments of high crisis to have the Emperor issue a rescript. Instances of this were his rescript of 27 March 1933 on Japan's leaving the League of Nations. Another was, of course, his broadcast of 15 August 1945 accepting surrender and urging the people to bear the unbearable. But these interventions were generally confined to emergencies. Recently there has appeared the maverick study of David Bergamini which argued that 'Hirohito and his faction planned step by step to force Japan into war against the west'.[15] This thesis rejected all existing scholarly thinking on this point. But it has in its turn been upset by countless writers. Such is the scope of the work that it will take a decade of scholarship to examine its more detailed evidence. It has been most persuasively tested in an article by Dr Charles Sheldon which rejects the whole concept. It is also by implication overturned by the careful study of David Titus, which takes the line that the scientifically-trained Emperor held the army in contempt and took a firm stand against the uprising of February 1936.[16] Certainly there is abundant evidence to show the Emperor's distaste for the army's conduct and ambitions. But, in the time of civil disobedience which was the thirties in Japan, the views of the Emperor were not always accepted. Though he was universally revered, the spirit of his messages, if it was not pleasing to a certain group, was attributed to the ill advice of his 'wrong-headed' advisers. In other words, a distinction was drawn by the disaffected between the Emperor to whom they professed loyalty, and the court which they criticised as devious and deceitful.

Much of the blame for Japanese expansion has conventionally been put at the door of the *zaibatsu*, the financial and business magnates who dominated Japanese industry and export–import trade on a vast scale. Later when the *zaibatsu* concerns were broken up in 1947–8, it was common to draw a distinction between the Old and the New Zaibatsu families; and this point is stressed in the memoirs of Prime Minister Yoshida. The Old Zaibatsu consisted of the predominant five families of Mitsui, Mitsubishi, Sumitomo, Yasuda and Okura. They came under attack in the 1930s for neglecting Japan's problem of poverty while pursuing their own prosperity. The New Zaibatsu were in origin the *narikin* of the First World War, the *nouveaux riches* who, having made vast profits, had difficulty in surviving in the depressed years of the 1920s. As a way of saving themselves, many came close to the military and favoured the pursuit of new sources of raw materials especially in Manchuria and in China as a whole. Most notable were perhaps Ayukawa Gisuke, president of Manchurian Heavy Industry Company, and Kuhara Fusanosuke, who as industrialist and minister was a noted publicist. He was a strong believer in pan-Asian views and a hostile opponent of Western imperialism especially in its economic manifestations. Kuhara and big business as a whole found it opportune not to keep too remote from the military leadership.[17] In short, there was in these circles the same division that there was elsewhere in Japanese society. It is well to record, however, the words of the wise Sir George Sansom in 1939, written shortly after he reached London from Japan on leave: 'There are among the so-called liberals and bankers and business men those who are afraid of and opposed to totalitarianism'.[18] It was the businessmen who looked for peace and profit that he saw as the best hope, admittedly not a great one, for collaboration with Western powers. He did not look to the Foreign Ministry or the other agencies of government.

In the first part of this enquiry we examined the many-sided war in which Japan found herself engaged in 1941. She had already experienced four years of hostilities with China—a war of fits and starts but in the long run a dreadful drag on the Japanese economy. The Japanese failed to cope with the type of resistance which the Chinese were putting up; they failed to end the fighting which only grew in scope; they failed to negotiate a settlement. With this uncomfortably behind her, Japan embarked on a dual exercise: the Greater East Asia war and the Pacific war. The first, if not a direct consequence of the China war, was related to it. Obviously it was closer to the China war than was the Pacific war. Any time after 1937 the South-East Asian countries felt themselves to be under threat of attack or at least the victims of propaganda warfare. The decision to embark on war against them was made in several stages but became a serious proposition in mid-1940. The Pacific war was in a separate category. The Japanese hoped and believed that war with the United States was avoidable, though the historian may consider this to have been wishful thinking and doubt whether the Japanese were really prepared to make the necessary down-payment in order to remove Washington's suspicions. The critical decision for war was in this case a late one, not before September 1941. Even though the two wars were linked, the thinking, the motives and the objects of the Japanese were different in each case.

In the second part we considered some of the factors which affected political stability in Japan in the 1930s. We saw how Japan included differing groups with widely differing ideas on policy and how consensus was difficult to achieve. There were many factors which brought government to the verge of breakdown. Most important for our present concerns were the failures in cool-headed decision making in the field of diplomacy. Throughout the 1930s Japan displayed an unbending quality, an inability to compromise and an incapacity for the give and take of negotiation. She had many opportunities for compromise: with the League of Nations in 1933 over the Lytton report; with the parties in China from 1937 onwards; and with the United States in the trauma of 1941. It would be wrong to suggest that the failure to compromise in these cases lay purely with the Japanese. Their counterparts were sometimes unyielding and obstinate, but it is not possible here to enter into the intricate diplomatic problems involved. The fact remains that in Japan decisions were scarcely influenced by moderate opinion ready to reach accommodations with overseas countries.

There is no simple explanation for the outbreak of war. The clue to the happenings of 7 December 1941 does not merely lie in slogans like fascism, militarism, ultra-nationalism, encirclement or over-population. Nor does it lie in the notion of a conspiracy of the Japanese leadership, as the judges of the International War Crimes Tribunal, Tokyo, concluded. It is difficult to be more positive because the considerations which apply to the Greater East Asia war do not invariably apply to the Pacific war. Thus, it can be said that the Japanese had been fortified in their attack on South-East Asia by the rightness of their cause, the New Order in Asia;

but this had no relevance to the attack on Pearl Harbor which was purely a pre-emptive strike. Or again, it can be argued that Japan had made comprehensive preparations for war in the colonial territories of South-East Asia and that these stood her in good stead. In the case of the United States, it must be said that the Pearl Harbor operation was well planned; but this can hardly be said of the war that must follow. Here the decision for war was based on the premise that war could not be sustained for more than six months. But this was an outrageous premise to accept Japan's planning—especially her assessment of the enemy's capacity to strike back—was as inadequate in the case of America as it was sound in the case of the French, British and Dutch. In the case of the last three, Japan made her decision for war fairly early which allowed due preparation. In the case of the United States, her decision was made comparatively late in the day and was influenced to a remarkable degree by bravado and miscalculation. Her military officers were inclined to admit the lack of preparation, boasting that their decision for war was 'an act of desperation' brought on by the provocative policies of their adversaries. Even here, there is a point of contrast for the 'provocation' of the colonial governments of South-East Asia was of an economic kind, whereas the provocation of Washington was presumably diplomatic in origin.

The sorely-tried examinee, confronted by the many-sided nature of the wars in Europe in 1914 and 1939, may take refuge by attributing them to German recklessness. By the same token, we, lacking the omniscience to formulate a satisfactory generalisation to account for the multifarious aspects of the war of 1941, may put much of it down to the recklessness of the Japanese. The wise historian—rather than the one who, by adopting psycho-analytic techniques, seeks to catch, and usually succeeds in catching, the reviewer's eye—is well advised to avoid explaining affairs solely in terms of national characteristics. Recklessness is not a normal characteristic of the Japanese. But, in the crisis of the first days of December, weak men, weighed down by testing events and puffed up by an artificial confidence, decided on a reckless gamble.

## Notes

1 J. H. Boyle, *China and Japan at War, 1937–45* (Stanford, 1972) p. 44, quoting Hata Ikuhiko, *Nitchu sensoshi*.

2 *Documents on British Foreign Policy, 1919–39* (London, 1955) 3 (ix), appendix 1, note by G. B. Sansom, 3 Aug 1939.

3 *Nihon Gaiko Nempyo narabi ni Shuyo Bunsho* (Tokyo, 1955) ii, broadcast statement by Arita, 29 June 1940.

4 Nobutaka Ike, *Japan's Decision for War* (Stanford, 1967) pp. 232–3.

5 *Dai To-A senso kiroku gaho* (June 1943) p. 39.

6 Tanahashi Toragoro, 'East Asiatic Resources and our Techniques', *Nippon Times*

*Weekly*, 16 Sep 1943, pp. 10.

7  *Nippon Times Weekly*, 16 Sep 1943, pp. 3, 5.

8  See J. W. Morley (ed.), *Dilemmas of Growth in Pre-war Japan* (Princeton, N.J., 1971) ch. 13.

9  D. Bergamini, *Japan's Imperial Conspiracy* (London, 1971) p. 422n.

10  J. B. Crowley, *Japan's Quest for Autonomy, 1930–38* (Princeton, N.J., 1966) p. xvii. S. E. Pelz, *Race to Pearl Harbor* (Cambridge, Mass., 1974) ch. 2.

11  Kurihara Ken, *Tenno, Showashi oboegaki* (Tokyo, 1955) ch. 7.

12  *Gaimusho no 100-nen* (Tokyo, 1969) Vol. ii, ch. 3 (2); Usui Katsumi, 'The Role of the Foreign Ministry', in Dorothy Borg and Okamoto Shumpei (eds.), *Pearl Harbor as History: Japanese-American Relations, 1931–41* (New York, 1973) pp. 127–8.

13  T. R. H. Havens, *Farm and Nation in Modern Japan* (Princeton, N.J., 1974) pp. 308–13.

14  Cf R. J. Smethurst, *A Social Basis for Prewar Japanese Militarism: the Army and the Rural Community* (Berkeley, 1974); R. P. Dore and T. Ouchi, 'Rural Origins of Japanese Fascism', in Morley (ed.), *Dilemmas of Growth*, ch. 6.

15  Bergamini, *Japan's Imperial Conspiracy*, which has the sub-title 'How Emperor Hirohito led Japan into War against the West'.

16  C. D. Sheldon, 'Japanese Aggression and the Emperor, 1931–41', *Modern Asian Studies*, Vol. x, 1 (Feb 1975); D. A. Titus, *Palace and Politics in Prewar Japan* (New York, 1974) pp. 328, 164–7.

17  A. Tiedemann, 'Big Business and Politics in Prewar Japan', in Morley (ed.), *Dilemmas of Growth*, ch. 8.

18  See note 2 above.

# 8 People's War and Top People's Peace? British Society and the Second World War

## ARTHUR MARWICK

'A People's War *and* A People's Peace' was the avowed aim of Common Wealth, the party founded by Sir Richard Acland and friends to urge the claims of social reform in face of the electoral truce maintained between the Labour, Conservative and Liberal members of Churchill's wartime Government. That the ending of the war in 1945 and the election of a majority Labour Government did indeed bring social revolution and genuine popular democracy was, till at least the end of the fifties, a view shared both by those who rather liked the idea, such as Liberal intellectuals and Labour politicians, and those who heartily disliked it, including many Tories. Historians, to begin with, paid most attention to the Attlee government's attempts, in difficult economic conditions, to make a reality of the People's Peace.[1] But by the sixties attention was being refocused on the People's War. The classic statement is the famous final paragraph of A. J. P. Taylor's *English History 1914–1945* published in 1965:

> In the second World War the British people came of age. This was a People's War. Not only were their needs considered. They themselves wanted to win. . . . Traditional values lost much of their force. Other values took their place. Imperial greatness was on the way out; the welfare state was on the way in. The British Empire declined; the condition of the people improved. Few now sang 'Land of Hope and Glory'. Few even sang 'England Arise'. England had risen all the same.[2]

Mr Taylor does not tell us what happened next (reasonably enough, since his book ends there). However when Ralph Miliband (writing in 1961) gave a not dissimilar view of the significance of the war in causing 'the emergence . . . of a new popular radicalism' his purpose was to prepare the way for an exposure of the failure of the Labour Government to exploit this mood and carry through a genuine social revolution.[3] By the end of the sixties the very notion of a 'People's War' was being opened to serious question. Much of Angus Calder's long, thoroughly documented, and subtly ironical *The People's War*[4] was taken up with showing how, through the medium of a political consensus into which upper-class Labour ministers (Sir Stafford Cripps is singled out) too readily entered, the power of traditional hierarchies was in fact preserved. Whereas another committed young man of the left, Anthony Howard, had earlier spoken of 1945 bringing a *restoration* of traditional values, Angus Calder declared that the war itself had *hastened* society's progress along the old grooves.[5] Then came the coolest debunking of all: a short chapter in which Henry Pelling contested the view that working-class participation in the war, in itself, had any significant effect on their social and economic status.[6] Thus 'A People's War *and* a People's Peace' had first become 'People's War and Top People's Peace' and now seemed on a fair way to being 'Top People's Peace *and* Top People's War'.

Re-revising the revisionists is one of the stalest ploys by which historians struggle to keep redundancy at bay. Nonetheless this paper sets out unrepentantly to show how the phrase 'People's War' can legitimately and without irony be used in regard to the Second World War, and to argue that the momentum of social change continued into the post-war period. Certainly the Attlee Government failed to do nearly as much as it might have done to exploit the psychological opportunity created by the war; it was also the prisoner of many of the developments that the war had brought about. But the root of the historiographical problem as I see it is that just as it has always been too easy to exaggerate the bulldog spirit, the patriotic unity, the self-sacrifice, and the speed and scope of social change during the war (as, of course, propagandists did), it has subsequently been equally easy to present an exaggerated view of an extreme reaction at the end of the war. It is the great strength of Calder's book that he does bring out the complexities of the war experience, the shabbiness and the selfishness, as well as the heroics. Here I too propose to stress the strong resistances which there were to social change during the war and the very slowness of the build-up of opinion in favour of change. To my mind the war was all the more a People's War for the fact that 'the people' did not have their gains handed to them on a plate; so too was the impetus for social change after the war had ended all the more powerful.

The first sense in which the Second World War was a People's War is the most straightforward and obvious one: throughout a critical period from the late summer of 1940 to the early summer of 1941 ordinary people in London, and in other population centres, were plunged by the blitz into a front-line situation of incendiaries and high explosives, yet they continued to turn up for work, to operate the war factories, to man the auxiliary services, and thus kept the war effort going.

On the Sunday night a large public shelter in Beaufort Street had received a direct hit. There were no survivors, and as soon as it got light on Monday morning, the ambulance girls from the adjacent post were sent to help the rescue and demolition squads to remove the human remains. They had to put what they could collect into blue waterproof bags and take them to the mortuary. She [a nurse] had seen a man pick up a head and put it in the sack, and another with his hand scrape a woman's scalp off the surface of a concrete block, where it had stuck when the head was smashed against it. She had seen a half-born dead baby attached to its dead mother.[7]

This record of London in the front line comes from the diary (typed some years later from notes) of an upper-middle class lady Diana Brinton-Lee, who for a time was a volunteer driver, while her husband was a captain in the Local Defence Volunteers (later the Home Guard) in Shepherd's Bush. The same diary mentions the pilfering of handbags in air-raid shelters; and, indeed, there was so much looting in the blitz that the maximum penalty for summary conviction was increased from three to twelve months. Social psychologists make a useful distinction between 'active' and 'passive' morale; the government itself, in one of the many excellent secret reports through which it kept a careful eye on civilian reactions, recognised a parallel one between the 'transient' and the 'durable' effects of raids.[8] Most of those who were bombed did not, quite understandably, go around smiling and singing, swearing eternal loyalty to Churchill and demanding a war to the death with Hitler. The first blitz on the East End produced a flood of distressed and bewildered evacuees: 'people wanted to be brave but found bravery was something purely negative, cheerless, and without encouragement or prospect of success'.[9] In other towns there was often complacency till the terrible shock of the arrival of the first mass bomb attack. In all bombed areas there was dismay and confusion, and no wonder, over the collapse of government and local services: voluntary services—fire, ambulance, nursing, and all the aspects of the W.V.S. stood out in contrast. Yet absenteeism was negligible, work did go on, and most people, when interviewed, expressed themselves in favour of carrying the attack to Germany, even though it was widely believed that this would simply provoke a more severe retaliation on British civilians. Passive morale—carrying on—was good. High active morale was less widespread, but can be clearly seen in police reports and censored letters, in the chirpy shop signs which were much photographed, in the observations of middle-class commentators now brought more closely in contact with the working class than ever before, and in the smaller number of direct working-class records. William Penny lived in Paddington, but drove his number 6 bus through the East End, and, when the Northern Line was bombed out, south of the river on an auxiliary route to Morden. Perhaps there is a touch of the newspaper headline about his diary entries, yet the feel is authentic enough, and in June 1941 (when the worst in fact was over) he does admit that 'No doubt everybody is somewhat down in "spirits" after the past months of Bombs':

> Although the past week has been very Trying with the Bombs and Sleepless nights we are still not 'Down hearted' for as it has been said: We are all in the 'Front Line' and we realise it . . . (12 September 1940)

> Several Day 'Alerts'. Some for several Hours. But nobody takes the slightest 'Heed' of these 'Alerts'. All Traffic on the Streets and all businesses 'Carry On'. . . (11 October 1940)

> . . . I was greatly shocked by the Huge amount of Damage that has been caused over South London . . . But it is surprising to see everybody going about the next morning all Merry and Bright taking the Raids as they come . . . (8 November 1940)

> This night's 'Raid' on London being the worst so far in this 'Total War'. But at no time did I see anyone in this district get depressed or grumble. Or even lose [sic] heart. For we all know our 'Own Boys' will repay in full as soon as we get the machines . . . (10 May 1941)[10]

Obviously there are differences between being a civilian under aerial attack and a soldier in the front line of a shooting war; yet the point about the People's War experience is strengthened by the fact that after the Dunkirk evacuation (which itself projected front-line casualties straight back into civilian hospitals—including the Emergency Hospital at Ashridge, now a depository of the Public Record Office—making them seem part of the war zone even before the blitz) many men in uniform were placed in much less hazardous circumstances than were civilians. A librarian conscripted into the Signal Corps wrote cheerfully from Redford Barracks in Edinburgh to a female colleague in Bethnal Green: 'Army life seems to be fag, fags, fun and food, in that order, I have never worked, smoked, laughed, and eaten so much in my life.'[11] At the height of the blitz the *Daily Telegraph* suggested that the army should knit socks and scarves for the civilians, and an aristocratic naval officer turned businessman, now back at the Admiralty, wondered 'why they haven't been employed assisting the A.R.P., Rescue or Demolition Services in London more'.[12] The thought was shared by Sir Warren Fisher who had recently emerged from decent obscurity as head of the inter-war Civil Service into a blaze of publicity, largely created by himself, as (in the phrase of the newsreels) 'London's Chief Cleaner-Upper'. In a crazy, but all too characteristic, comic opera played out amid the ruins of London,

Fisher failed to get either the navvies he required, partly because the local authorities insisted on operating only through private contractors, or as many Pioneers as he requested, because of Churchill's insistence that 'it should be brought home to public opinion that our Army could not be properly trained for war if it was continuously used for work that could be done by navvies.' However Ernest Bevin made it clear to Sir John Anderson that he thought the main problem was Fisher's incompetence.[13] As late as May 1944 the Director of Education for Dumbartonshire, J. P. McHutchison, was secretly grousing about the tendency to 'spoil and mollycoddle the soldier . . . men and women who are having the time of their lives'.[14] In fact civilians (McHutchison had toured the devastation of Clydebank together with Davie Kirkwood) and servicemen were in it together in a way which simply was not true of the First World War—and most servicemen anyway were simply civilians in uniform.

To say that, of course, is not to say that the rich cheerfully abandoned their privileges and the snobbishness which went with them. Some, in perfect, if naive, good faith, did help to foster that very myth. As early as the second day of war one middle-class spinster from Putney, who had volunteered to work in her local A.R.P. Report Centre, was telling herself:

> There is one good thing, and one only, about this war—it is an instant and complete leveller of 'classes'. Everyone mixes and talks to anyone and I think we all find that the other is really quite a normal and interesting person and not a bit different from ourselves. About 30 of us are in the Centre, taken from widely divergent walks of life and we all get along very well indeed.[15]

But a wealth of published and unpublished material testifies to the persistence of upper-class nonchalance and detachment. W. H. Haslam, owner of Hundridge Manor, Chesham, Buckinghamshire, and director of several companies, wrote a regular series of letters throughout the war to relatives abroad. In a preface which he himself provided for the collected letters, which were deposited with the Imperial War Museum, he records that the staff at Hundridge during the war years included: 'Ada Baker (Nannie); Marion Hersee (Cook); Mary Walbling (Housemaid); Terese Kneschauer (Ladies' Maid); Mercer (Parlourmaid); Sandford (Butler); R. A. Rumens (Handyman and general factotum); Alfonso Gibbs (Assistant Gardener).'

At the beginning of 1941 Haslam took some days off from his office in Moorgate because the blitz had destroyed the heating. The heating restored, he took the 9.11 a.m. train as usual from Amersham to Marylebone, and thence on to the city. His thoughts are illuminating:

It is of course infuriating that Wren churches and the Guild Hall and City livery Companies halls should be destroyed or mauled about but we shall ultimately not regret the destruction of piles of antiquated buildings in the St. Paul's area. No legislation could have got rid of them without hideous sums of compensation and yet most of them were antiquated, many partially empty, and few of them susceptible to modernisation, as I well know from being a director of the Sackville Estates which has had a number of properties raised [sic] to the ground.[16]

Haslam regarded Attlee (whose name he consistently misspelled) as 'insignificant' and Kingsley Wood (perhaps with some justice) as 'specially dreary and bourgeois'; he also recorded, in June 1942, his 'feeling that it will do well to break up the Trade Union system.'[17] There is a nice example too of class war from above in a report compiled in April 1942 by the major in charge of the Security Control Office in Glasgow, who also happened to be the son of the managing director of Scott's Ship Building and Engineering Company: Major Brown created quite a ripple through the War Office, the Foreign Office, and right up to the War Cabinet, with his allegations of 'slackness' on the part of Glasgow dockers, until the whole business was thoroughly squashed by the Ministry of War Transport and the Lord President, Sir John Anderson.[18] If caught in an attack, of course, the rich had to mix with the poor in air-raid shelters; but most continued to prefer the luxury of their own private arrangements. For many middle-class Londoners in 1940 and 1941, and again in 1944, a constant preoccupation was that of finding safer accommodation among the villages of the home counties.

Still, even if the very rich continued to try to go their own way, the middle class—the class which, though better-off and more secure than the working class in the thirties, in reality had very little more real power and influence—did, give or take a few perks and a slightly easier access to rural bolt-holes, join the working class in a full involvement in the war. Whatever Buckinghamshire village the Brinton-Lee's fetched up at, he, though he in fact worked at the Denham film studios, always turned up for Home Guard duty in Shepherd's Bush; and the middle class throughout were the readiest volunteers for the various auxiliary services. But there is a more specific sense in which certain professional people became involved in the war effort, giving them a direct influence over opinion, and perhaps even policy, of a kind that they had never exercised in peacetime: this is the second sense in which this was a people's war. Dons (who are people, after all) entered government: D. N. Chester, for instance, lecturer in Public Administration at Manchester, and a man of modest background, entered the Economic Secretariat of the Cabinet. Journalists, film-makers, scientists: many were given a new role and a new purpose. There is much about the public image of British society in the war that is reminiscent of the public image of the Soviet Union: civil servants eating at canteens, ballet dancers explaining their steps to engineering workers, music coming to the factory, films about the importance and future prospects of the worker. The anti-establishment of the thirties joined the wartime establishment. British propaganda films at the beginning of the war were offensively out of touch with popular sensibilities, and probably pretty ineffectual. Soon, with the blessing of the Ministry of Information, the documentary film-makers of the thirties, almost all men of the left, began to take over. Much of their output now seems patronising; it was quite powerful left-wing propaganda all the same. But perhaps the most effective propaganda of all was the feature film *Love on the Dole*, ready, but unreleased, in 1939 because of the unfavourable view it gave of life under Baldwin and Chamberlain; in 1941 it was released, with a message flashed on the screen at the end in which the Labour First Lord of the Admiralty, A. V. Alexander, declared that such conditions must never be allowed to return.

And this takes us to the third justification for speaking of a People's War: the steady emergence of a mood of popular radicalism favouring reform. Mass Observation reports, published and unpublished, give a reliable chart of the changing working-class mood, from 'bewilderment, uncertainty, insecurity and hope for the best' in 1938, to the 'less selfish' mood of 1940–2 when the main concentration was on the war, to the period after 1942 and the publication of the Beveridge report, when a shift in focus towards the period beyond the peace could be detected: if there was nothing specially new about people's responses, they were now much more specific in defining the changes which they expected to be brought about. 'Faith in the future', the published report, *The Journey Home*, summed up, 'is being pinned more and more on the ability of ordinary people to build it, less on official actions, treaties, promises'.[19] In the forces, the Army Bureau of Current Affairs, in particular, fostered an interest in social and political questions, and, in contrast with the previous war, there was a constructive interaction between civilians and soldiers on leave. The Reverend James Mackay, Methodist Minister at the Archway Central Hall in a working-class and lower-middle class area of London, is an interesting witness since his own faith was in a 'strong vital Church' and not at all in social reform:

> I have been greatly interested in talking to many of those who have been home on leave recently, to find how their thinking is widening and deeping, and to find what sort of pictures are in their minds of the world after the war. Most of them are thinking of a world where there will be better opportunities for everyone, and more economic security than there has been since the early ages of mankind.[20]

If this evidence of growing working-class commitment (in or out of uniform) seems too impressionistic it is always worth remembering that the number of days lost due to strikes, after dropping in 1940 and 1941, went up in every war year from 1942 to 1944, and even in 1945 the number was still double that of 1938.

The change in sections of middle-class opinion is often linked with evacuation, which brought respectable households into contact with children of the slums for the first time. Actually the evacuations of 1939 and 1940 were probably as significant for the way in which they revealed class hostilities as for the way in which they brought about a mixing of classes; however by the time of the V-bomb evacuation in 1944 many of the former tensions had disappeared. Again it is unwise to look for the sudden shedding of ingrained habits. Evacuation, anyway, is best seen as a part, though a very important one, of a wider and steadily developing set of circumstances in which middle-class people were drawn into activities, official and voluntary, which both involved them directly with working-class people and their children (in pioneer play-schools and adventure playgrounds, for example), and brought home to them the terrible inadequacies of existing social institutions. An unpublished Mass Observation report of August 1944, concerned mainly with middle-class outlook, noted the following changes: 'greater sociability and tolerance, with a decrease in class prejudice', and 'more interest in politics than before the war with a general movement from Right to Left'.[21] The mood was reflected by many high up the social scale who never gave up their unrepentant Toryism. In June 1942 W. H. Haslam noted that: 'There is much thought and speculation going on as to what may be the face and structure of post-war Britain.' Although he then continued, 'because I feel concrete planning or earnest speculation rather premature my leisure moments are less exercised about this than many who have time to think . . .', he did express quite strong views after the Beveridge report finally made its appearance in December 1942:

> The Report has so far only been previewed; it has not been debated in Parliament. No doubt vested interests are marshalling their opposition but the country and the Press as a whole are for it. It does promise a different state of affairs for the service-men when demobilised and if it were to get on the Statute Book it might rank in historical importance with the Reform Bill of 1832 and the Repeal of the Corn Laws. Personally I don't think it will become operative but only because time and change are running too fast for any great code to be established. The great point is that the public will never release the prospect that Report opens up. (5 January 1943)

> The Government in my view has made a great mistake in not endorsing the Beveridge Report to the extent of creating a Ministry of Social

Security. Such an institution would be an earnest of their intention that unemployment and want shall not prevail on demobilisation. I feel sure such a gesture would have appealed to the services. Surely the first two calls on the National financies for the future are maintainence of defence and freedom from want. Financial consideration must be subservient to both necessities. (5 March 1943)[22]

Even Commander Yates noted: 'The Beveridge "New Britain" plan is engaging the attention of the Home Front at the moment. It undoubtedly has something on the right lines, but is very expensive.'[23]

Changes in outlook, then, are detectable in upper- and middle-class elements outside the main circle of politics, among servicemen, and among the broad mass of the people. What of the central circle of politics and administration? Obviously, the inclusion of Labour ministers in positions of importance helped to move official policy in a leftward direction, and the great series of reconstruction White Papers published in the later years of the war is well known. As early as June 1940 there is a neat example of a new attitude towards education in wartime, and one which contrasts sharply with that apparent in the First World War. Certain local authorities had sought the release of children from the public elementary schools so that they could undertake agricultural work, and, in some cases, even munitions and other work of national importance. The Conservative President of the Board of Education (Ramsbotham) had strongly resisted this, and he was given the overwhelming support of the Home Policy Committee, chaired by Attlee—only Ernest Bevin was prepared to countenance the idea of children being released for temporary farm work. The one local authority which had continued to defy the President of the Board of Education was threatened with a cut in its education grant.[24] But other points also stand out, in particular the Tory revolt over Ernest Bevin's Catering Wages' bill, and the hesitancy and bumbling obstructionism over the publication, debate and implementation of the Beveridge report. Apart altogether from Churchill's own personal reservations, hostility, naturally, was particularly strong in the Treasury. The Lord President's Office file on the report shows very clearly the tremendous fight put up by D. N. Chester (who acted as Secretary to the Beveridge Committee) on behalf of the report against the Treasury mandarins and the Chancellor of the Exchequer, Kingsley Wood.[25] On the fringes, Lord Dudley Gordon, President of the Federation of British Industries, Lord Croft, Sir Edward Mountain and Mr Percy Rockliffe (both the latter representing insurance interests), various spokesmen for the B.M.A., the *Daily Telegraph*, the *Sunday Times*, and the Conservative newsheet, *Onlooker*, all attacked the report, more or less openly.

The powerful resistance in high places to any talk of social reform and social levelling brings out in fact the real strength of the popular mood for social change. For those who believed in a People's War and a People's Peace there were no easy victories to be won. On the other hand there is no doubt that the war, irrespective of the decisions and actions of individuals, did directly bring about a situation favourable to social change.[26] Furthermore the war also brought about a direct immediate improvement in living standards for most working-class civilians. Certainly it should not be forgotten that, even though there is much evidence, particularly among middle-class diarists, of moods and moments of exaltation and deep moral purpose, much of the war was grindingly boring, with patched-up housing, monotonous food, and vexatiously inadequate transport. Nevertheless the basic situation in the labour market, where unemployment gave way to a manpower shortage, and the introduction of food subsidies, rationing, and a national nutrition policy all operated in favour of labour. Earnings were up 80 per cent at the end of the war, whereas the cost of living had only gone up by 31 per cent. No historian has denied this improvement in basic standards (though Dr Pelling doubts whether it can be attributed to the war); here we have a fourth reason for speaking of a People's War.

The Labour victory of 1945 was no surprise for those who had followed the steady evolution of opinion throughout the war period. The working class now voted more solidly Labour than it had ever done before, and, as John Bonham once calculated, perhaps a third of the middle-class vote also went to Labour.[27] Had there been a general election in 1940 it is as certain as these things are that Labour would not have won it.[28] Turning our heads in the other direction, we should recall too that Labour's popular vote increased both in 1950 and 1951; it was due as much to the nature of the British electoral system and to the failings and illnesses of Labour's top leadership, as to any tide of resentment against, or disillusionment with Labour's handling of the first five years of peace, that there began, in 1951, 'thirteen years of Tory rule'. Equally, it is true, Labour's 1945 victory was not greeted by great gusts of brotherly goodwill from the working class: within weeks there were dock, gas, and bus strikes. Nor was upper-class nonchalance any more shaken than it had been by the reorganisations of war:

> Apart from the effect that this election will have on our credit abroad and on Russia, India and U.S.A., where it may be interpreted as a defeat for Churchill's foreign policy, which it is not, I am not unduly alarmed at the moment. At home in the persons of Bevin and Morrison we have had a labour government for five years, as Winston hardly touched the home front and that's why he is out. They have learned a lot—those two. . . . Bevin . . . mobilized the man and woman power of the easy-going liberty-loving English to an extent that no other

country (including Russia) of the United Nations ever approached. It
made him unpopular, but I think on the whole he did a good job, and
we were fighting for our existence.

There is a tendency to prophesy that the government won't last two
years. Personally, without having analysed or even seen the detailed
returns, I give it ten. The first few will be difficult at home. Wages will
have to come down and the labour leaders are the best people to
explain this . . .[29]

Commander Yates, as well as Harold Nicolson, and 'Chips' Channon
and his like, were remarkably unaffected by the early years of Labour
rule: 'At the fashionable, carefree Cartano-Edman wedding reception I
remarked to Emerald how quickly London had recovered from the war
and how quickly normal life had been resumed.'[30] But the Labour
government, whatever its failings, certainly never became the agents of
the rich in forcing down wages.

Nonchalance, naturally, did not extend to active Conservatives, nor,
more significantly, to the substantial sections of the middle class who
had not moved left. Conservatives viewed the overflowing Labour
benches with dismay: 'just like a crowd of damned constituents' said one
M.P.[31] 'We were certainly staggered by the election result especially as I
live and worked in a very Conservative atmosphere—the end of the world
would have occasioned only a little more alarm', wrote one middle-class
lady to her father in South Africa. Her husband, so his brother-in-law
wrote: 'is particularly depressed. I think he regards the Labour Government and the atom bomb as two inescapable evils, either being certain to
bring about his premature demise.'[32] As a civil servant in the Ministry of
Agriculture, the brother-in-law himself presented a slightly different
point of view, though corroborating the picture of deep suburban
middle-class gloom:

> The gloom and despondency that prevailed in Hinchley Wood could
> not have been greater if we had lost the war . . . Being a Civil Servant, I
> have no politics, but I must confess I was somewhat amused at this
> local depression . . .
>
> Viewed from the inside, the Civil Service takes an impressive view of
> the drive of the new Labour Ministers. Our own man in particular has
> pleased the farmers with his forthright manner and energy. I don't
> know he has pleased *us* so much, as new legislation means more work,
> and we are continually losing our staff, a large percentage being tem-
> porary married women.
>
> The fear of nationalisation seems to be very real. Why, I do not
> know. I can imagine people's misgivings if it were proposed to hand
> over a big national undertaking like the Post Office to a private com-
> pany yet these same people, during the war would be heard to say of a

private undertaking 'The Government ought to take it over'![33]

The nature of the developments which followed the war must be assessed against the limited, but precise and real, definition of the People's War which I have already given. After 1945 there was no fundamental change in the allocation of political or economic power: but there had been none during the war. There was no workers' control, though there was a continuation of some of the modest experiments in worker participation undertaken during the war. There was no great rational re-planning of the entire community in accord with the lights of pure efficiency; but then, as Calder points out, there had been a great deal of muddle during the war: the historian who seeks the kind of rationality and efficiency demanded on the front pages of the *New Statesman* might as well give up studying human societies altogether. The privileges and self-indulgence of the rich continued; but then they had continued throughout the war. Undoubtedly the Attlee Government could have done much more than it did—abolishing the public schools and experimenting much more boldly in the management of the nationalised industries, for instance. But Attlee, Cripps, Dalton—chosen leaders of the Labour party—were prisoners of their own upper-class backgrounds; still more were they prisoners of the planning structure of co-operation between government and business and of the apparently fruitful collaboration with the civil servants, both of which had seemed to work well in wartime.

The change, then, is not in basic structures, but in ideas and in social attitudes and relationships, in how people and classes saw each other, and, most important, in how they saw themselves. Three fundamental points must be made. First the baseline of working-class demands had shifted: 'both work and maintenance became not aspirations but fixed expectations.'[34] Second, the 'consensus' (in industry as well as politics) which emerged towards the end of the war, real, but flawed by much powerful opposition, was far more humane and genuinely democratic than the attitudes of industry, government and Civil Service in the 1930s. Third, the Labour Government in many of its policies was in fact ahead of this consensus, and frequently had to fight against bitter opposition both inside and outside parliament.

The People's War left a legacy of improved industrial relations, eventually to be satirised in the film, *I'm All Right Jack*, and doubtless in some respects a hindrance to economic growth when compared with the totally new structure of industrial relations created in Germany; still the contrast with the patronising and uncomprehending arrogance of so many employers in the thirties was a marked one. The record of the blundering and futile activities of the Land Settlement Association, a privately sponsored body supported by the government which sought to convert unemployed miners and other industrial workers into small-holders, provides (to our eyes) a laugh a line: the film they made to publicise their activities literally has to be seen to be believed. The funda-mental administrative morality of the thirties was the morality of the Means Test. The tone was set by the notorious Board of Education circular no. 1421 which in the autumn of 1932 sought to end the system whereby secondary schools subsidised by the state had to provide *at least* 25 per cent of their places free to pupils from the public elementary schools who had passed a special scholarship exam: free places were to be replaced by 'special places' with a scale of fees based on means. Voluntary hospitals throughout the decade charged according to means; and this established principle was appealed to by those who wished also to introduce differential rents based on means into public housing. The sorry story of Public Assistance and the Means Test is well known. The key idea underlying the Welfare State legislation of 1946–8 was that of 'universality'—social provision was to be made for rich and poor alike, so that there would be no stigma attached to the receipt of benefits or treat-ment, and so that there would not be second-rate services for the poor only. Full universality was never attained, a Means Test element being built into National Assistance from the start. In more recent times, when the social problem has become one of deep pools of deprivation in the midst of relative affluence rather than one of whole sections of the work-ing classes perched on the verge of insecurity, universality no longer car-ries the potency it did in 1945. Yet the fact that it was built into the very structure of the original Welfare State legislation helped to set a new code of social and administrative morality, a function of legislation too often ignored by historians who, as in the all too familiar textbooks, tend to hail acts of parliament as in themselves major concrete achievements, or else reject them altogether because in the real world the very letter of the law is seldom achieved.

As a last example in my comparison of the thirties with the later forties I leave this little account of establishment attitudes towards the 1936 hunger marchers (the entire file[35] can be studied at leisure in that famous former wartime hospital at Ashridge) to speak for itself. Sir John Simon, Home Secretary, wished the government to issue a formal statement con-demning the marches, and hoping 'that the law-abiding public through-out the country will discourage and discountenance .any such proceedings in any possible way.' Simon tried to consult Sir Kingsley Wood (Haslam's 'insignificant bourgeois'): however as he was out of town, his permanent officials were able to stop Simon making an ass of himself. Instead, 'they thought there was much to be said for the Govern-ment leaving this kind of exhortation to the leader writers who can use weapons of irony from which the official draftsman is debarred: see the excellent leader in the Western Mail attached.'

Attached was this masterpiece of snide obscurantism published as a leading article in the *Western Mail* on 24 September:

An eminent scientist, dipping into the near future, predicted that the pedestrian would soon be as extinct as the dodo and that conducted parties would then be led round the museums to study the remains of this lost species. But he reckoned without giving due consideration to the modern tendency of bodies with grievances setting out on a March to London in the hope of wringing concessions from harassed Ministers. If this new craze becomes much more prevalent, it will rival the attempts to swim the Channel, and steps will have to be taken to prevent head-on collisions between marchers. It may even be necessary to construct new roads to accommodate them.

We suppose that many marches are organised as a diversion for people who have nothing else to do. They are believed to have a certain propagandist value as they attract crowds of spectators at various points who wonder what on earth the marchers hope to achieve. Usually collections are taken en route, and thus on arrival in London the pilgrims are able to have a fairly good time. In other cases misguided local authorities have seriously contemplated making the cost of these expeditions a charge on the rates, despite warnings regarding the illegality of the proposal. Is it not high time that public opinion condemned this new stunt and refused to afford it the slightest encouragement? Nothing useful has ever been achieved by past marches. The procession usually sets out without invitation; it arrives with no plans for its reception; no responsible person regards it as anything more than mere propaganda; and after a few days sight-seeing in the Metropolis and some entertainment in the soup kitchen the marchers return without ever meeting the Minister whose flesh they wanted to make creep . . .

The formal ministerial reply was, 'Sir Kingsley himself thinks that it would be better to induce the friendly newspapers to take this line themselves and on their own responsibility, and he believes that a considerable number of the papers would do so.'

But it took another phone call finally to persuade Simon that he could not make statements implying that the marchers themselves were not 'law abiding'.

The main argument of this paper can be summed up by reference to that most topical of all topics, the position and status of women. Women were not suddenly emancipated by the war, as much propaganda suggested. Often they were simply doing the same old 'feminine' jobs in different surroundings, or in uniform. The Women's Land Army actually advertised for 'women who like doing housework'; at the other extreme great stress was placed on the importance of women as 'pinups'. But in spite of deeply ingrained attitudes and much resistance, the war did create new demands and provide new opportunities. In the thirties it was still common practice in many jobs to sack women as soon as they married. In the wartime labour market, married women had to be employed, and the old prejudices about their unreliability as employees were exploded. A government questionnaire to various employers, public and private, at the end of the war showed a considerable swing round in opinion on the employment of married women.[36] With women, as elsewhere, there was no sudden appearance of total equality in wartime, followed by an equally sudden reaction back to the old ways at the end of the war. Instead a new baseline (to repeat a metaphor I have already used) was, with some difficulty, established. During the war, while many women had a taste of economic freedom, others, dependent on the miserable allowance paid to soldiers, were badly off: but in general the war meant an enhanced status for women, the effects of which were never dissipated.

There were, then, no great revolutionary changes after 1945—some of the older writers are quite wrong here. But if it is unhelpful to speak of a 'social revolution' it is positively misleading to speak of 'a restoration of traditional values' or of society sweeping along 'the old grooves'. Change resulted more from the mechanisms touched off by total war (I have defined these elsewhere)[37] than from the deliberate actions of politicians. But it must always be remembered that throughout the war and well into peacetime there were plenty of powerful people ready to emulate their predecessors of 1918 in attempting to restore the lost golden age of the Means Test and insecurity. The clock could have been put back in 1945; it may not be the most glorious of achievements, but the Attlee Government did not put it back.

There are two major reasons why the changes initiated in the war years tend to seem less significant in the 1970s than they did in the 1950s. First the whole set of new changes in the late fifties and early sixties, summarised under the blanket heading of 'affluence' and involving such key developments as the diffusion of the contraceptive pill, rather threw the wartime changes into the shadow. Second, we find ourselves in such a terrible mess in the seventies, with neither an efficient economy nor an effective welfare state, that it is hard to believe that any constructive changes at all took place in the forties. But then in human affairs few problems have complete solutions, and those that do are inevitably replaced by new problems. This is not a counsel of despair, but rather a plea for eternal vigilance, and constant action. A platitude no doubt: but which of us would really like to be back in the world of the 1930s?

# Notes

1  See, e.g., E. Watkins, *The Cautious Revolution* (London, 1950); Robert Brady, *Crisis in Britain* (California; Cambridge, 1952); and C. F. Brand, *The British Labour Party: A Short History* (Stanford; Oxford, 1965).

2  Oxford, 1965, p. 600.

3  *Parliamentary Socialism* (London, 1961) pp. 272, 275–6.

4  London, 1969.

5  A. Howard in M. Sissons and P. French (eds), *The Age of Austerity* (London, 1963) p. 31; *The People's War*, p. 17.

6  Henry Pelling, *Britain and the Second World War* (London, 1970) ch. 12.

7  Diary of Mrs Brinton-Lee, 4th week, 8–14 Sep (typescript, Imperial War Museum) p. 53.

8  'Air-raids on London, September-November 1940: Memorandum by Home Secretary and the Minister of Home Security', CAB 67/9(41)44 (5 May 1941). For active and passive morale see F. C. Iklé, *Social Impact of Bomb Destruction* (Norman, Okla., 1958) p. 121.

9  Mass Observation, 'Evacuation and Other East End Problems', unpublished typescript, file no. 392 (10 Sep 1940). I am most grateful to Mr Tom Harrisson for granting me access to the invaluable Mass Observation archive, now housed at the University of Sussex.

10  MS. diary of Henry Alexandra Penny, Imperial War Museum.

11  Gunner Jack Luck to Miss E. Evans, 30 Mar 1942, Evans Collection, Imperial War Museum.

12  Commander (later Captain) A. V. S. Yates to R. E. Gillmor (his business associate in New York), 6 Nov 1940. Yates Collection, Imperial War Museum.

13  The whole funny story can be read in the Lord President's Office, 'Clearance of Debris, Labour Requirements For', CAB 123/1 (4 Oct 1940).

14  Diaries of J. P. McHutchison, 7 May 1944, MSS, Imperial War Museum.

15  Diary of Vivienne Hall, entry for 4 Sep 1939, Imperial War Museum.

16  W. H. Haslam to J. Winder, 5 Jan 1941, Haslam Collection, Imperial War Museum.

17  Haslam to Winder, 19 Jan 1941, 9 June 1941.

18  The report entitled 'Morale of Allied Seamen', dated 27 Apr 1942, was circulated to the War Cabinet as W.P. (42)234. The complete file is in the Lord President's Office: 'Morale of Allied Seamen', CAB 123/198.

19  Mass Observation, 'The Mood of Britain—1938 and 1944', by Tom Harrisson, unpublished typescript, file no. 2067 (20 Apr 1944); Mass Observation, *The Journey Home* (1944) p. 19.

20  J. Mackay, 'Archway letter', 8 Apr 1942, Mackay Collection, Imperal War Museum.

21  Mass Observation, 'Report on Changes of Outlook During the War', file no. 2149 (Aug 1944).

22  Letters from Haslam to Winder.

23  Yates to Gillmor, Dec 1942.

24  CAB 75/5/H.P.C.(40), 20th meeting, 18 June 1940.

25  Lord President's Office: 'The Beveridge Report', CAB 123/45. See also Beveridge Papers, VIII, 26–53, British Library of Political and Economic Science.

26  I have discussed this fully in my *Britain in the Century of Total War* (London, 1968), and *War and Social Change in the Twentieth Century* (London, 1974).

27  John Bonham, *The Middle Class Vote* (London, 1954) p. 168.

28  See David Butler, *The Electoral System in Britain* (London, 1963) p. 184.

29  Yates to Gillmor, 28 July 1945.

30  *Chips: The Diaries of Sir Henry Channon*, ed. R. Rhodes James (London, 1967) p. 414.

31  Viscount Kilmuir, *Political Adventure* (London, 1964) p. 138.

32  Doris King to Herbert E. Strong, 28 Oct 1945; Eddie Lawrence to Herbert E. Strong, 23 Dec 1945, H. E. Strong Collection, Imperial War Museum.

33  Lawrence to Strong, 23 Dec 1945.

34  W. G. Runciman, *Relative Deprivation and Social Justice* (London, 1966) p. 77.

35  H.L.G. 30/61.

36  Appendix to *Report on Pensionability of Unestablished Civil Service*, Cmd. 6942 (London, 1946).

37  See note 26 above.

# 9 Journey to the Centre: Churchill and Labour in Coalition, 1940–5

## PAUL ADDISON

In spite of the work of historians on the war years, there is still a powerful myth to the effect that party politics stopped in May 1940 when Churchill became Prime Minister at the head of a Coalition government. We naturally regard the five years which followed as a period when the political world, reflecting the will of the British people, was united by a common purpose—the defeat of the enemy. By and large we are not surprised to learn that politicians and civil servants spent much of the time locked in personal and departmental rivalries, for ambition and rivalry never cease, and indeed thrive in wartime. But it is more difficult to understand these years as a time of rapid party political change, since party warfare was almost entirely suspended. But the co-operation of the Conservative and Labour parties changed British politics far more radically than the shadow-boxing of government and opposition which had gone on since 1931.

After May 1940 the initiative in politics began to pass from the Conservatives to Labour. (The Liberals had an interesting career during the war, but they have been omitted from the present discussion.) The ultimate result was Labour's decisive victory at the general election of 1945, a subject which would involve us in a discussion of propaganda and popular opinion on the home front. But Labour's achievement *during* the war was of equal importance. For Labour, the Churchill Coalition offered the first opportunity of exercising a lasting influence upon social and economic policy from inside the system. The Labour movement as a whole were conscious of the fact that by taking an important part in the war effort, they were also putting themselves in a position to influence the future. They shared with the Conservatives the conviction that the overriding aim of the war was military victory. But they differed from most Conservatives in insisting from the start that the war entailed a secondary purpose: social and economic reform. In the Labour view, the mobilisation of the British for total war was an exercise which itself required new standards of welfare and social justice. The larger purpose of

Labour was to secure, during the war, a commitment from the Conservatives to accept a new basis for peacetime society. The task was all the more urgent since few people in the Labour movement expected a Labour government after the war. Curious as it may seem, the political strategy of Labour was directed less towards post-war power than towards the reformation of the traditional governing class before the war was over.

A minority of Conservatives, like R. A. Butler, or R. M. Barrington-Ward, the editor of *The Times*, favoured a wholehearted response to Labour's demands for reconstruction. They were for grasping the nettle and enunciating a bold forward policy in domestic affairs, perhaps in part to prevent the initiative from passing to the left. The majority of Conservatives, while too intelligent to oppose aspirations for social change on principle, persistently dragged their feet over the question. In the years 1931 to 1940 they had exercised a near-monopoly of power in a society which seemed to expect little from them apart from government as usual and the piecemeal consolidation of social benefits. In wartime they were very conscious of the extent to which victory depended upon the efforts of factory workers and servicemen. With hindsight, there is every reason to assume that the British people would have fought the war just as effectively without the promise of a post-war new deal, which most of them were in any event too sceptical to believe in. But Conservatives at the time felt themselves to be under strong pressure. Popular left-wing broadcasters and lecturers were striving to raise expectations for the future: to puncture entirely the talk of a new Britain was to run an unacceptable risk both to the war effort and the credibility of the Conservative Party. Nor was the problem solely one of trimming Conservative sails to a real or imagined breeze of popular opinion. Organised labour—the trade unions and the Labour party—had to be treated by the Conservatives as a virtual equal in high politics for the duration of the war. Flexibility over reconstruction was essential.

The Conservatives were determined to prevent the introduction of 'socialist' measures—i.e., nationalisation—but they were in no position to resist plans to reform capitalism by attacking poverty and unemployment. Most Conservatives would never have taken the initiative in pushing forward such ideas, for they were set in the mental habits of the 1930s and hardly believed that any major improvement in the social system was possible. In practice they were obliged to accept a major new commitment to improve the efficiency and social standards of capitalism. Above all, they found themselves committed to the maintenance of a high level of employment, and a large expansion of social welfare, including the provision of a National Health Service.

It may seem that the increased bargaining power of the Labour movement in wartime was bound to lead to a result of this kind, on the common-sense assumption that political history moves broadly in step with social development. But the world of high politics depends so much upon the idiosyncrasies and manoeuvres of a handful of leading personalities that nothing is inevitable. Until December 1942, in spite of considerable moral pressure from Labour, social reconstruction was barely beyond the stage of rhetoric and tentative blueprints of uncertain status. Perhaps most of the ideas for post-war Britain would have remained in suspense but for a sustained flight of egotism on the part of one formidable public servant, William Beveridge. The Beveridge report of December 1942, although disguised by its author as a report to the government on social insurance, was a personal manifesto outlining a new relationship between the state and society. It was also a sublime example of political opportunism. Beveridge happened to say the right thing at the right time, in a blaze of publicity which swept the Coalition into a new channel of activity. After Beveridge, a government which had so far been overwhelmingly preoccupied with the war acquired a vigorous, if still secondary, identity as a government of social reform. Indeed, the Coalition initiated the largest programme of change since the heyday of the Liberal Government of 1905–14. Post-war plans acquired a high priority in the administrative machine. The agenda included comprehensive social security, family allowances, the National Health Service, the maintenance of employment, town and country planning, the relations of the state with industry and agriculture, and the acceleration of R. A. Butler's proposals for educational reform: all major questions at the heart of peacetime politics. In all these areas, Labour and Conservative ministers sought to achieve agreement, and in many of the most fundamental aspects they succeeded. By the time of the general election of 1945, the party leaders on both sides were spokesmen for the new consensus which had arisen since 1940. Rhetorically speaking, the election was presented to the public as an argument about the desirability or otherwise of state control over big business. The real disagreement was much narrower, though genuine enough. Perhaps the best index of the gap between Conservative and Labour leaders is the fact that during the war some of them were ready to sink even these differences in the hope of continuing the Coalition into peacetime. The Coalition ended primarily because the rank and file of the Conservative and Labour parties reasserted themselves and obliged their leaders on the front bench to resume partisan behaviour. At the parliamentary level, consensus tends to imply a tacit understanding about the conduct of affairs which unites the government and opposition front benches against the partisan and doctrinaire elements among their supporters. Consensus of this variety reached an apogee as the result of the Second World War. From an abstract point of view, the Coalition was very largely about the permeation of Conservatism by the social and economic aspirations of Labour.

(Perhaps Labour were permeated at the same time by the military and great power attitudes of the Conservatives, but a discussion of this would take us too far afield.) But the Coalition was also about the erosion of party boundaries by friendship, flattery, or mutual esteem. Politicians on opposite sides in peacetime began to understand one another better. As early as March 1941, Churchill told a Conservative Party meeting:

> . . . some of the ties and friendships which are being formed between members of the administration of all parties will not be very easy to tear asunder . . . the comradeship of dangers passed and toils endured in common will for ever exercise an influence upon British national politics far deeper than the shibboleths and slogans of competing partisans.[1]

If the war between Britain and Germany had petered out in the spring of 1940, as some commentators expected, the political scene would hardly have been changed. The Conservatives, with a majority of about 200 in the House, still monopolised power under the thin disguise of a 'National' government. Although the ruling circle of the 1930s had been forced, at the outbreak of war, to invite Churchill into the War Cabinet as First Lord of the Admiralty, the 'old firm' of Chamberlain, Simon, Hoare and Halifax still controlled the machine. The Labour opposition led by Attlee held only 165 seats, to the 402 commanded by the government. The Conservatives would only be compelled to share power with Labour if the war began in earnest.

Early in April 1940 the Germans invaded Denmark and Norway, and the Chamberlain Government replied by mounting an expeditionary force to dislodge the Germans from the ports they had seized on the Norwegian coast. Ever since 1931, when the National Government was formed, its critics had been dreaming of the crisis which would bring it down: the collapse of the British expeditionary force to Norway did the trick. Opposition to the Chamberlain Government came to a head in the parliamentary debate of 7 and 8 May 1940. On the second day of the debate the Labour Party plucked up the courage to challenge a division by opposing the government's motion for the adjournment—thus, in effect, moving a vote of no confidence in Chamberlain's conduct of the war. In the division on 8 May, 40 supporters of the government rebelled and voted with the opposition, while about 36 (so recent research suggests) abstained.[2] After the Munich agreement of September 1938, Chamberlain had triumphed with a majority of 222, which now plummeted to 81, a decisive moral defeat. On all sides the cry went up for a genuinely national government. Chamberlain made feverish efforts to set up a coalition under his own auspices, but Labour had scores to settle with a number of ministers whom they regarded as arch-appeasers of fascism in previous years: Simon, Hoare and Chamberlain himself. Chamberlain was at last forced to resign on 10 May when he received a telephone message from Attlee reporting that Labour would not serve under him. Meanwhile the inner ring of the Conservative Party—Chamberlain, Halifax, Churchill and Margesson the Chief Whip—had decided at a meeting on the previous day that if Chamberlain had to go, Churchill should succeed him. On both the Conservative and Labour front benches, the favoured candidate for the job was Lord Halifax, the high Anglican foreign secretary, a personality who thoroughly lived up to his nickname of the 'holy fox'. Churchill was widely regarded as a brilliant creature flawed by lack of judgement and a reckless streak, a figure more safely employed in the engine-room than as captain of the ship. However, when Churchill asserted his claim, Halifax failed to put in a counter-bid, perhaps through loss of nerve at the last moment. The Labour leaders for their part took no hand in the decision, and made no effort to ensure a Halifax government. In the event, they seemed equally content to accept office under Churchill.

Churchill and Labour had reasons for distrusting each other. There was a legend in the Labour movement, which always has a long memory for grievances, that as Home Secretary in 1910 Churchill had ordered troops to fire on miners who were on strike at Tonypandy in the Rhondda valley. Churchill had in fact authorised the stationing of troops in the valley, but he had also insisted that the handling of rioters should be strictly a matter for the police. However, both at Tonypandy and during the railway strike of 1911, he was open to the charge of seeking to intimidate workers by displays of military force. In the general strike of 1926 Churchill, as Chancellor of the Exchequer in the Baldwin Cabinet, was plainly the most belligerent and melodramatic figure on the government side. Although Churchill and Labour drew together in the late 1930s on the common platform of resistance to Hitler, there remained some feeling that he was a class enemy. After the Munich crisis of September 1938 there were rumours of an arrangement between Churchill and Labour. Ernest Bevin, the General Secretary of the Transport and General Workers Union, issued a vigorous counterblast in his union journal:

> Those who made this suggestion do not understand the Trade Unions, nor do they give us credit for memory.
> Winston Churchill restored the gold standard and upset every wage agreement in the country.
> He was the chief protagonist in starving the miners into submission when he was Chancellor.
> He was the sponsor of the Trade Disputes and the Trade Unions Act of 1927.

He was responsible for breaking the civil servants away from the Trades Union Congress.

He took office in the Baldwin Government on the pledge to reduce Income Tax; to do this he cut down the defences of the country below those fixed by the Labour Government of 1924.

He also raided the reserves of the Approved Societies. Is it any wonder that he makes no appeal to us![3]

At the Labour Party's annual conference in June 1939 the deputy leader of the party, Arthur Greenwood, could still speak of 'the grim figure of Mr. Winston Churchill, the man who tried to beat us in the general strike.' On the very eve of Churchill's premiership in 1940, Attlee is said to have argued that Labour would not accept Churchill because of Tony-pandy.[4] Churchill's record in international affairs also inspired left-wing hostility. He had crossed swords with the Labour movement in 1919–20 by campaigning for increased military intervention against the Bolsheviks. Later he praised Mussolini's achievements in Italy, ridiculed Mahatma Gandhi's crusade for the independence of India, and (striking a most painful Labour nerve) condemned the Republican side in the Spanish Civil War for the licence it gave to Communists and anarchists. After Munich, we find the editor of the *Daily Herald*, Robert Fraser, writing to Hugh Dalton:

> There is only one danger of Fascism, of censorship, the unification of parties, of national 'discipline', and that will come if Chamberlain is overthrown by the Jingoes in his own Party, led by Winston, who will then settle down, with his lousy and reactionary friends, to organise the nation on Fascist principles for a war to settle scores with Hitler.[5]

In spite of the lingering suspicion of him as a sinister Colonel Blimp, Churchill did acquire considerable respect on the left towards the end of the 1930s. From 1936 onwards he linked his championship of a strong line against Germany with a campaign to revive the League of Nations and the Covenant, the lodestars of Labour's foreign policy. To support the campaign there arose an informal private grouping known as 'Focus' which, significantly, included certain Labour M.P.s, the General Secretary of the Trades Union Congress, Sir Walter Citrine, and the editor of the *New Statesman*, Kingsley Martin.[6] By the spring of 1938, Kingsley Martin was canvassing the idea of an anti-appeasement coalition with Churchill as Prime Minister, Eden as Foreign Secretary, and Labour and Liberal representation in the Cabinet. Attlee and Greenwood had been interested in the idea, Martin claimed, and Morrison even more so: 'It was said that Bevin would be willing, if offered the Ministry of Labour.' There was further talk after Munich of a common front between Labour, Churchill and Eden, though once again the idea evaporated. When at last war broke out, and Churchill and Eden entered the Chamberlain Government, Labour regarded their presence in office as the main guarantee against some kind of attempt by the 'men of Munich' to patch up peace with Hitler.

Churchill in the course of his career had said many contemptuous things about the Labour Party. On the eve of the first Labour Government in 1924 he had declared: 'The enthronement in office of a Socialist Government will be a national misfortune such as has usually befallen great states only on the morrow of defeat in war.'[8]

What party politicians say about their opponents, especially in the heat of battle, need not be taken very seriously. Churchill, like all men of the right, affected to regard Labour as a party with some moderate elements which were always in danger of being swamped by extremists. The instincts of the British working man might be sound, but he was liable to be led astray by working-class agitators like Aneurin Bevan, and socialist intellectuals like Sir Stafford Cripps. For the left-wing intelligentsia, with their imported ideas, pacifism and self-questioning introversion, Churchill had a truly Orwellian distaste. But for the mass of manual workers, stoically coping with oppressive conditions and passing their lives in physical toil, he revealed a certain imaginative sympathy, coloured by a vision of the typical working man as a sturdy patriot at heart. As Minister of Munitions in the First World War, Churchill had worked closely with David Kirkwood, a Clydeside shop steward who later became a Labour M.P.—a classic example of the rebel tamed by the embrace of the House of Commons. When Kirkwood published his memoirs in 1935, Churchill contributed a remarkable preface in which he extolled working-class values, rounding off his tribute on a prophetic note:

> David Kirkwood and the strong type he represents are the natural foes of tyranny. Gripped in the iron regimentations of the Continent, they would resist with an indomitable, or at the worst desperate, tenacity. Many of his [Kirkwood's] readers have disapproved of his views and actions in the past, and will probably do so in the future. But should the life and freedom of our race again be called in question we shall find ourselves together heart and hand.[9]

From 1931 to 1935 the Labour Party had been led by the pacifist George Lansbury, and permeated by the revolutionary sayings of Sir Stafford Cripps, who had picked up Marxism as his doctrine of the hour. About 1935 major changes began to work their way through the party. Lansbury was forced to resign, and as Churchill notes in his war history, 'Major Attlee, who had a fine war record, reigned in his stead.'[10] Cripps fell out of step and into the shadows. The bosses of the T.U.C., Bevin and Citrine, began to swing the party towards rearmament, and the scaling down of its domestic programme. In the House, the Labour front bench was fortified by the return of two tough political operators, Dalton and Morrison. As Chamberlain embarked upon the policy of appeasement, Churchill found the Labour leaders increasingly in step with his own views. He began to praise the sturdy responsibility of the trade unions.[11] The working-class patriotism of which he had written in 1935 was marching to the forefront of Labour politics. By 1940 Churchill could trust entirely in Labour's will to win the war.

Perhaps this explains why Churchill gave Labour so much scope within the Coalition when it was set up. (Perhaps, also, Halifax would have done the same: there is no way of telling.) The House of Commons was an overwhelmingly Conservative assembly, but in the War Cabinet the parties were nearly on an equal footing. The five members consisted of Churchill himself, Chamberlain and Attlee as leaders of the Conservative and Labour parties, and the number two figures in each party, Greenwood and Halifax. From the Labour side, Charles Edwards became joint Chief Whip, Morrison Minister of Supply, Dalton Minister of Economic Warfare, A. V. Alexander First Lord of the Admiralty, and William Jowitt Solicitor-General. Churchill personally invited Bevin to become Minister of Labour, necessitating his entry to the House of Commons and thus incidentally providing Labour with a powerful recruit for its parliamentary team.

What was the balance of forces within the Coalition? Arguably, politicians should altogether have forgotten about party claims in this dark hour, leaving selection for office to be decided solely on grounds of personal merit. Churchill's plan was more realistic: a fair division of patronage. Thus there was a Conservative Secretary for War, a Liberal Secretary for Air (Sir Archibald Sinclair), and a Labour First Lord of the Admiralty. In the government as a whole, including junior political offices, Labour began with sixteen jobs and over the period of the war worked their way up to twenty-seven. The Conservatives and their allies, the small National Liberal and National Labour parties, began with fifty-four jobs and ended with fifty-five. The main reason why Labour gained ground was simply that Attlee won a number of junior offices for his side.

In terms of the distribution of *jobs* the Coalition always represented a fair division, given the relative strengths of the parties in the House of Commons. But if we examine the distribution of *power* the story is very different. The flow of power was towards two groups: Churchill, and the circle through which he directed the war; and the politicians of the home front, namely the Labour ministers in conjunction with certain powerful non-party technicians. And by the same token the flow of power was away from the orthodox Conservatives of the 1930s, who were experienced in home affairs. If we look behind the façade of the Coalition of

May 1940 to examine the committee structure, the new pattern of power is already apparent. Churchill, as Prime Minister and Minister of Defence, was Chairman of the Defence Committee, through which he planned to run the war. On the home front there were to be four key committees. As Lord Privy Seal, Attlee was Chairman of the Food and Home Policy committees while Greenwood, as Minister without Portfolio, took the chair of the Production Council and the Economic Policy Committee. The Civil Defence Committee was in the hands of Sir John Anderson, a former civil servant of magisterial mind and pompous demeanour, appointed by Chamberlain as Home Secretary and Minister of Home Security. In the calculations of politicians, Anderson, although personally conservative in outlook, ranked as a non-party functionary holding office as a technical virtuoso. The Conservatives proper had only one committee chairman: the Leader of the party, Chamberlain, was responsible as Lord President for a small steering body designed to co-ordinate the other committees on the home front.[12]

Attlee and Greenwood failed to make a success of their opportunities. Greenwood, overshadowed by a drink problem, was incapable of significant administration: the Production Council met only once a month in the last quarter of 1940, while the Economic Policy Committee dealt with trivia. In January 1941 both committees were abolished, the work of the Production Council being handed over to a production executive under Bevin. Greenwood remained in the War Cabinet in charge of a new committee concerned with reconstruction problems, a relative backwater at that grim period in the war. Again he was unable to take a grip on the proceedings, and in February 1942 Churchill dismissed him. Attlee was hard-working as a committee chairman, but no one regarded him during the war as an impressive or powerful figure. The editor of *The Times*, Barrington-Ward, was sympathetic to Labour, but his reaction to Attlee in March 1942 may be quoted as typical of many: 'He is worthy, but limited. Incredible that he should be where he is. Impossible to discuss any matter of policy with him. He would be too unsure of himself, too doubtful about being given away.'[13]

This was a harsh judgement, for Attlee had his moments, but in the main he owed his position to the fact that he was Leader of the Labour Party. In February 1942 he was made Secretary for Domions and given the title of Deputy Prime Minister, thus authorising him to chair the War Cabinet in Churchill's absence. The reshuffle of September 1943 made him Lord President, so that after all he ended the war as the principal minister in home affairs, though still not regarded as more than a bantam-weight in the political contest.

In effect, Bevin and Morrison came to occupy the place originally reserved for Attlee and Greenwood. Churchill took Bevin into the War Cabinet in October 1940, and Morrison in November 1942. Bevin, as

Alan Bullock's life of him testifies, was a man of wide-ranging mind, sure sense of direction, and massive presence in Cabinet. Always prepared to say what he thought, he was never afraid of precipitating a blazing row. He bore himself as the one true representative of organised labour in the government, and Churchill, seeing in him the working-class John Bull of his imagination, supported Bevin's pretensions and treated his opinions with especial deference and care.[14] Churchill and Bevin had in common an authoritarian streak which led them to agree on the imposition of conscription in Ulster (a folly prevented by the War Cabinet), the suppression of the *Daily Mirror* for creating despondency (also averted), and the putting down of the Communist-inspired resistance movement in Greece. But the main reason for Bevin's power was his success in building up the Ministry of Labour into a key factor in the war effort. He won for his department the exclusive right to find and supply manpower for industry and the services alike. As manpower became the critical scarce resource in the economy, the task of allocating labour for different purposes assumed central importance, and by the end of 1941 the chief instrument of economic policy was the 'manpower budget'. The budget was framed by Bevin in close collaboration with Sir John Anderson, the Lord President. The Treasury had slipped into the background: Bevin and Anderson were virtually joint dictators of a planned economy.[15]

Herbert Morrison was not a success in his first office as Minister of Supply. But in October 1940 Churchill appointed him Home Secretary and Minister of Home Security. As Home Secretary Morrison was responsible for law and order and (a delicate political issue in wartime), civil liberty. As Minister of Home Security it was his job to end the chaos in the organisation of the Civil Defence services laid bare in the first blitz on London, and to maintain the morale of the population in bombed areas. These were big responsibilities but Morrison shouldered them successfully, drawing upon his greatest gifts—an understanding of the common touch, a genius for organisation, and the know-how of a practised wire-puller and fixer. There was indeed little personal *rapport* between Churchill and Morrison, the dashing Hussar from Blenheim and the blackcoat ex-pacifist from Brixton. They sometimes clashed. But Churchill told one trade union leader that Morrison's mind was the best of all the Labour ministers in the government. Morrison for his part was somewhat in awe of the Prime Minister. Under pressure from Churchill in November 1943, he released from internment the British Fascist leader, Sir Oswald Mosley. In serving his master, Morrison was taking on the entire Labour movement, which erupted into organised protest.[16] His reputation in the Labour Party suffered a considerable setback.

The two other important Labour ministers were Hugh Dalton, especially after he was moved to the Board of Trade in February 1942 and became involved in home affairs, and Tom Johnston, appointed by

Churchill as Secretary of State for Scotland in February 1941. Johnston is still regarded in Scotland as the most successful of all holders of the office. Alone among Labour ministers he was in a position to initiate a broad programme of reconstruction, which he organised by setting up a Scottish version of the Coalition—a Council of State composed of all living ex-secretaries of state. One of Johnston's tactics was to lecture the War Cabinet on the dangers of Scottish nationalism unless more help was given to Scotland.[17] Whatever his method, he turned the war to Scotland's advantage as well as Scotland to the advantage of the war: a depressed country was given a new lease of industrial prosperity.

Sir Stafford Cripps, we have to recall, had been expelled from the Labour Party before the outbreak of war, and did not rejoin it until early in 1945. From May 1940 until the New Year of 1942 he was out of politics altogether, as British Ambassador in Moscow. Returning to Britain, he enjoyed an inflated reputation as a champion of Russia, and was even supposed to have brought Russia into the war (Hitler could claim the credit for this). Entering the War Cabinet, he was Lord Privy Seal from February to November 1942, but after quarrelling with Churchill over the central direction of the war, he was demoted to the Ministry of Aircraft Production, where he remained for the rest of the war. Cripps sometimes aligned himself with his Labour ex-colleagues, but there is good evidence to show that at the height of his influence in 1942 he believed that both main parties were out of date and would have to give way to a progressive centre grouping.[18] He was therefore not a direct element in Labour's strength. But it is fair to say that his social and economic ideas chimed well with those of Labour ministers and in this sense reinforced Labour's position.

The personal relations among Labour ministers were not very satisfactory. Morrison had a poor opinion of Attlee as a leader; Bevin consistently ran a vendetta against Morrison. When Beaverbrook was asked by Lord Halifax in the spring of 1942 what relations were like between Attlee and Bevin, he replied: 'Oh, very good indeed—like two high and distant mountain peaks, and both with snow on them.'[19] But in spite of these problems, Labour were an effective force within the Coalition. The same was true on a broader front. The Labour movement—the left-wing intelligentsia, the constituency activists, the trade union organisers—were an army torn by quarrels, but nonetheless advancing. In the 1930s they had been relative outsiders in public life. In wartime they formed a kind of proto-Establishment on the march, pitching their tents far inside Conservative territory. If it was their duty to share in the organisation of the war effort, it was also their chance to build up the left.

Even at the grassroots, the war broke up the Conservatives' influence in small ways. The Ministry of Information had encouraged the setting up of local information committees, voluntary bodies run by town clerks, trade unionists, newspaper editors, local politicians and so forth. There was considerable friction between these committees, which often regarded themselves as representative of the area, and local M.P.s, especially when the M.P. was a Conservative. The M.P. for Oxford, Quintin Hogg, asked the Minister of Information in October, 1940:

> whether his attention has been drawn to a public speech in Oxford by Mr. A. J. P. Taylor, a member of the local Information Committee appointed by the Ministry of Information, to the effect that a withdrawal from Egypt would not be a major disaster; and whether he is prepared to take steps to prevent members of committees from committing themselves to irresponsible public statements . . .[20]

After a tour of the regions early in 1941, Nicolson reported that local information committees were often exploiting the opportunity to discredit and undermine Conservative M.P.s, who were particularly angry when prominent left-wing speakers were invited to address meetings.

For several reasons, among them the need to keep the public informed about the progress of the war, and the idea that lectures and discussions were good for morale, the progressive intelligentsia of the 1930s came into their own at the height of the war effort as quasi-official publicists. They began to work for the B.B.C., the Ministry of Information, and the adult education service in the forces, the latter being greatly expanded in 1941 with the setting up of the Army Bureau of Current Affairs, a scheme whereby officers were to lead their men in weekly discussions of the war and world affairs. Whether as radicals or socialists, the intelligentsia were active in propagating the assumption that the social system of the 1930s had in certain respects failed, and ought to be reformed or replaced. The first of the wartime prophets to create an impact was of course the Yorkshire novelist and playwright J. B. Priestley, in his series of broadcast Sunday evening 'postscripts' in the summer and autumn of 1940. Other prominent figures in the movement were Ritchie Calder, Harold Laski, Julian Huxley and Cyril Joad. George Orwell summed up the change when he wrote:

> The British Government started the present war with the more or less openly declared intention of keeping the literary intelligentsia out of it; yet after three years almost every writer, however undesirable his political history or opinions, has been sucked into the various ministries or the BBC and even those who enter the armed forces tend to find themselves after a while in public relations or some other essentially literary job . . . No one acquainted with the Government pamphlets, Army Bureau of Current Affairs lectures, documentary film and broadcasts to occupied countries which have been issued during the

past two years can imagine that our rulers would sponsor this kind of thing if they could help it.[21]

The Establishment was becoming bipartisan. As the literary left tumbled in at one door, the trade unionists were pouring in at another. The general secretary of the T.U.C., Sir Walter Citrine, built up his organisation into almost an auxiliary department of state. Ever anxious to reinforce the principle (conceded by Chamberlain in October 1939) that Whitehall departments should take the trade unions into consultation whenever necessary, Citrine was vigorous in obtaining trade union representation on government commissions and committees. A Treasury official complained to the Prime Minister's office in January 1945:

> He is always prone to claim that the T.U.C. have a right to be represented as such on these bodies. Ministers often wish to constitute them not on a representative basis. Even when they are not on this basis the T.U.C. may have no claim to representation as compared with other bodies. For example, they have claimed that where consumers' interests are to be represented they ought to be asked to nominate. Several Ministers have specifically rejected this claim.
>
> Even where it is not a question of representation, Citrine tends to insist on the nomination, i.e., he will not put forward two or three names for the Minister to choose from but puts forward only as many names as there are vacancies and insists that those names and no others should be accepted.[22]

Naturally enough, Labour politicians also wished to push forward their own nominees. As Home Secretary and Minister of Home Security, Herbert Morrison saw to the appointment of at least a dozen Labour men, including a number who were to be prominent politicians after the war, in the regional offices of the Civil Defence organisation.[23] As leader of the parliamentary party, it fell to Attlee to protect Labour's interests in the government. One day in February 1942 Dalton asked Attlee whether there was to be another reshuffle. Attlee replied: 'Oh yes, we are going to get rid of some more of these bloody Tories!'[24]

The Labour movement comprised many shades of opinion. While all were agreed that the war had a progressive character, they differed wildly about the measure of change which was to be expected. In particular there was a gulf between the socialist intelligentsia, who at first regarded the fall of France and the battle of Britain as harbingers of the millenium, and the practical politicians, who assessed the prospects for useful gains in the short or medium term.

Millenarian expectations are too easy to mock in retrospect, when the excitements of the hour have died away. We know now that although France collapsed in 1940, a France recognisably the same was restored after 1945; that although large parts of London perished in the blitz, a more ugly and disenchanting London was to spring up again. A thoroughly sober realist might have foreseen all this at the time, but anyone of imagination found it hard to remain intellectually sober. The old world, like Humpty Dumpty, seemed to be crashing down, and it was difficult to imagine how it would be put together again. Few escaped disorientation. One day in June 1940 even the War Cabinet, overwhelmed by the collapse of France, packed their bags for a new world. They proposed an indissoluble union of Britain and France as one nation with a common constitution and joint citizenship, a vision as illusory as the social revolution anticipated by left-wing commentators. The socialist illusion derived from the belief, fostered during the 1930s by the world slump and the rise of Fascism, that an inherent contradiction between capitalism and the needs of the masses had precipitated European civil war. Fascism represented the last-ditch attempt of capitalism to protect itself by force and repression. The rise of class conflict was everywhere rendering the old compromise of liberal democracy out of date: even in Britain the choice would have to be made between socialism and Fascism. The Second World War was bound to develop into a socialist counter-revolution against Hitler and Mussolini, for only the power of the working classes could liberate Europe. Britain, therefore, must range herself on the side of a European revolution, thus completing on the Continent the work which the Bolsheviks had begun in 1917. The British working classes would themselves have to take the lead, commanded and inspired by—the Labour party. These views were the common coin of the left, but their chief exponent was undoubtedly Professor Harold Laski, a member of the National Executive of the Labour Party. Laski argued that Labour could achieve during the war a 'revolution by consent'. The theory was that the governing classes would be forced to recognise the necessity of mobilising the British working classes, without whose aid they would be defeated. According to Laski, whose grasp of political reality was slender, the British worker would only put his full weight behind the war effort if he knew he was working for a socialist Britain. Hence it followed that Churchill himself, rather than lose the war, would accept a substantial instalment of socialism. At the end of May 1940, when British attention was riveted upon the fate of the British Expeditionary Force at Dunkirk, Laski was calling in the *Daily Herald* for a declaration of British war aims:

> Labour is fighting for victory for a new Britain, it is not fighting for Tory Britain. The justification of the sacrifice it makes—and let us be clear that Herbert Morrison and Ernest Bevin have called for great sacrifices—lies in great measures of social reform now.
>
> In education, in old age pensions, in workmen's compensation, in

the restoration of trade union rights taken away vengefully in 1927, there is room for measures now which prove that the governing class of Britain recognises that victory depends upon the effort of the working class.[25]

The Labour leaders regarded Laski as a doctrinaire—a significant figure at party conferences, but a liability in the corridors of power. Dalton recorded in his diary during the battle of Britain:

I preside at a meeting of the Labour Party Policy Committee, when little Laski has a bad time from several of our Trade Union members. He has produced an academic little paper urging that, in order to raise the morale of the people, the Bank of England and the land should be nationalised. It is replied that, whatever the arguments in favour of this may be—and they are well known to all of us—raising morale is not one of them. This is better done by Air Force victories, by full employment, by better dependant's allowances, by improvements in Workmen's Compensation, and by modification of the Means Test. He goes away with his little tail between his little legs.[26]

Dalton's words are useful to dwell upon. The Labour leaders refused to accept a doctrinaire package labelled 'revolution by consent', which they would then have to lay upon the War Cabinet table. As practical politicians, they knew it was better to take one issue at a time, arguing each point on its merits when the moment was ripe. They also judged that wage-earners would respond to material incentives rather than symbolic measures of nationalisation. But in many respects they *accepted*, in a pragmatic way, arguments which Laski presented in undigestible, theoretical form. The activities of Labour ministers between May 1940 and November 1942, the uphill phase of the war effort, reveal three rule-of-thumb assumptions of great significance. Firstly, the working classes deserved better treatment both for the sake of raising their morale, and for the sake of greater social justice. Secondly, the state-directed wartime economy was not merely an emergency apparatus, but an opportunity for the vindication of Labour policies. The third assumption grew naturally out of the first two: the war was not to be understood as a military event alone, but as a chapter in the rise of Labour. This time Labour must use its leverage in the war effort to insist upon pledges of social reconstruction, and thus obtain the 'fit country for heroes to live in' which had been promised by Lloyd George in 1918.

At the very moment when Labour were becoming a coherent force with definite aims on the home front, the Conservatives were poorly organised and on the defensive. Perhaps the main reason why they lost ground was the simple one: having monopolised power, they were now obliged to share it. But they also appeared to go to pieces at the same time. They were in difficulties at a number of levels, not least of all at the top. Stanley Baldwin and Neville Chamberlain had in different ways been strong party leaders, acutely aware of problems of organisation and strategy. In October 1940 Chamberlain was succeeded as Leader of the party by Churchill. Although a Conservative by temperament, Churchill had kicked over the party traces on a number of occasions in the past, had no reason to love the party which had cold-shouldered him in the late 1930s, and was too absorbed in the war to regard the party as much more than a convenient vehicle for his triumph. His intimate circle were as deficient in solid party sentiment as himself. His closest advisers were the proprietor of the *Daily Express*, Lord Beaverbrook, a figure widely detested among Conservatives, but introduced into the government as Minister of Aircraft Production in May 1940; Churchill's mysterious acolyte Brendan Bracken, owner of the *Financial News*, who became Minister of Information in 1941; and the Oxford scientist Professor F. A. Lindemann, the head of the Prime Minister's statistical section. (Lindemann was made Lord Cherwell in 1941 and took office as Paymaster-General at the end of 1942.) All three owed their wartime influence exclusively to Churchill's favour. None of them had worked his way up through the Conservative ranks. None was even English by origin: they had rocketed into the governing circle from beginnings in New Brunswick (Beaverbrook), County Tipperary (Bracken) and Alsace-Lorraine (Lindemann). To all of them, Conservative politics were at best a wartime hobby, useful to their master. When the party was defeated in 1945, Beaverbrook and Bracken returned to Fleet Street, Lindemann to Oxford. From 1922 to 1940 the Conservatives had been managed by a tightly-knit oligarchy with green fingers in domestic politics. After 1940 they were discredited as the 'guilty men' who (supposedly) had neglected rearmament and bungled foreign policy. There was no new circle to take their place as a Conservative high command, apart from the eccentric court of Churchill himself. In 1941 the Chairman of the party, Douglas Hacking, confided privately that he seldom saw Churchill, who would take advice only from his mysterious personal entourage. In March 1942 the right-wing journalist Collin Brooks happened to meet both Hacking, and the incoming party Chairman, Thomas Dugdale, for lunch. Brooks noted in his diary: 'Both agreed that Winston is a difficult leader, and is not a Conservative at all, or even, perhaps, by normal standards a statesman—being a creature of 'Palace' favourites, of moods and whims and over-riding egotism under his charm and geniality. Dugdale is fearful of what Max Beaverbrook may do . . .'[27]

To some extent the Conservatives were weak because they were simply absent: 136 Conservative M.P.s were usually away on active service (which was true of only fourteen Labour M.P.s), and no fewer than 246 Conservative constituency agents were with the forces. The Conservatives who remained were ineffectual partly because circumstances were so much against them. The Conservative magazine *The Onlooker* buzzed with complaints about the volume of left-wing propaganda in the speeches of Labour ministers, the broadcasts of J. B. Priestley, and so forth. But what could be done about it? The Conservatives could have tried to reply, but they had nothing attractive to say, and no one to say it for them. When Conservatives wrote to Churchill complaining about the speeches of Labour ministers, he replied that the political parties were still free to express their ideas.[28] When Priestley returned to the air in January 1941 and called for a declaration of British war aims, Churchill was angry, and wrote to the Minister of Information, Duff Cooper:

> I am very sorry you have got Mr. J. B. Priestley back, and that his first broadcast should have been an argument utterly contrary to my known views. How many more has he got to do? Have you any control over what he says? He is far from friendly to the Government, and I should not be too sure about him on larger issues.[29]

Nonetheless, Priestley completed his series. The limitations of Churchill's authority were demonstrated when he issued a minute instructing that the Army Bureau of Current Affairs should be wound up: nothing happened. Perhaps the Conservatives would have had more impact had they been led clearly in any particular direction. But Churchill alternated between Whig sympathy with a progressive policy at home, and moods of impatient reaction. A disgruntled Conservative M.P. summed up the party's situation in a letter to the Chief Whip in October 1942:

> Throughout the country the Conservative Party has become a cheap joke; the press and the BBC treat us with the contempt that we have earned and deserve.
>
> You yourself are well aware of what the P.M. thinks of the Tory Rump: he may not say so himself, but R. C. [Randolph Churchill] B.B. [Bracken] and his other satellites are not so careful of their tongues.
>
> You must agree with the fact that as an effective body of opinion either in the House or the Country, the Conservative Party have ceased to exist.[30]

Churchill was fairly negligent about the promotion of a Conservative voice in home affairs. Attlee tried in vain to persuade him that the Foreign Secretary, Anthony Eden, who displayed considerable sympathy for social reform, should be given a job in domestic affairs. When Churchill moved R. A. Butler from the junior post at the Foreign Office in 1941, he wanted him to take a diplomatic post abroad: only on Butler's insistence did he appoint him Minister of Education. In September 1943 the office of Chancellor of the Exchequer fell vacant with the death of the Conservative, Kingsley Wood. There was an obvious Conservative candidate for the job in the person of Oliver Lyttelton, who was also a close friend of Churchill. Instead, Churchill called Lyttelton to the telephone to explain that Sir John Anderson would be much distressed if he were not appointed: 'Having started life as a civil servant', Churchill said, 'it would crown his career to be head of the Treasury.'[31]

The origins of the Coalition programme of reconstruction can be traced back to the period after Dunkirk. At first the question was largely one of rhetoric and propaganda. In the summer of 1940 the War Cabinet discussed the need for a counterstroke to Nazi propaganda, which had begun to proclaim a 'new order' in Europe. A War Aims committee was set up to devise a statement of the domestic and international objects for which Britain was fighting. The committee's terms of references included the following hint of a post-war Coalition: 'To consider means of perpetuating the national unity achieved in this country during the war through a social and economic structure designed to secure equality of opportunity and service among all classes of the community.' The life of the committee was brief, gaseous, and inconclusive. Harold Nicolson eventually drew up a statement proposing federalism abroad and social reform at home, but Churchill turned it down in January 1941 on the grounds that 'precise aims would be compromising, whereas vague principles would disappoint.'[32]

While social reconstruction was thus barred from the front door, it crept in through various side entrances. The presence of Labour in the government was often decisive in encouraging changes. When Reith became Minister of Works in October 1940, Attlee and Bevin played a part in securing for him some responsibility for post-war town and country planning—a decision from which much was to flow later in the war.[33] The rhetoric employed by Labour ministers was also significant in creating that mysterious entity, a 'climate of opinion' in Whitehall. Attlee struck a typical note when he declared, in the New Year of 1941: 'We are never going to move back to pre-war 1939. We have got to move forward to a new world.' At the same moment the deputy Secretary at the Board of Education, R. S. Wood, observed in a note on post-war educational policy:

There are straws to be found in Cabinet papers and elsewhere which indicate the way the wind is blowing, and we may assume that responsibility for the direction of the nation's effort in the immediate post-war years will remain in the hands of a National Government prepared to face radical changes in our social and economic system and contemplating not merely restoration or a return to normality, but reconstruction in a very real sense . . .

While policies will have to command the support of the main elements in all parties, it is clear that the war is moving us more and more in the direction of Labour's ideas and ideals, and the planning for a national 'New Order' will be more towards the Left than may generally be imagined now.[34]

The drive for a new education bill began in earnest with the appointment of R. A. Butler to the Board of Education in July 1941. One of the curious features of the movement for reconstruction is that although Labour aspirations set the guidelines, and the political muscle of Labour ensured that action would eventually be taken, no Labour minister with the exception of Dalton produced detailed proposals himself. The Labour ministers were too busy: Reith, Butler, Beveridge and the Keynesian economists produced the plans as if by a tacit understanding that Labour would champion them. Butler, for instance, in drafting proposals to bring about secondary education for all schoolchildren, was implementing a policy which Labour had campaigned for in the 1920s, and the Conservatives rejected as impractical. Much was contributed to the new bill by Ernest Bevin, and according to Butler's Parliamentary Secretary, the Labour ex-schoolteacher James Chuter Ede, it was largely because of Bevin's support that the bill was passed during the war.[35]

Although Churchill had vetoed a statement about war aims, discussion on the subject continued. Bevin made an important speech in November 1940 in which he said: 'I suggest that at the end of this war, and indeed during the war, we accept social security as the main motive of our national life.' The phrase 'social security' quickly passed into general currency. The great economist John Maynard Keynes, who now occupied a room at the Treasury, used it in a draft of war aims which the Ministry of Information had requested from him. The Foreign Secretary, Anthony Eden, spoke of social security as an important allied war aim in a speech of May 1941. When Roosevelt and Churchill met later that month to draw up the Atlantic Charter, a statement of Anglo-American aims for the future of the world, the War Cabinet under Attlee's chairmanship asked for a clause on social security to be inserted.[36] The government were now committed to the principle. Largely by accident, it was taken up by a formidable personality who managed to translate it into a broad and irresistible demand for reform.

William Beveridge was a distinguished public servant of great eminence and vanity. But although he had great experience of high administration, and had been Permanent Secretary of the Ministry of Food at the end of the First World War, he had left the Civil Service in

1919. In Whitehall during the Second World War, he was an over-mighty figure with no fixed place in the system, but commissioned to carry out various inquiries into the war effort. Early in 1941 the T.U.C. approached Greenwood, who was responsible for reconstruction, to call for an inquiry into the anomalies of the existing pattern of social insurance benefits. The various schemes of insurance had grown up in piecemeal fashion, and obviously required ironing out into a uniform scheme. Beveridge at this point was a temporary civil servant at the Ministry of Labour, much to the chagrin of Bevin, who disliked him and wanted him out of the way. Bevin therefore telephoned Greenwood and suggested that Beveridge be put in charge of the Committee on Social Insurance. As Alan Bullock explains:

> The last thing Bevin or anyone else expected was that Beveridge's investigation would produce not just a technical report on social insurance, but a new declaration of human rights brought up to date for an industrial society and dealing in plain and vigorous language with some of the most controversial issues in British politics.[37]

Greenwood and Beveridge were lost souls together, debarred by their colleagues from the limelight. Their recovery was dramatic. Greenwood was the first to see the potential of the committee. No sooner was Beveridge appointed than Greenwood began to predict that sweeping changes were to be expected. He alerted the press, and repeated the story in a broadcast to the United States. Beveridge, however, initially regarded the committee as an unrewarding chore: perhaps it was his secretary and future wife, Janet Mair, who persuaded him that it presented a golden opportunity. On 11 December 1941, a few days after the Japanese attack on Pearl Harbor, Beveridge circulated to his officials the outline of a set of major proposals. Social insurance would henceforth be reorganised to achieve the goal of which the Webbs had dreamed before 1914: a national minimum. Equally important were the assumptions which Beveridge claimed must necessarily be attached to the insurance scheme—a National Health Service, family allowances, and the maintenance of employment, all major innovations. Warming to the task, he prepared to offer a still more comprehensive vision. By July 1942 he had discovered that want, the main subject of his labours, was only one of 'five giants to be destroyed—Want, Disease, Ignorance, Squalor and Idleness.'[38] By this time Greenwood had lost his job in the government, a casualty of the reshuffle of February 1942. Beveridge, however, displayed an equal talent for handling the press. Gradually, he rehearsed and tuned up the Fleet Street orchestra, ready for the moment when the curtain should rise to reveal the report to the public.

The Beveridge report was published on 2 December 1942. By 18

February 1943 the government had accepted the great majority of its recommendations and established a high-powered reconstruction priorities committee to plan the peace. Historians have discussed this celebrated turning-point in some detail, and are generally in agreement about their findings.[39] The Cabinet records and other newly available material have tended to sharpen the picture of a division between Conservative and Labour. Before the report's publication, the Chancellor of the Exchequer, Sir Kingsley Wood, produced for Churchill a memorandum which raised such a large number of objections as to amount to a complete rejection. He wrote:

> Many in this country have persuaded themselves that the cessation of hostilities will mark the opening of the Golden Age (many were so persuaded last time also). However this may be, the time for declaring a dividend on the profits of the Golden Age is the time when those profits have been realised in fact, not merely in imagination.[40]

After the publication of the report it was no longer feasible to take such a negative line. It so happened that the report appeared within a few days of the battle of El Alamein, and the successful Anglo-American invasion of north Africa. For people in Britain it was as though the fog of defeat had suddenly lifted to disclose the high road to victory running clear ahead: and there, like a mirage on the horizon, was the promise of social security for all contained in the Beveridge report. The fanfare of welcome which the report received from most of the press, and the evidence of its stunning popularity, made it impossible to reject out of hand.

So much has been written about the Beveridge affair that instead of rehearsing the story it may be more useful to cut briskly through to the implications for party politics. Beveridge's proposals, though put forward by a non-party figure (it was later that Beveridge joined the Liberals), were in effect Labour policy, recently endorsed at the 1942 Labour Party conference.[41] But Labour stalwarts had been passing resolutions with no effect since the dawn of the century. They received the Beveridge report rather as we may imagine a man who has spent forty years doing the football pools receives a cheque for a sum beyond his dreams. His first reaction is to bank the cheque at once, before it vanishes in front of his eyes, or the pools company discover that they have made a mistake. Overwhelmed with gratitude, Labour were also profoundly apprehensive that the Tories would sabotage the plan. Beveridge was not in fact proposing a redistribution of income from rich to poor, merely a scheme whereby the working classes (and the middle classes too) pooled their risks. But the rates of benefit proposed looked like a substantial workers' windfall, a prize to be secured while the time was ripe. In the War Cabinet, Attlee and Morrison argued eloquently for immediate action committing the government to the report; at the grassroots, Labour activists demanded:

'Beveridge Now!'

The Conservative response to the Beveridge report takes us at once to the heart of modern Conservatism. Churchill and the majority of Conservatives at first distrusted the Beveridge plan, but once obliged to accept it as a fact of life they embraced it and sought to turn it to advantage. Disraeli had said of Sir Robert Peel that he 'caught the Whigs bathing and walked away with their clothes.' In 1952 Aneurin Bevan observed, in more contemporary vein: 'Capitalism proudly displays medals won in the battles it has lost.'[42] The Conservatives were too astute to blunder into outright opposition to the report, but initially they deployed three main arguments to weaken it. Firstly they said that Britain had a limited taxable capacity: there would be many claims on the exchequer after the war, of which the most important was defence. Whether Britain could afford the report was therefore a matter of sorting out priorities. Secondly they argued that Britain would depend for its prosperity after the war upon the profitability of industry, particularly the export trades. In consequence, any extra burden of taxation on industry like the increased employers' contributions to social insurance would lead to high costs and unemployment. Thirdly, the national minimum would be bad for the British character, acting as an incentive to spongers and idlers who would prefer to live off the state than do an honest day's work.

All these objections gradually withered into insignificance. When the Beveridge report was debated in February 1943 it appeared for the moment that the Conservatives had succeeded in frustrating the project. Government spokesmen, following the line laid down by Churchill beforehand, announced that although they accepted most of Beveridge's proposals in principle, they could not commit themselves to legislation or to the expenditure involved. The final decision would remain open for the first post-war government to take or leave.

In practice the Beveridge band wagon was unstoppable. Churchill and his advisers realised that in view of the popularity of the report, scepticism was not enough. In March 1943 Churchill devoted a broadcast for the first time to social reconstruction, promising the working out of a four-year plan to be ready when the war was over. This oration, with its broad prospectus for the future incongruously expressed in Churchillian vocabulary, marked the virtual fusion of the parties in domestic affairs. Before Beveridge, reconstruction was a twilight zone inhabited mainly by failures, journalists and intellectuals. After Beveridge, important people began to devote their time to the subject. A break occurs in the sequence of Cabinet records early in 1943, with serious high-level committees beginning to prepare plans for social insurance, family allowances, a National Health Service, the maintenance of employment, and the location of industry. In December 1943 Lord

Woolton, a philanthropic businessman who had made a great success of the Ministry of Food, was appointed by Churchill as Minister of Reconstruction. At the same time he was made Chairman of a new reconstruction committee of the Cabinet which comprised four Conservatives (Lyttelton, Butler, Crookshank and Cherwell), four Labour ministers (Attlee, Bevin, Morrison and Jowitt) and Sir John Anderson.

Just as Churchill confided the home front to Labour in 1940, so he was content to award them the lion's share of post-war planning from 1943. For most of the time he neither knew, nor greatly cared, what was happening in the Reconstruction Committee. One of the great landmarks of recent history is the 1944 White Paper on Employment Policy, in which the government committed itself to maintain a high and stable level of employment. This document was the subject of lengthy discussion by the Reconstruction Committee before it reached the War Cabinet in May 1944. When it did so, Churchill had neither read it, nor a memorandum which Lord Cherwell had prepared to guide him: but as he had read the first sentence of Cherwell's paper, which recommended the White Paper, he was content to see it approved.[43] Sometimes Churchill suspected that Labour were getting too much of their own way in the Reconstruction Committee. He once drafted a letter (apparently not sent) in which he told Attlee:

A solid mass of four Socialist politicians of the highest quality and authority, three of whom are in the War Cabinet, all working together as a team, very much dominates this Committee . . .

I feel very much the domination of these Committees [Churchill was referring also to the Lord President's Committee] by the force and power of your representatives, when those members who come out of the Conservative quota are largely non-Party or have little political experience or Party views.[44]

When proposals from the Reconstruction Committee were ready for decision by the War Cabinet, Churchill would sometimes cast a spanner into the works by obtaining a second opinion from Beaverbrook and Bracken, a practice of which Attlee complained in a stinging letter:

The conclusions agreed upon by a Committee on which have sat five or six members of the Cabinet and other experienced Ministers are then submitted with great deference to the Lord Privy Seal [Beaverbrook] and the Minister of Information [Bracken], two Ministers without Cabinet responsibility neither of whom has given any serious attention to the subject. When they state their views it is obvious that they know nothing about it. Nevertheless an hour is consumed in listening to their opinions.[45]

Churchill and Labour had their quarrels from time to time, but these were less akin to party strife than to disputes within a marriage. When Attlee was asked whether there had been disagreements between Churchill and himself during the war he replied: 'I remember we had a bit of a talk one night about India. We used a few words. Quite all right in the morning.'[46] In spite of his grumbles, Churchill never overturned decisions of the Reconstruction Committee, or challenged the powerful position which he had conferred on Labour in this sphere. More likely he thought the Reconstruction Committee was a useful rehearsal for continuing the Coalition into peace, an option which politicians considered fairly seriously from time to time.

In January 1941 Lord Halifax noted after a talk with Morrison: 'He does not look forward immediately to getting back to party fighting after the war.'[47] Greenwood hinted at a post-war coalition in a speech in June, and in August Halifax found that Churchill was also turning over the idea in his mind: 'He discussed very freely the pros and cons of trying to get a common programme with Labour, and said with evident sincerity that he would be in a much stronger position than L.G. had been in 1918.'[48] As has been pointed out, Cripps was also thinking of a cross-party combination—but in his version it would be led by Cripps.

Churchill reopened the discussion in his reconstruction broadcast of March 1943, suggesting that his four-year plan could be presented to the country at a general election 'either by a National Government, formally representative, as this one is, of the three parties in the State, or by a National Government comprising the best men in all parties who are willing to serve.'[49] Something of a veil has been drawn over the lively interest in a post-war coalition displayed in 1943–4 by Attlee, Bevin, Dalton and Morrison. Morrison actively propagated a scheme whereby all three parties would campaign on a basic agreed programme, pledged to reform the Coalition after the election, but allowing party contests in the constituencies so that voters could decide which party's representation would be strengthened.[50] The main reason, of course, why Labour ministers wanted to go on with the government was their conviction that a return to party politics would mean a sweeping victory for Churchill at the head of the Conservative Party. In the midst of the fruits of office and achievement, they would be cast out again into the wilderness. Needless to say, Labour backbenchers and the rank and file of the Labour movement looked at matters differently. There was never a genuine possibility of continuing the Coalition after the war, or of reforming it after a general election: neither the Labour nor the Conservative parties were prepared to tolerate the frustration of their main purpose by a handful of ministerialists. But the talk of coalition at the top is indicative of the mutual understanding which had developed there.

On the Conservative side, Eden, Halifax, and the leaders of the back-bench Tory Reform Committee were all supporters of a post-war coalition. Halifax told Dalton in September 1943 that it would be very dangerous for the Tories to hold power on their own after the war. The economic and financial situation would soon be so bad that they would be 'violently swept out again.'[51] Not long before D-Day, Eden and Bevin discussed the idea. Bevin said that if Churchill were to retire, he would be happy to work with Eden: 'He would not care which office either of us held. I replied, "Neither would I".' Bevin said the coalmines would have to be nationalised. General Smuts, hearing of this from Eden, commented: 'cheap at the price.'[52]

The Tory Reformers felt isolated in the Conservative Party, and believed they would lose such influence as they had if the party regained a monopoly of power. Lord Winterton, a member of the group, explained to Dalton in May 1943 that the Tory reformers

> are determined to hold in check the reactionary elements in their Party. They would be quite prepared for a continuance of controls [wartime controls over private industry and commerce], for much state action and some state ownership, if we could agree to a strong defence and Empire development policy. I said I thought there would be little difficulty on these last. We, particularly the Trade Union leaders, were most firm now upon defence.[53]

Churchill was usually for a post-war coalition, but sometimes against. Bracken and Beaverbrook both favoured the restoration of an independent Conservatism with fire in its belly—in other words the rapid post-war liberation of private industry from state control, and a swift return to the market economy. By playing on Churchill's more reactionary instincts they sometimes worked him up to a state of partisan belligerence. More often, he liked to feel that he was above party, and would unite the British in peacetime as he had during the war. In his memoirs he wrote of his feelings in May 1945, when the Coalition was about to break up: 'I was myself deeply distressed at the prospect of sinking from a national to a party leader.'[54] After October 1944, when the Labour Party issued a statement announcing that it would fight the next general election as an independent party, leading politicians seem to have realised that a post-war coalition was no longer on the cards. Conservative and Labour partisans united in proclaiming that a great issue separated the parties, and that only an election could resolve it. Labour activists urged that the system of wartime controls over industry should be maintained after the war and consolidated by measures of nationalisation, thus establishing a planned socialist economy. As has already been mentioned, the Conservative cry was for a free enterprise crusade. The Coalition was not immune from these tensions, but working politicians knew that in practice a middle way was being found. Halifax and Eden in partnership with

Bevin and Morrison would have worked out a compromise if allowed to do so: fortunately for the health of British politics, party feeling reasserted itself. When the Coalition was about to dissolve in May 1945, Churchill determined on a last effort to hold it together. The war with Germany was over. Churchill invited Labour to continue in office until the defeat of Japan, which it was then estimated would take another year to eighteen months. Churchill's offer was not a tactical manoeuvre designed to show Labour in a bad light when they refused to maintain national unity, but a *bona fide* invitation which he hoped and expected Labour would accept. President Truman had sent him a telegram urging resistance to the designs of General Tito, the Yugoslav Communist leader, on Trieste. Churchill was anxious to fight the Cold War as a national leader, writing to Eden: 'If there is going to be trouble of this kind the support of men like Attlee, Bevin, Morrison, and George Hall is indispensable to the national presentation of the case.'[55] Attlee was probably in favour of accepting Churchill's offer: but the National Executive firmly instructed him to turn it down, offering only (in the belief that a postponement of the election would be to Labour's advantage) to carry on until October. Churchill preferred a July election, and the Coalition broke up to be replaced by a caretaker Conservative government.

The 1945 general election was hard fought, and will always be remembered for Churchill's self-evidently bogus allegation that Labour would introduce some form of Gestapo or political police. Labour's landslide victory, the reasons for which are outside the scope of this particular discussion, upset Churchill profoundly, but without destroying his sense of perspective. In his first major speech as leader of the Opposition, he concluded by saying:

> . . . it is evident that not only are the two Parties in the House agreed in the main essentials of foreign policy and in our moral outlook on world affairs, but we also have an immense programme, prepared by our joint exertions during the Coalition, which requires to be brought into law and made an inherent part of the life of the people. Here and there there may be differences of emphasis and view, but in the main no Parliament ever assembled with such a mass of agreed legislation as lies before us this afternoon.[56]

How, then, are we to sum up the effect of the Second World War on party politics? We can do so very simply. After the war a number of the most powerful politicians understood each other personally better than in 1939; and agreed with each other on what should be done over three-quarters or more of the field of government action. There are various levels at which political history can be discussed, and they need to be taken together. In one aspect, politics *is* a game of personalities, played by a handful of creative manipulators for jobs and careers, dominated by tactical considerations, and influenced by loves and hatreds which owe nothing to ideas or principles. In peacetime some external rationality is imposed on the process by the existence of political parties to which politicians are responsible. In a coalition party pressures are weakened. We can learn something about the effect of the Coalition from the fact that in 1941 Lord Beaverbrook used to invite the Labour First Lord of the Admiralty A. V. Alexander (who was known as the 'parliamentary grocer' because of his connection with the Co-operative movement) to accompany himself in simple ballads at the piano at Cherkley Court, Beaverbrook's home.[57] Something too can be gleaned from Herbert Morrison's feelings about Churchill, expressed to the editor of *The Times* in December 1944: 'Thinks Winston treats his colleagues with magnanimity and is unlikely ever to forget the part they have played together. He (H. M.) cannot imagine himself 'getting spiteful about the old man.'[58] Many examples could be given of cross-party alliances and friendships within the Coalition: Labour ministers invariably hated someone on their own side and made up to someone in the Conservative team. The high degree of consensus in the post-war years was certainly due in part to the existence of an invisible old comrades' association in the House.

In a loftier sense political history has also to be read as the high-level reflection and resolution of social and economic change. In pre-war Britain, the leverage and influence of Labour in relation to the Conservatives had been weak for many years. Trade unionism suffered the defeat of mass unemployment and the defeat of the general strike. The Labour Party never won a parliamentary majority, and the two minority Labour governments made little impact, the second collapsing in a demoralised heap in 1931. In spite of a top dressing of Marxism, the bulk-of the Labour Party in the 1930s wanted from the next Labour government a series of measures to increase employment, improve the social services, and broaden educational opportunity. The wartime Coalition gave Labour the moral and political power to obtain a more comprehensive programme of reform than had been envisaged in the 1930s. The leading edge of the Conservative Party—Conservative ministers in touch with Labour through the Coalition—and the minority of Tory reformers, either accepted or welcomed the change. Perhaps the majority of Conservatives were only converted in their hearts by the defeat of 1945, and the need to accept the legislation of the post-war Labour government as a fact of life. The new centre of the war years was not the Conservative-based centre which has so often been advocated in recent years, but a Labour-based centre in which the right of the Conservative party was pushed into isolation. The millenarian hopes of the romantic left were defeated as the dream of 'the people's war' faded after 1940. But so far as the internal affairs of Britain were concerned, and in a less dramatic sense, Attlee's prophecy to the Labour Party conference on 13

May 1940 was to prove correct: 'I am quite sure that the world that must emerge from this war must be a world attuned to our ideals.'[59]

## Notes

1 Winston S. Churchill, *The Unrelenting Struggle* (London, 1943) p. 85, speech of 27 Mar 1941.

2 Jorgen S. Rasmussen, 'Party Discipline in War-Time: the Downfall of the Chamberlain Government, *Journal of Politics*, 32 (1970) 379–406.

3 *The Record* (Dec 1938) p. 128.

4 *Report of the 38th Annual Conference of the Labour Party 29 May to 2 June 1939*, p. 330; L. S. Amery, *My Political Life* (London, 1955) Vol. III, p. 371.

5 Fraser to Dalton, 20 Oct 1938, Dalton Papers.

6 Eugen Spier, *Focus* (London, 1963).

7 Dalton Diary, 8 Apr 1938.

8 Quoted in Robert Rhodes James, *Churchill: A Study in Failure* (Harmondsworth, 1973) p. 194.

9 David Kirkwood, *My Life of Revolt* (London, 1935) p. vi. I owe this quotation to Dr Angus Calder.

10 Winston S. Churchill, *The Gathering Storm* (London, 1948) p. 137.

11 Winston S. Churchill, 'The Ebbing Tide of Socialism', *Step by Step* (London, 1942) p. 140; 'England Learns about Labour', *Collier's Weekly* (24 Sep 1938).

12 Attlee gave the details of the new structure to the Home Policy Committee at the end of May. See H.P.C. (40) 17th meeting, 28 May 1940. The clearest account of the committee system on the home front is D. N. Chester, 'The Central Machinery for Economic Policy' in D. N. Chester (ed.), *Lessons of the British War Economy* (London, 1951).

13 Barrington-Ward Diary, 8 Mar 1942.

14 Alan Bullock, *The Life and Times of Ernest Bevin*, Vol. II: *Minister of Labour 1940–1945* (London, 1967) p. 112.

15 For a good account of the Bevin/Anderson axis see John W. Wheeler-Bennett, *John Anderson Viscount Waverley* (London, 1962) pp. 265–7.

16 Bernard Donoughue and G. W. Jones, *Herbert Morrison* (London, 1973) pp. 313, 304–5.

17 Unfortunately I do not have permission to quote the source for this story.

18 See my account of wartime politics, *The Road to 1945* (London, 1975) ch. 7.

19 David Dilks (ed.), *The Diaries of Sir Alexander Cadogan 1938–1945* (London, 1971) p. 444, note 1.

20 House of Commons Debates, Vol. 365, Col. 1143, 24 Oct 1940.

21 Ian Angus and Sonia Orwell (eds), *The Collected Essays, Journalism and Letters of George Orwell* (Harmondsworth, 1970) Vol. II, p. 381.

22 PREM 4/82/2, J. A. Barlow to Leslie Rowan, 9 Jan 1945.

23 Donoughue and Jones, *Herbert Morrison*, p. 287.

24 Dalton Diary, 20 Feb 1942.

25 *Daily Herald*, 31 May 1940; for Laski's views about the war see Harold Laski, *Where Do We Go From Here?* (Harmondsworth, 1940) and *Reflections On The Revolution of Our Time* (London, 1943). On 'revolution by consent' see Chapter 12 of Herbert A. Deane, *The Political Ideas of Harold J. Laski* (New York, 1955).

26 Dalton Diary, 16 Aug 1940.

27 Collin Brooks Diary, 11 Dec 1941, 12 Mar 1942.

28 PREM 4/65/1, Sir G. Broadbridge to Churchill, 18 Feb 1941; PREM 4/57/7, Churchill to Erskine-Hill, 11 Mar 1944.

29 PREM 4/57/7, minute by Churchill of 29 Jan 1941.

30 Philip Goodhart, *The 1922* (London, 1973) p. 124.

31 *Clem Attlee,* The Granada Historical Records Interview 1967, p. 20; the *Listener,* 28 July 1966, p. 112; Samuel Brittan, *Steering the Economy* (Harmondsworth, 1971) p. 189.

32 The minutes of the War Aims committee are to be found in CAB 87/90; and see Nigel Nicolson (ed.), *Harold Nicolson: Diaries and Letters 1939–1945* (London, 1967) p. 387.

33 J. C. W. Reith, *Into the Wind* (London, 1949) pp. 407–8.

34 ED 136/217, memorandum by R. S. Wood, 17 Jan 1941.

35 Alan Bullock, *The Life and Times of Ernest Bevin* (London, 1960) Vol. II, p. 237, quoted in Patricia Strauss, *Bevin & Co* (New York, 1941) p. 98.

36 PREM 4/100/5, memorandum by J. M. Keynes, Jan 1941; Anthony Eden, *Freedom and Order* (London, 1947) p. 154; Winston S. Churchill, *The Grand Alliance* (London, 1950) p. 392.

37 Bullock, *Bevin*, pp. 225–6. I would also like to thank, for interviews which touched on the background to the Beveridge report, Lord Clitheroe, formerly Sir Ralph Assheton, Bevin's Parliamentary Secretary at the Ministry of Labour; and Sir Norman Chester, Warden of Nuffield College, Oxford, who was the Secretary of the Beveridge committee and a member of the Economic Section of the War Cabinet.

38 Sir William Beveridge, *Pillars of Security* (London, 1943) p. 42.

39 See the accounts by Calder, Marwick, Bullock; also Henry Pelling, *Britain in the Second World War* (London, 1970).

40 PREM 4/89/2, memorandum by Kingsley Wood, 17 Nov 1942.

41 See the valuable article by Arthur Marwick, 'The Labour Party and the Welfare State in Britain 1900–1948, *American Historical Review,* LXXIII, no. 2 (1967) 380–403, and in particular 398.

42 Quoted in Michael Foot, *Aneurin Bevan,* Vol. II *1945–1960* (London, 1973) p. 105.

43 Dalton Diary, 19 May 1944.

44 PREM 4/88/1, Churchill to Attlee (unsent) 20 Nov 1944.

45 Undated memorandum by Attlee, probably May 1944. Attlee Papers, Churchill College, Cambridge.

46 *Clem Attlee*, p. 23.

47 Halifax Diary, 3 Jan 1941, Hickleton Papers.

48 *News Chronicle,* 23 June 1941; Halifax Diary, 30 Aug 1941.

49 Winston S. Churchill, *Onwards to Victory* (London, 1944) p. 38, broadcast of 21 Mar 1943.

50 Paul Addison, 'The By-Elections of the Second World War', Chris Cook and John Ramsden (eds), *By-Elections in British Politics* (London, 1973).

51 Halifax Diary, 16 Sept 1943.

52 *The Eden Memoirs: the Reckoning* (London, 1965) p. 454.

53 Dalton Diary, 26 May 1943.

54 Winston S. Churchill, *Triumph and Tragedy* (London, 1954) p. 512.

55 Ibid., p. 514.

56 Winston S. Churchill, *Victory* (London, 1946) p. 238, speech of 16 Aug 1945.

57 Dalton Diary, 12 Mar 1941.

58 Barrington-Ward Diary, 21 Dec 1944.

59 *Report of the 39th Annual Conference of the Labour Party*, 1940, p. 124.

# Index